PLAT
DU JOUR

PLAT DU JOUR

FRENCH DINNERS MADE EASY

SUSAN HERRMANN LOOMIS

The Countryman Press
A Division of W. W. Norton & Company
Independent Publishers Since 1923

For information about permission to reproduce selections from this book, write to
Permissions, The Countryman Press, 500 Fifth Avenue, New York, NY 10110

For information about special discounts for bulk purchases, please contact
W. W. Norton Special Sales at specialsales@wwnorton.com or 800-233-4830

Manufacturing by ToppanLeefung
Book design by Allison Chi
Production manager: Devon Zahn

Library of Congress Cataloging-in-Publication Data

Names: Loomis, Susan Herrmann, author.
Title: Plat du jour : French dinners made easy / Susan Herrmann Loomis.
Description: New York : The Countryman Press, an imprint of W. W. Norton & Company,
Independent Publishers since 1923, [2021] | Includes index.
Identifiers: LCCN 2020035170 | ISBN 9781682684504 | ISBN 9781682684511 (epub)
Subjects: LCSH: Cooking, French. | LCGFT: Cookbooks.
Classification: LCC TX719.L665 2021 | DDC 641.5944—dc23
LC record available at https://lccn.loc.gov/2020035170

The Countryman Press
www.countrymanpress.com

A division of W. W. Norton & Company, Inc.
500 Fifth Avenue, New York, NY 10110
www.wwnorton.com

978-1-68268-450-4

10 9 8 7 6 5 4 3 2 1

Venite ad me, omnes qui stomacho laboratis,
et ego vos restaurabo.
Come all to me, you whose stomachs cry with misery,
and I will restore you.
—Written above the first restaurant in Paris.
After the Gospel of Matthew.

I dedicate this book, *Plat du Jour*, to my mother,
Doris Bain Herrmann. She provided all of us—
seven hungry people—with her delicious plats du jour
every single day for years on end with a variety, vivacity,
and comfort that knew no bounds. Today, at nearly
100 years old, she is still cooking and her vivacity hasn't
diminished. Thanks, Mom, for my first plats du jour.

CONTENTS

INTRODUCTION
THE PLAT DU JOUR "FORMULA"

Plat du jour, three familiar words in the French language that seduce, excite, and comfort.

Plats du jour are the dishes you find on handwritten menus outside bistros or cafés, the dishes that beckon everyone inside to sample a restaurant's irresistible, mouthwatering menu. They change daily, a litany to the abundance in the French culinary repertoire.

Most plats du jour are classics lifted from the heart of French regional cuisine, dishes that evoke the essence of France, the spirit of farm, terroir, and Grandmère. They remain relevant to chefs worldwide, who continue to refine and adapt them because they are the fundament of cuisine and pleasure, of everything that is right with the world as seen on the plate.

You know many of them, from Boeuf Bourguignon and Blanquette De Veau to Bouillabaisse and Croque Monsieur. Dishes like these reflect the history of France itself and all the permutations of its cuisine. They evoke nostalgia, romance, emotion, and even today, chefs prepare them with reverence as they tweak and create whole new dishes based on the old. This makes for lively variety and flavor and a constantly evolving selection, which you will find within the pages of this book.

Plats du jour are hearty yet elegant, absolutely seasonal, calculated to give pleasure. Each makes a perfect one-pot lunch or dinner along with a *bal-lon* or a carafe of red wine and a basket of freshly cut baguette. Yet the plat du jour is always offered as part of a *formule* that includes a first course or dessert. For every French chef and cook knows that even the heartiest plat du jour is made better with more.

The plats du jour I've chosen for this book are generous, authentic, delicious touchstones in an ever-changing world. They reflect the classics, the tweaking, my creations, and those of many a chef. They are simple to make, offered with joy, always welcome. Each recipe calls for easily available ingredients, offers substitutions, and includes methods that have been streamlined without sacrificing an iota of quality. As you prepare the dishes, they will teach you, without you even realizing it, the natural economy of the French chef and cook, who relies on the season for inspiration. Each will nourish you, and each will take you to the lively cacophony of the café and bistro, then on a culinary tour of France and its regions. More than all that, though, even the simplest plat du jour in this book will lend your meal a festive air, whether it be for a crowd or for a busy family that sits down together before returning to whatever activities each is involved in. Why? Because every plat du jour speaks of caring, which includes time in the kitchen preparing dishes with delicious and simple ingredients, those that are in season and are filled with flavor.

Enjoy your journey through *Plat du Jour* and profit from all the flavors and colors, the side dishes, the first courses, and the desserts. Remember the carafe of wine and the freshly sliced baguette. I wish you all a hearty *bon appétit!*

A Little History of the Plat du Jour

When the first public eating establishment—called a *bouillon*—was opened in the 18th century in Paris by a M. Boulanger, there was one dish on offer, also called a bouillon, which was generally chicken boiled with root vegetables (similar to *poule au pot*). It was intended as a restorative to the weak and for pregnant women, and M. Boulanger hung a sign in front of his restaurant (a term that in itself meant "restorative") which stated, "*Venite ad me, omnes qui stomacho laboratis, et ego vos restaurabo* [Come all to me, you whose stomachs cry with misery, and I will restore you]."

In fact, he was prevented from offering anything but bouillon to avoid competing with the union of *traiteurs*, the caterers of the time. But, eventually, he transgressed by serving lamb's foot in white sauce, which he advertised in front of his bouillon so potential clients knew what the dish included and its price. This was arguably France's very first plat du jour. Some say the caterers took him to court for his audaciousness, others say they didn't. Whatever the legal ramifications, it wasn't long until the French Revolution divested the country of its royals, and the chefs who had been in their employ were without work. They opened restaurants throughout the land, serving all manner of luscious dishes that went far beyond anything resembling bouillon, or lamb's foot in white sauce, for that matter. And as we see today, restaurants and caterers—the charcutiers

of today—live in harmony. From bouillon to the plat du jour, the French culinary road has been long and fragrant but not so winding, for we still find plats du jour that would have been perfectly at home in the restaurant of the 18th century. (I apologize right off for not offering a recipe for lamb's foot in white sauce.)

Cooking Plats du Jour

The French cook strives for ultimate flavor, and he or she thinks ahead. This means that for many—though not all—plats du jour, long, slow cooking is the answer. Please note the preparation and cooking times for each recipe so that you can plan ahead. You will also find a list that specifies the equipment needed to make your plat du jour. Note, too, that whenever possible, I've mentioned components that can be prepared in advance so that you can get a jump start on your plat du jour!

Another thing about plats du jour—the ingredients list can be long, but don't be daunted. Most of the ingredients are no more complicated than cabbage or olive oil. Before allowing yourself to be intimidated, read through the list and you'll see. There is nothing to fear!

There is a final chapter here called "Basics." Basics are the French cook and chef's secret weapon: the sauces and seasonings that make plats du jour so delectable. You'll find the very best here, which you'll use over and over.

ASTUCES

What is an *astuce*? It's a tip, a trick, a little secret that you need to navigate a recipe safely and surely. We all need astuces when cooking, and I've included these for many of my recipes. It's my way of helping you be the best chef/cook you can be.

Good-Quality Ingredients for Good-Quality Food

WHAT DOES "GOOD QUALITY" REALLY MEAN?

Good quality means fresh, from freshly harvested to freshly made. It means choosing the best ingredients you can find, even those staples that appear in so many dishes, which we often take for granted in terms of their potential quality. What the French chef knows, and what I believe, is that the quality of every single ingredient you use is important to the quality of the finished dish and, ultimately, to your enjoyment. What follows explains the quality attributes of certain key ingredients.

GARLIC is generally harvested in July and is really good and firm until just about Christmas. Then it starts itching to grow, and a green germ—which is the nascent garlic plant—begins to form inside the clove. There isn't anything wrong with this germ, but its texture is tougher than the clove. So I always recommend removing it. When you see garlic called for in a recipe, remove the green germ from the clove, unless the clove is being left whole.

BAY LEAVES—I'm in love with them. They offer a delicate perfume and a balance to the flavor of every dish they touch, so I suggest using them often. When I do, I am referring to the *laurier-sauce* (sauce bay) herb, *Lauris nobilis*. Don't mistake bay leaf for the California bay, *Umbellularia californica*, also called Oregon myrtle, which is unpleasantly pungent. If you don't have fresh bay at your disposal, you can also get dried imported bay leaves. They're from *L. nobilis*, too! When you see bay leaf called for in a recipe, it is always referring to *L. nobilis*.

EXTRA VIRGIN OLIVE OIL is the only type of olive oil you want to cook with, ever. Olive oil without the label "virgin" is widely available, but it can be of dubious origin, whereas extra virgin olive oil is certain to actually come from an olive. That said, you don't need to spend your family fortune on olive oil. Buy a respectable brand of extra virgin olive oil—Lucini is one of my favorites—and use it both raw and for cooking.

SALT is so basic we mostly don't think about its quality. But there is salt and salt. I insist on using sea salt, and my favorite is from Guérande in Brittany. I choose it because the only processing it goes through, once it is raked from the salt marsh, is sifting. Nothing is added nor taken from it, and it has the finest, most subtle flavor of any salt I've ever tasted. In contrast, a commercial table salt, which was sea salt millions of years ago, is mined and highly processed, and usually has a bitter, acrid taste. Why such distinction? The taste of the salt you use affects the final taste of your dish.

BLACK PEPPER—There are so many varieties available now that you simply have to taste and choose. And you may find several you love. My favorite? Voatsiperifery from Madagascar. But I don't use it on everything, nor all the time, because its flavor is so unique that it can become less special if overused . For a good, wonderful, basic black pepper, I recommend Tellicherry from India. Whichever or how many pepper varieties you choose to have, you should really grind the corns as you use them, which means you will need to have several pepper grinders on hand, for pre-ground pepper has very little flavor and that which it does have diminishes quickly.

SPICES—Ground spices have a shelf life. My rule of thumb is to check them every six months. If their flavor isn't what it should be, I replace them. Buy smaller rather than larger amounts so you are using the freshest possible spices. For very high-quality spices, I recommend Penzeys.

VINEGAR—My go-to vinegar is sherry vinegar, because it is delicate yet adds a requisite tartness where that is necessary. I also use a homemade red wine vinegar because it is robust without being too acidic. Balsamic vinegar is good in certain dishes because it is roundly sweet, and you may make it your go-to, though beware that it has such personality that it can take over. Whichever vinegar you choose, get one that is good quality, such as a product that lists the grape variety on the label. This sounds snobby but it isn't—a good-quality vinegar will enhance every recipe that calls for it, and since quantities required are usually small, a good bottle will last a long time. For variations, try apple cider vinegar (from a local orchard, if possible) or, for very special recipes, try raspberry vinegar.

Seasonality and Cooking

We gather around the idea of seasonality as though it is something new and precious. But rural people have always lived with the seasons. In France, eating seasonally is as ingrained as singing "La Marseillaise" at a national event, or dipping a buttered *tartine* (a baguette cut in half) into a steaming bowl of coffee. Beyond the reverence accorded to seasons in France, though, is simple good sense. Seasonal foods have more taste, are more abundant, and are more cost effective. And there is another element: When the season is over and you've had your last bite of scallop, or strawberry, or rhubarb, or oyster, then it's on to something new.

And you're left with the delicious nostalgia of what you've just lost.

Around this seasonality hovers the lunar cycle. If you live in France long enough, you will come to take for granted that most people around you check out the moon before they till the soil, plant seeds, water and fertilize plants, cut their hair, shave their legs, make cakes, do a detox, wash their windows . . . We all sense the importance of a lunar cycle—think: moodiness at the full moon—but in France it is an active, guiding principle to the seasonality of foods, as everything is planted and harvested according to lunar cycle, one of the keys to seasonal foods.

Being in season is one thing; timing during the season is another. Take the tomato, which needs sun and water to develop flavor. This means that in the Northern Hemisphere the tomato is a late summer fruit, ideal from July through September, depending on the year. A June tomato is exciting because we haven't seen a tomato for eight months. But if you really taste it, a June tomato will be more fun than flavor. Consider the strawberry, too, which has become a fruit of spring and summer, thanks to botanical tinkering. But no lab work so far has produced a strawberry that tastes spectacular during the winter months.

Seasonality affects meat and poultry, too. Chefs and butchers consider that pork, beef, veal, and lamb are best from March through September, because at that time they are out to pasture or mountainside where they graze on fresh grass, which enhances their flavor. As for poultry, its quality is constant throughout the year and depends directly on the quality of food it eats. Wild game is best in the autumn (which coincides with hunting season) because its food is most rich at that time. Large birds, such as black turkeys and capons, are best around the holidays, but this is more about tradition than season, for it is typical to serve these birds for Christmas and

New Year's. As for foie gras, it is best from autumn through early summer. Although it can be produced year-round, it mostly isn't in the summer heat, because then the birds have little appetite, let alone the energy to convert their food into buttery liver. The humane foie gras producer takes a warm-weather hiatus, giving the geese and ducks time and place to "chill."

SEASONALITY AND SEAFOOD

Seasons are perhaps most obvious when it comes to seafood, because most of the seafood we eat is wild. Each species has its moment of abundance, peak health, reproduction. This, and much more, affects what we see at the fish market.

Seafood seasons in France might be compared with holiday seasons. Seriously. French eaters look forward with anticipation to that day in November, for example, when the first scallop appears at the market in its gorgeous, pale pink and ivory shell. From November to May, we can all luxuriate in fresh scallops, which we will eat raw, sautéed in butter and garlic, baked with cream, set atop a puree of Jerusalem artichokes, braised in fish broth for a beautiful soup or stew. Then, come May 15, there won't be another French scallop to be had. Why? Because once the waters warm, the scallop needs to be left alone to reproduce, sending energy from its meat to its bright, orange egg sacs.

In France, fishing is subject to governmental regulations, in an effort to protect both stocks and fisheries. For instance, to protect and maintain the scallop population, the regulations are strict. Fishing licenses are doled out each year in accordance with the strength of the population. When stocks are low, fewer licenses are given out. Those with licenses must fish according to their license restrictions, which allot them just forty-five minutes per day to haul in scallops. French fishermen respect this natural cycle, and in doing

so they help protect shellfish to keep it on our tables for years to come.

For the most part, all wild fish stocks are protected by these types of government regulations, which tend to respect the natural cycles of the species. In theory, imposed seasons work, but every country has different laws, and there aren't enough "sea police" to make certain that all boats respect all laws. As a result, fish stocks are often overfished. Many organizations monitor this and publish lists of which species have healthy populations. A good list comes from the Monterey Bay Aquarium and can be found at www.seafoodwatch.org.

When it comes to fish farming, we consider that seasons don't exist, but they do for some species. Take oysters. They are farmed; their life cycles controlled. And they're on offer year-round. But the oyster remains a wild creature, with a cycle of its own. It's easy to farm because it has a natural instinct to survive—when the tide is out and it's exposed to the air, the muscles of the oyster clamp its shell shut, keeping sea water inside so it can survive. When the water warms, the oyster wants to reproduce, so it develops spawn and becomes very soft. Some people don't mind eating a soft "spawny" oyster, which is why oyster vendors can sell them year-round. But their natural "season" isn't respected. And if you've got crisp oysters on your mind, then you want to pay attention to the oyster and to eat it when the water is cold, during the months with an "R" in them. The season is the same for mussels.

Aqua farming erases seasons, because fish are available by simply dipping them out of the water at will. Thus, farmed fish provide constant and relatively inexpensive protein to a wide population. But fish farming is controversial. Take salmon, which is farmed throughout the Northern Hemisphere, making it one of the top four farmed fish (along with tilapia, catfish, and carp).

Environmental issues swirl around the effect of salmon farms on the environment, including changes in water temperature, high concentrations of waste, the use of pesticides to combat parasites, and farmed species that escape and mate with wild species. It's a can of worms, so to speak. All of this is watched by various governmental and other organizations, which impose rules and regulations. Yet, yet, yet ... if you can, opt for wild fish. It may be around less often, but when it is, *quel plaisir* (what a treat)!

Eating seasonally is a sustainable practice, as is establishing strict regulations in the fishing industry aimed at sustainability. I always encourage eating as seasonally as possible, no matter what it is you're eating.

Now that we've addressed seasonality in seafood, how do you know whether what you're buying is of the utmost quality? There are simple signals to look out for. If you smell any fish aroma, stay away. If a whole fish is missing scales in patches, has dull eyes, or—the most important—has off-color gills, it's not fit to eat. Fish must be firm, with all its scales and bright pink gills. A cloudy eye isn't necessarily a problem. For fillets, they must be bright and appetizing, with no gaping and no off-colored juices.

Garnishing the French Way: Edible Embellishments

I often suggest garnishing a dish with one or another blossom or herb sprig. I didn't invent this; it's been a French practice since the Middle Ages. Even before that, the knowledgeable were using edible blossoms and herbs in everything from healing teas to liqueurs, not to mention to dress up a plate. An edible flower or its petals, an herb sprig or leaf does wonders to make a dish "pop," charming and exciting the palate of the person who is going to eat it.

They can add subtle flavor, too, particularly herbs. I suggest using a fresh sprig from an herb that is already in the dish, to echo its flavor. Do remember that when it comes to a flower blossom, while it may be edible and beautiful, it won't necessarily be delicious. For example, the chicory flower is a lovely and elegant blue blossom that is quite bitter; lavender is pretty, fragrant, and chic, but has an overwhelmingly intense taste; and beautiful royal blue borage livens up any dish visually, but it does have a distinct oyster flavor.

Before garnishing with flowers, be aware which blossoms are edible and which aren't—including whether or not they have been treated with pesticides or preservatives. It isn't advised to buy an edible flowering plant from a florist and use the blossoms for culinary purposes because, unless the establishment claims it's organic, the flowers are most likely covered with chemicals. You don't want to eat them.

In the case of garnishing with fresh herbs, their leaves are often sufficient as garnish—if you can use their flowers, too, so much the better.

To assist you, here is a non-exhaustive list of edible garnishes to get you started.

BLOSSOMS

Anise hyssop	Chrysanthemum
Apple	Cornflower or bachelor
Arugula	button
Bean flower	Dandelion
Bee balm	Day lily
Begonia	Elderberry
Borage	Geranium
Broccoli	Hibiscus
Calendula	Honeysuckle
Carnation	Lavender
Chamomile	Lettuce
Chicory	Lilac

Linden

Phlox (perennial: *Phlox paniculate*)

Marigold

Mint

Mustard

Nasturtium

Okra flower

Pansy

Pea

Pea flower

Purslane

Rose

Sweet woodruff

Violet

Zucchini blossom

HERBS

Basil

Chervil

Chive

Cilantro

Fennel (and the pollen is great)

Garlic

Garlic chive

Lemon verbena

Mints

Rosemary

Sage (*Salvia officinalis*)

Salad burnet

Savory

Thyme

CHOPPING HERBS

You will notice that my recipes give a separate step in the instructions for chopping herbs right before they are to be added to the other ingredients. There is a very specific reason for this. Once herbs are chopped, their essential oils (which contain their taste and scent) begin to release flavor, which goes into the air if you chop them in advance. Thus, chopping herbs should be done at the *very* last minute . . . which is what I'm training you to do with my recipes.

Food Labels

The French care, deeply and primordially, about the quality of their food. They want to be reassured that, for instance, when they buy a Camembert de Normandie it is made in and around the town of Camembert, with milk from the Norman cow that has been treated and fed and cared for in a specific way, and that the cheese its milk produces, which has also undergone stringent and codified preparation, will have the flavor and texture they expect. To ensure the quality of their food, the French invented a classification system that champions ingredients of note from a specific region, requiring its producers to adhere to strict quality standards before they are awarded a label. This applies, in France, to everything from wines and peppers to butter, walnuts, and chestnuts. This codification system has been so effective in allowing producers to do their best, and in reassuring the French consumer, that the whole of Europe has adopted it. I've included the information on food labeling here because I find that people often have questions about what these labels—which are often on ingredients found in specialty shops outside France, or which they encounter on reading about or visiting France—actually mean and why they are important. In many ways, they are the fundament of the French philosophy of food, for they demonstrate the constant desire the French have for excellence in eating.

Regionality and the notion of *terroir*—where an ingredient or preparation comes from—are primordial to the French. They are absolutely loyal to the diversity and quality of their agricultural and culinary products, and the chauvinism involved in their loyalty is second to none. The French government is no exception, having applied for and obtained the status of a UNESCO "world intangible heritage" for French cuisine in 2010. But since 1936, the French government has been busily protecting French products by codifying their cultivation and production methods with a label, AOC (Appellation d'Origine Contrôlée). This label still stands, though it has been diversified into a variety of categories adapted for legitimacy in Europe. Here is a roundup of food labels, for whether you are in France or anywhere else in the world, you are likely to come across them.

AOP: L'Appellation d'Origine Protégée is an official European label. It designates a product where each step of its production is done in a geographically limited area (terroir)—according to traditional, regional know-how, or *le savoir faire des hommes* (the know-how of men), which give the product its characteristics. The AOP is the highest standard for food production, serving to maintain quality and traditional methods and know-how, as well as reassuring the customer about a product's quality. The AOP label is valid throughout the European Union.

AOC: L'Appellation d'Origine Contrôlée is the French equivalent of the AOP. Some say it was originally created in the 15th century for Roquefort. It wasn't called AOC then, but there was a quality label attached to the cheese since kingdoms were won and lost fighting for the rights to its production. Since 2012, the AOC label—which is very hard won and requires reams of documentation and years of process—is the first step in a product's journey toward an AOP. Once a product has earned its AOP, it no longer has the right to carry the AOC label, with the only exception being wines.

IGP: L'Indication Géographique Protégé is similar, but less stringent than AOC or AOP. It nonetheless establishes a strong link between a product and its terroir.

STG: La Specialité Traditionelle Garanti ensures that a product is made following a traditional recipe. This label isn't related to terroir.

AB OR BIO: Designates organic production and is a Europe-wide label that stipulates products contain no GMO ingredients and no synthetic additives.

LABEL ROUGE: Designates food products that are higher in quality than similar products available on the market. Label Rouge is a quality label unrelated to terroir.

CHAPTER 1
APPETIZERS

NO MATTER WHAT the meal, occasion, or venue, one cannot enjoy food in France without appetizers. You might meet a colleague for lunch, a friend for supper, a group for a drink before a meal—no matter. There will always be something on offer, whether it be the ubiquitous bowl of peanuts or olives, homemade chips, or a more elaborate savory "cake." Regardless of what it is, the appetizer—eaten along with the aperitif—is vital to any notion of sitting down at the table to eat. And that, sitting down to eat, is what this book is all about. For a plat du jour demands a table, a chair, silverware and a napkin, at least one glass of wine (perhaps two), but most of all, time. Perhaps not a lot of time, but enough to enjoy the ritual of the meal, to honor its preparation, to benefit from the moment, the flavors, and the aromas. *Au plaisir!*

Cheese Puffs with Thyme

GOUGÈRES AU THYM

When you bite into this little thyme and cheese–scented puff, you are tasting history. A *Gougère* is in evidence as far back as 1571, when it was mentioned in a wedding menu in Burgundy, offered among the varied desserts at that time. Even earlier, though, in 1316, a Gougère was mentioned in a book written by the Comte d'Anjou. These early iterations of gougères were most likely sweet because salt was such a rare and costly seasoning at the time.

Today, Burgundy calls the Gougère its own, and it is in this wine-rich region that the history of the Gougère has flourished. Today, one cannot sample a kir or a glass of white or red in Burgundy without a Gougère alongside.

MAKES 35 TO 40 GOUGÈRES

EQUIPMENT: 2 baking sheets, medium saucepan, pastry bag with ½-inch (1.3 cm) round tip or a 1-inch (2.5 cm) ice cream scoop

PREPARATION TIME: about 15 minutes

COOKING TIME: 20 to 35 minutes, depending on your oven, so check after 20 minutes

DIFFICULTY LEVEL: medium

1¼ cups (170 g) unbleached all-purpose flour

2 teaspoons fresh thyme

1 cup (250 ml) water

7 tablespoons (105 g) unsalted butter, chilled, cut into chunks

¼ teaspoon fine sea salt

4 large eggs

2 ounces (60 g) Gruyère or Comté, to give ¾ cup grated

1. Preheat the oven to 400°F (200°C). Line two baking sheets with parchment paper.

2. Sift the flour onto a piece of waxed or parchment paper. Add the thyme to the flour and mix it in with your fingers.

3. Combine the water and butter in a medium saucepan and bring to a boil over medium-high heat. Let the mixture boil for 30 seconds. Then remove it from the heat and add the flour and salt all at once. Beat the mixture vigorously with a wooden spoon. It will come together easily, creating a sort of thick paste. Continue to beat until the mixture comes away from the side of the pan and forms a homogenous ball of dough, 20 to 30 seconds. The dough should not be sticky—it will be slippery from the melted butter—but it should hold together well and not stick to the pan or the wooden spoon. If it does, return it to the heat and continue to beat until it dries out.

4. Remove the pan from the heat and let the dough cool slightly. Then add the eggs, one at a time, beating well after each addition. When they are incorporated, beat in the cheese.

5. Fit a pastry bag with a ½-inch (1.3 cm) round tip, then fill the bag with the dough. Pipe walnut-size portions of the dough on the prepared baking sheets, leaving about 1 inch (2.5 cm) between them. Alternatively, you can use a small ice cream scoop or 2 teaspoons to make the little rounds of dough—they'll be less uniformly shaped, but this doesn't matter. Bake in the center of the oven until the gougères are puffed, golden, and crisp, 20 to 35 minutes.

6. Remove from the oven, remove from the parchment paper, and let cool on a wire rack before serving. Gougères also freeze beautifully and can be enjoyed later. To thaw, heat them in a 400°F (200°C) oven for about 10 minutes.

ASTUCE: The only trick to a gougère is mixing the eggs into the ball of dough that is created by the flour, water, and butter. Persist—it all comes together perfectly.

Avocado, Cherry, and Chive Salad

SALADE D'AVOCAT, CERISES, ET À LA CIBOULETTE

What is avocado doing with cherries in the same dish, seasoned with a touch of sugar and served as an introduction to a gorgeous spring plat du jour? Cherry season corresponds with the last month of the Spanish avocado season, so it seemed perfectly natural to combine them here.

If you don't have chive blossoms, use a single chive balanced atop the mixture. I love a beautiful white Burgundy with this.

SERVES 4

EQUIPMENT: small nonreactive bowl, small bowl, 4 wine or cocktail glasses

PREPARATION TIME: 15 minutes

COOKING TIME: none

DIFFICULTY LEVEL: simple

---

1 cup (about 160 g) cherries, pitted and cut into quarters

2 teaspoons white wine vinegar

¼ teaspoon Vanilla Sugar (page 339)

¼ teaspoon fine sea salt

1 large avocado (about 9 ounces; 280 g), pitted and peeled

1 small bunch fresh chives

2 tablespoons best-quality olive oil

1 generous teaspoon fresh lemon juice

Fleur de sel

2 tablespoons pistachio nuts, shelled and minced

4 chive blossoms for garnish (optional)

1. Place the cherries in a small nonreactive bowl. Cover with the vinegar, toss so they are combined, then sprinkle with the sugar and the fine sea salt. Toss until all is thoroughly blended, then set aside.

2. Cut the avocado into ¼-inch (6 mm) pieces.

3. Mince the chives and place them in a separate small bowl. Immediately cover them with the oil and mix together.

4. Reserving 12 avocado cubes, evenly divide the remaining cubes among four wine or cocktail glasses. Drizzle each with about ¼ teaspoon of the lemon juice. Sprinkle lightly with fleur de sel and, reserving 1 scant teaspoon of the chive mixture, drizzle equal amounts of what remains over each glassful of avocado cubes.

5. Drain the cherries. Top the avocado cubes with equal amounts of cherries, turning some of the cherries so their bright skins show. Divide the reserved avocado cubes atop the cherries. Drizzle with the remaining chive mixture, then sprinkle each with 1½ teaspoons of the pistachios. If you have a chive blossom, separate its individual blossoms and sprinkle a few over each glass. Serve immediately.

ASTUCE: I always call for the weight of fruit that you need to buy, rather than the weight you'll end up using, which makes it easy. So the cherries are weighed *before* being pitted.

Salted Spanish Almonds

DES AMANDES D'ESPAGNE SALÉES

This is an ideal appetizer to serve before your favorite plat du jour because it is that perfect little salty, crisp nugget that tastes so good but won't fill you up. If you like a lot of spice, simply increase the amount of paprika, though I suggest you try this first to see how it suits your palate. The Marcona almond, which is wide and flat with a very intense almond flavor, is terrific here, so use it if you find it, but know that other almond varieties are delicious, too. Serve these along with a chilled glass of rosé, a Spritz, a Cinzano, or a Tío Pepe. Whatever you serve these with, know one thing—you can never make enough of them!

MAKES 2 CUPS (270 G) ALMONDS

EQUIPMENT: medium saucepan, nonreactive baking sheet

PREPARATION TIME: 10 minutes if blanching the almonds

COOKING TIME: 20 to 30 minutes

DIFFICULTY LEVEL: simple

---

2 cups (500 ml) water

2 tablespoons coarse sea salt

½ teaspoon hot paprika

2 cups Spanish or other almonds (9.5 ounces; 270 g), blanched

ASTUCE: To blanch an almond, plunge it into boiling water and leave it for about 30 seconds, then drain. Squeeze the almond and it will slip right out of the skin.

1. Preheat the oven to 325°F (165°C). Note the oven temperature is quite low for the almonds, so they will bake all the way through and become completely dry and crunchy. Don't try to rush them, because they burn easily.

2. Bring the water, salt, and paprika to a boil in a medium saucepan and boil, stirring, until the salt is dissolved. Add the almonds, stir, and boil until the almonds begin to look translucent, about 8 minutes. Drain the almonds and spread them evenly on a nonreactive baking sheet. Bake in the center of the oven until the almonds are pale golden and crisp, 20 to 30 minutes. Do not let the almonds get toasty brown, as they will be too toasted at that point.

3. Remove the almonds from the oven and let them cool before eating.

4. These will keep in an airtight container for about 1 week. They can also be successfully frozen.

Fig and Hazelnut Bread with Cocoa Nibs

CAKE AUX FIGUES ET AUX NOISETTES AU ECLATS DE CACAO

When you sit down in a bistro or café at mealtime and place your order, your drinks will come first, and often they may be accompanied by small pieces of *cake* (pronounced "kek"), a savory bread that pairs perfectly with whatever you are drinking. The cake is a throwback to the 1970s, when it was the traditional accompaniment for the aperitif. Serve this at your next dinner, before your favorite plat du jour. This goes with a white or a red, but my preference is a Sauvignon Blanc or a Pinot Gris.

MAKES 1 LOAF; 10 TO 12 SERVINGS

EQUIPMENT: 8½-by-4½-by-2½-inch (21-by-11.5-by-6.5 cm) loaf pan, fine-mesh sieve, wire rack

PREPARATION TIME: 15 minutes without the hazelnut toasting time; 24 minutes with

COOKING TIME: 40 to 45 minutes

DIFFICULTY LEVEL: simple

Unsalted butter and flour for baking pan

1½ cups (200 g) unbleached all-purpose flour

1 tablespoon baking powder

1 mounded teaspoon fine sea salt

¼ mounded teaspoon freshly ground black pepper

6 large eggs

8 tablespoons (1 stick; 125 g) unsalted butter, melted and cooled

8 dried figs (7 ounces; 210 g total), hard stem end removed, coarsely chopped

6 ounces (180 g) Gruyère or Emmental, finely grated (to give 2 cups)

½ teaspoon fennel seeds, crushed

1 tablespoon cocoa nibs

½ cup (2 ounces; 60 g) hazelnuts, toasted and skinned

1. Preheat the oven to 425°F (220°C). Butter an 8½-by-4½-by-2½-inch (21-by-11.5-by-6.5 cm) loaf pan. Line it with parchment paper, butter the parchment paper, and dust it lightly with flour.

2. Using a fine-mesh sieve, sift the flour, baking powder, salt, and pepper onto a piece of parchment paper.

3. Place the eggs in a large bowl or the bowl of an electric mixer fitted with the whisk attachment. Whisk the eggs until they are combined, then slowly whisk in the flour mixture. Stir in the melted butter until it is thoroughly blended, then fold in the figs, cheese, fennel seeds, cocoa nibs, and hazelnuts, making sure they are well distributed throughout the batter.

4. Pour the batter into the prepared pan, rap it sharply on a work surface to release any air bubbles, and bake in the center of the oven until the top of the bread is golden and a sharp knife stuck in the center comes out clean, 40 to 45 minutes.

5. Remove the bread from the oven and turn it out onto a wire rack. After about 10 minutes, peel off the parchment paper. Let cool, then serve.

ASTUCES:

- By sifting dry ingredients onto either parchment or waxed paper, you can easily pick up the edges of the paper and let the dry ingredients slide into the mixing bowl.
- To skin hazelnuts, remove them from the oven after they have toasted at 350°F (180°C) for about 9 minutes. Tip the hazelnuts onto a cotton tea towel, wrap, and let them sit for about 10 minutes, then rub them vigorously with the towel. Not all their skin will come off, but work at it until they are almost entirely skinless.

Cucumber Puree with Herbed Fresh Cheese

CERVELLE DE CANUT, CONCOMBRE EN PURÉE

When it's warm and the palate needs a refreshing opener, this is the ideal appetizer. I first tasted this in Normandy at a country café, and it has become a standard part of my repertoire. I guarantee that you, your guests, and your family will love it. I like to serve this in glasses so you can see the layers, so get creative with serving receptacles, too! Pair this with a dry Muscat from Domaine de Barroubio, or use the drained cucumber juice from the recipe to make a special cocktail!

SERVES 8

EQUIPMENT: food processor, fine-mesh stainless-steel sieve, 8 small glasses

PREPARATION TIME: 10 minutes, with 1-hour chill time for the cucumber

COOKING TIME: none

DIFFICULTY LEVEL: simple

---

2 long European cucumbers, peeled and cut into chunks

1¾ cups (435 ml) Fromage Blanc (page 312)

1 tablespoon (15 ml) white wine vinegar

Sea salt and freshly ground black pepper

1 bunch fresh chives

1. Puree the cucumbers in a food processor. Transfer the puree to a fine-mesh stainless-steel sieve and set the sieve over a bowl. Chill for at least 1 hour.

2. In a separate bowl, whisk the cheese until it becomes slightly light. Whisk in the vinegar and season with salt and pepper to taste.

3. Reserving a few stalks for the garnish, mince the rest of the chives and fold them into the cheese. Correct the seasoning and set aside until you are ready to serve. If you prepare this the night before you plan to serve it, store it in the refrigerator in a covered container.

4. To serve, drain away (but reserve—it is delicious to drink!) the juice from the cucumber puree. Whisk in a pinch or two of salt to the cucumber to taste, then evenly divide the cucumber puree among eight small glasses. Top with an equal amount of the seasoned cheese, being very careful to spread the cheese in an even layer. Garnish each serving with a chive and serve immediately.

Grilled Shiitakes

SHIITAKES GRILLÉS

Shiitakes, those oddly shaped mushrooms that look a little bit like brown, velvety elephant ears, have, in the past five years, taken the French palate by storm. Shiitakes have a slightly earthy flavor underlined with the taste of toasted walnuts. They are also nutrition bombs, with notably high amounts of vitamin B_5, copper, riboflavin, zinc . . . and the list goes on. In France they are "prescribed" as an antioxidant and often included in cancer treatments. Everything about shiitakes is good, and this preparation simply makes them more incredible, served with a glass of white Sancerre or a lovely, buttery Chardonnay.

SERVES 2 TO 4

EQUIPMENT: large bowl, heavy skillet or grill pan

PREPARATION TIME: 5 minutes

COOKING TIME: 8 minutes

DIFFICULTY LEVEL: simple

---

1 pound (500 g) shiitakes, stems removed, wiped clean, cut if necessary

¼ cup toasted sesame or extra virgin olive oil

Fine sea salt and freshly ground black pepper

1. Place the shiitakes in a large bowl, drizzle with the oil, season with salt and pepper, and toss so the mushrooms are oiled and seasoned.

2. Heat a heavy skillet over medium heat. When the pan is hot, add the shiitakes and cook, stirring and shaking the pan, until the shiitakes soften and turn golden on all sides. This will take from 5 to 8 minutes. If the shiitakes aren't turning golden, increase the heat to medium-high and sauté and shake them in the pan until they are golden.

3. Turn them out into a serving dish and serve immediately with an extra shower of salt and pepper.

ASTUCE: If the shiitakes you have are small, leave them whole. For larger ones, think "large bite-size pieces" and cut them before cooking.

Oysters on the Half Shell with Two Mignonettes

LES HUITRES À LA SAUCE MIGNONETTE

Oysters on the half shell are a near-obligatory opener to a plat du jour, especially from September to April, when they are at their best. They can also be a plat du jour on their own, a perfect meal on a crisp fall or winter day. Depending on the circumstance, remember that three oysters per person is a tease; six is fun; twelve is almost a meal; and eighteen is a meal. Go from there. And sauce mignonette is the traditional accompaniment.

Since perfecting my sauce mignonette, I've learned what ingredients can be varied. I like the mignonette made with either red wine vinegar or sherry vinegar; sherry vinegar is just slightly softer than red wine vinegar. What is equally important is the way you cut the shallots. They must be precisely cut, because the size of the shallot affects the mignonette's flavor and texture. I know this is very picky, but it's true. The next time you're in Paris, have oysters at Le Select, taste its mignonette, and talk with me afterward. An Entre-Deux-Mers is wonderful here.

The difficult part of this recipe might be opening the oysters. So either get your fishmonger to do it, or do as I do: invite a friend over who loves to shuck oysters and share the task!

SERVES 6 AS AN APPETIZER OR 3 AS A PLAT DU JOUR

EQUIPMENT: oyster knife, kitchen towel or oyster glove, shaved ice

PREPARATION TIME: 15 minutes or more, depending on how many oysters you're opening

COOKING TIME: none

DIFFICULTY LEVEL: simple

---

36 oysters

2 shallots

⅓ cup (80 ml) best-quality red wine vinegar or sherry vinegar

Coarsely ground black pepper

ASTUCE: Ultimately, vinegar will "cook" or soften the shallots. So make your mignonette no earlier than an hour in advance of when you'll serve it, not the night before.

1. Shuck the oysters (see "Shucking Oysters" on the following page) and put them in the refrigerator. Prepare a platter of ice and keep that in the freezer. Right before serving but no earlier, transfer the oysters to the ice.

2. Carefully mince the shallots so the pieces are as even as you can get them.

3. Add the shallots to the vinegar, stir, and set aside.

4. Just before serving, transfer the shallot mixture to serving dishes. Grind black pepper over each dish.

5. Serve the oysters with the mignonette alongside.

SHUCKING OYSTERS

To shuck an oyster: Rinse the oysters under cool running water, to remove any sand or loose bits on them. Now, get yourself an oyster knife and an oyster glove. Or you can use a towel; whatever you do, protect your hand. Holding the oyster cupped side down in your protected hand, go into the oyster on the side with the knife blade, wiggling it as you apply steady—but not hugely strong—pressure. If the knife doesn't go into the oyster on the side, you can try slipping it in more toward the back of the shell—each oyster species is slightly different; some are more accessible from the side, others from the back. Just keep checking around; don't give up. Once you've shucked a couple of oysters, you'll be an expert. (And if you don't want to fool around with shucking oysters, get someone else, such as the fishmonger, to do it for you!)

If you need more help, a great many videos online can provide further instruction and a visual on how to do this. Simply jump on the Internet and do a quick search; it's easy to learn with just a little research.

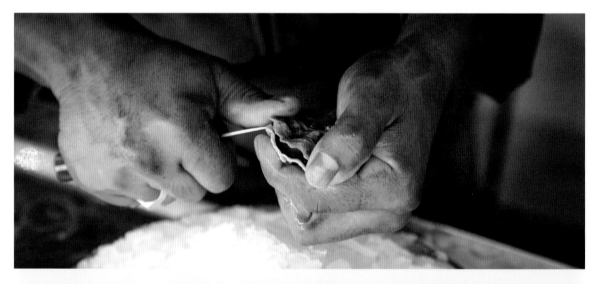

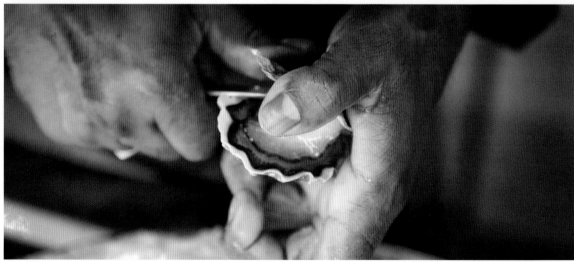

Tapenade with Green and Black Olives

TAPENADE AUX OLIVES VERTES ET NOIRS

Nothing says "Provence" more than this savory, flavorful combination of the region's finest ingredients—olives, garlic, anchovies, and olive oil! Of course, tapenade has infiltrated all of France, and is often served as an appetizer with the aperitif, with toasts or crudités (fresh vegetables), to whet the pre–plat du jour palate. Your favorite rosé goes particularly well with tapenade!

SERVES 12

EQUIPMENT: shallow nonreactive bowl (optional), mortar and pestle or food processor

PREPARATION TIME: 15 minutes (30 minutes if soaking the anchovies)

COOKING TIME: none

DIFFICULTY LEVEL: simple

---

8 top-quality anchovy fillets, preferably those from Collioure, or packed in salt

¼ cup (60 ml) dry white wine, such as Sauvignon Blanc (optional)

2 cups (400 g) best-quality, brine-cured green and black olives, pitted

1 tablespoon capers, preferably packed in salt, rinsed

1 teaspoon Dijon mustard

2 garlic cloves

4 to 6 tablespoons (60 to 90 ml) olive oil

Freshly ground black pepper

Thyme flower blossoms for garnish

ASTUCES: Best-quality olives can be found in olive bars in grocery stores or at specialty shops, either in the olive bar or in jars. My favorite olives for tapenade are either Niçoise, Lucques, or Tanche (from southern France); a black olive called Beldi that is cured and then called "Greek olive"; or a good cured green olive, ideally from Spain.

To pit olives (if you don't have an olive pitter), line up several on a cutting board, smack them with the flat of a chef's knife, and the pit will practically walk out on its own.

1. If using anchovy fillets in oil from Collioure or other excellent-quality anchovies, there is no need to soak the fillets in the white wine, which is done simply to remove some of their salt. If using anchovy fillets packed in salt, the soaking is necessary. Place the anchovies in a shallow nonreactive bowl and cover them with the wine. Let them sit for 15 minutes, then drain and pat dry.

2. Place all the ingredients, except the oil and pepper, in a mortar and pestle and grind until the olives are ground to a thick puree. Alternatively, this can be done in a food processor. Slowly add the oil until it loosens the puree just slightly and is fully incorporated. Season to taste with freshly ground black pepper.

3. Transfer to a serving dish, garnish with the thyme blossoms, and serve with freshly toasted bread or high-quality crackers. Tapenade will keep in an airtight container in the refrigerator for at least a week. You may need to "top up" the garlic.

CHAPTER 2
POULTRY

POULTRY IS ONE OF THE STARS of the plat du jour, and French poultry—from the guinea fowl to the duck, goose, quail, or pigeon—is a star in its own right. France is a rural country with an economy heavily based on agriculture; even in the biggest cities, a farm is never far away! And lucky for us, this means that high-quality poultry is readily available. The "average" farm-raised fowl in France is a thing of beauty, for it offers texture and flavor yet cooks to an astonishing tender juiciness. Some, such as the famed *poulet de Bresse* or its cousin, the *pintade de Bresse* (guinea fowl), sport a quality label and can cost the equivalent of higher education. But even the humbler varieties are pure heaven on the plate. For the recipes here, find the best poultry you can and enjoy!

Golden Roast Chicken with Shallots and Apples

POULET ROTI AUX ÉCHALOTES ET POMMES

This is a gorgeous plat du jour for an autumn or winter family dinner night, or for a group of friends who gather for a hearty, relaxed, delicious meal. It's easy to prepare, and everyone—and I mean everyone—loves it. It's a very typical sort of plat du jour: simple, unassuming, yet so scrumptious you can't believe it took so little energy to put together. And while I say this is a homey dish, it dresses up very well, so don't hesitate to serve it to the boss when she comes for supper!

I like to serve a rich and buttery white here, such as a white Burgundy or a lovely white from Gaillac. Both are made from the Chardonnay grape and will enhance this dish.

SERVES 6 TO 8

EQUIPMENT: kitchen twine, roasting pan, cutting board that collects juices

PREPARATION TIME: 20 to 25 minutes, depending on your trussing skills!

COOKING TIME: 1 hour

DIFFICULTY LEVEL: simple

One 3½- to 4-pound (1.8 to 2 kg) chicken with giblets

Coarse sea salt and freshly ground black pepper

2 fresh or dried imported bay leaves

1 orange or 2 clementines, cut into quarters

1 to 2 cups (250 to 500 ml) water

6 ounces (180 g) shallots, kept whole, peeled

¼ cup (60 ml) red wine vinegar

4 medium tart apples (5.5 ounces; 145 g), such as Cox's Orange Pippin or Pink Lady, peeled, cored, and cut into eighths

1 cup (10 g) fresh flat-leaf parsley leaves

1. Preheat the oven to 425°F (220°C).

2. Remove the giblets from the chicken. Season the cavity with salt and pepper, return the giblets to the cavity, and add the bay leaves and orange quarters. Truss the chicken.

3. Place the chicken in a roasting pan and pour ¾ cup (185 ml) water around the chicken. Place the pan in the center of the oven and roast until the chicken is turning golden, about 30 minutes. Check to be sure the bottom of the pan is wet and add more water if necessary.

4. Add the shallots to the pan around the chicken, shaking the pan to roll them around in the liquid, and return the pan to the oven, adding water regularly, enough to keep the juices from burning on the bottom of the pan. Roast the chicken until the juices run golden when you pierce the thigh joint with a sharp knife, about 30 additional minutes. About 10 minutes before the chicken is finished roasting, pour the vinegar over the chicken This will crisp the skin and add a touch of welcome acidity to the sauce.

(continued)

ASTUCES: Trussing the chicken holds the wings and the legs of the bird to the body, allowing everything to roast evenly and emerge from the oven moist and delicious. I also recommend stuffing the chicken with either an orange or a lemon, because I love the slight additional flavor they add during roasting. Then squeeze them over the chicken right before serving.

5. When the chicken is roasted, transfer it from the roasting pan to a cutting board that collects juices, breast side down.

6. Add the apples to the shallots in the roasting pan, season with salt and pepper, shake the pan to roll the shallots and apples in the juices, and return to the oven. Roast until the apples and shallots are golden, stirring once or twice so they roast evenly, and making sure to add just enough water to keep the juices from burning to the bottom of the pan, about 20 minutes.

7. Cut the chicken into serving pieces. Squeeze the orange quarters over the chicken (use tongs to remove from the cavity—the fruit will be *hot*).

8. Remove the apples and shallots from the oven.

9. Mince the parsley, add it to the apples and shallots, stir, then pour over the chicken and serve immediately.

Roast Chicken with Fresh Tarragon

POULET ROTI À L'ESTRAGON

This is a traditional recipe from the Loire Valley, where the soil is rich; the air, soft; and the crops and herbs, abundant. Issue from this sort of terroir is the tender-fleshed, farm-raised chicken which, when roasted, turns mouth-melting. Add fresh tarragon and a dollop of cream and you've got a wonderful dish that is quick and easy to make. Serve this with a lightly chilled Sancerre Blanc.

SERVES 4 TO 6

EQUIPMENT: kitchen twine, roasting pan, cutting board that collects juices

PREPARATION TIME: 15 minutes

COOKING TIME: 1 hour 15 minutes

DIFFICULTY LEVEL: simple

One 3½- to 4-pound (1.8 to 2 kg) chicken, with giblets

Coarse sea salt and freshly ground black pepper

About 5 large fresh tarragon stems

½ cup (125 ml) dry white wine, such as sauvignon blanc

⅓ cup (80 ml) crème fraîche or heavy cream

⅓ cup loosely packed (about 3 g) fresh tarragon leaves

Fresh tarragon sprigs for garnish

1. Preheat the oven to 450°F (230°C).

2. Remove the giblets from the cavity of the chicken. Season the cavity with salt and pepper, return the giblets to the cavity, and stuff the tarragon stems into the cavity to infuse the meat. Truss the chicken and place in a roasting pan. Roast until the skin is golden, puffed, and crisp and the thigh joint moves easily in the socket, 1 hour to 1 hour 15 minutes, depending on the size of the bird.

3. Remove the chicken from the oven, season it all over with salt and pepper, then transfer, breast side down, to a cutting board that collects juices. The chicken needs to rest for at least 20 minutes and will stay hot for up to 40 minutes.

4. To make the sauce, place the roasting pan over medium-high heat. Add the wine and deglaze the pan, scraping up any browned bits. Cook until the wine is reduced by about one-third, about 5 minutes. Pour any juices from the bird into the sauce and reduce by about half. You should have several tablespoons of juice.

5. While the cooking juices are reducing, cut the chicken into serving pieces and arrange them on a warmed serving platter.

6. Whisk the cream into the cooking juices and heat it just to the boiling point.

(continued)

7. Coarsely chop the tarragon leaves and whisk them it into the sauce. Taste for seasoning and adjust.

8. Serve the chicken, garnished with the tarragon sprigs, and the sauce separately; alternatively, pour the sauce over the chicken and garnish with the tarragon sprigs.

ASTUCES: When the recipe says to heat the cream once it is added to the sauce, be sure to do so *just* to the boiling point. You don't want the cream to boil, because it will lose some of its fresh flavor if it does.

Remember to chop herbs for the sauce right before you use them, so you get the fullness of their flavor.

Placing herbs in the cavity of the chicken allows them to infuse its meat with flavor.

Cider-Braised Duck with Onions, Shallots, Leeks, and Carrots

CANARD FAÇON BOUCHER

Duck—roasted, braised, sautéed—is a plat du jour mainstay in France, a favorite for any day of the week. I get mine either from the market, where Loïc Metrot sells those from his farm, or from my next-door neighbor, butcher Stephan Coutard. M. Coutard knows that I write books about food and is always ready to give advice and suggestions, and he happily gave me this recipe one day when I asked him for duck legs and thighs. He is precise with his instructions, since his goal in life is to make sure that what people buy from his shop is perfectly cooked. I guarantee this recipe fits the bill, and it's a perfect one for a cool summer or fall day, or for a cozy moment around the fire in winter. And best of all, this cooks on its own. Just check on it every 20 minutes to turn the duck pieces. Serve this with hard cider, preferably dry (brut).

SERVES 4

EQUIPMENT: large heavy saucepan or Dutch oven

PREPARATION TIME: 15 minutes

COOKING TIME: 1 hour 50 minutes

DIFFICULTY LEVEL: simple

---

1 tablespoon olive oil or duck fat

4 duck legs and thighs (1¾ pounds; 875 g total), with skin

Coarse sea salt and freshly ground black pepper

4 medium onions (about 5 ounces; 150 g each), cut into eighths

3 large shallots (2 ounces; 60 g each), cut in half lengthwise

1 pound (500 g) carrots, trimmed, very thinly sliced on the diagonal

2 fat leeks (18 ounces; 540 g total), trimmed and cleaned, cut into thin rounds

2 cups (500 ml) hard apple cider, white wine, or water

2 garlic cloves, cut in half

2 fresh or dried imported bay leaves

About 10 fresh thyme branches

Fresh flat-leaf parsley sprigs for garnish

1. Heat the oil in a large heavy saucepan over medium-high heat until it is hot but not smoking. Add the duck legs and thighs and brown on the skin side. Season them with salt and pepper. Once the skin is golden, about 5 minutes, remove the duck from the pan and drain away all but 1 tablespoon of fat in the pan. Return the duck to the pan, then add the onions, shallots, carrots, and leeks. Stir so all is blended, season with salt and pepper, then add the cider, garlic, bay leaves, and thyme. Shake the pan so the ingredients settle into the pan.

(continued)

2. Bring the cider to a boil, then lower the heat so it is simmering merrily. Cover and cook until the duck is tender, about 1½ hours, turning regularly (about every 20 minutes) so that the duck cooks evenly.

3. When the duck is tender, remove it from the pan. Increase the heat under the pan to medium-high and reduce the cooking liquid by about one-third, about 5 minutes.

4. To serve, remove the vegetables from the pan, discarding the bay leaves and thyme. Place the duck in the center of a shallow soup bowl, top with equal amounts of the vegetables, and drizzle with the sauce. Garnish with the parsley and serve.

ASTUCES:
- You can purchase duck legs and thighs online from D'Artagnan Foods or in certain specialty markets.
- Get creative and cut the vegetables in different shapes to add to your presentation.
- You may have some juices and vegetables left over after the meal; they make a fantastic soup. Simply add 1 cup each (250 ml) of hard cider and water, or just water. Bring to a boil, lower the heat, and cook for about 30 minutes. Taste for seasoning. I like to add a couple of tablespoons of red wine vinegar, too, if I've used additional cider for the soup because it makes it just slightly sweet-and-sour. To serve it, I toast country bread, rub it with garlic, and place a slice in the bottom of each shallow soup bowl before adding the soup. So good.

Braised Guinea Hen with Morel Cream

PINTADE BRAISÉE À LA CRÈME AU MORILLES

This elegantly simple recipe is so delicious it could be fit for royalty, which may have been part of its origin. Imagine—a dish made for a queen, and still fit for one!

The traditional version of this recipe calls for vin jaune, a wine of the Jura region, which is east of Dijon. And while I love vin jaune, it's difficult to find and usually expensive. So instead I use a wine from the Loire made with the Pacherenc grape, or a Chenin Blanc, both of which have rich minerality. Serve plenty of fresh baguette alongside this dish.

SERVES 4 TO 6

EQUIPMENT: heatproof bowl and cheesecloth (if using dried morels), large heavy-bottomed saucepan, large heavy skillet with lid

PREPARATION TIME: 15 minutes

COOKING TIME: about 35 minutes

DIFFICULTY LEVEL: simple

FOR THE MORELS:

2 cups (about 200 g) fresh morels (about 5 small per person), or 1 cup (100 g) dried

FOR THE GUINEA HEN:

1 tablespoon olive oil

1 tablespoon unsalted butter

One 3½- to 4-pound (1.8 to 2 kg) guinea hen or chicken, cut into serving pieces

Fine sea salt and freshly ground black pepper

2 medium onions (6 ounces; 180 g each), thinly sliced

4 large shallots (1 scant ounce; 25 g), thinly sliced

1 cup (250 ml) white wine

1 cup (250 ml) Chicken Stock (page 332) or water

1 Bouquet Garni (page 338)

TO FINISH THE MORELS AND SAUCE:

1 tablespoon unsalted butter

Fine sea salt and freshly ground black pepper

1 cup (250 ml) crème fraîche

2 large egg yolks

FOR GARNISH:

Fresh flat-leaf parsley sprigs

1. Prepare the morels: If you are using fresh morels, clean them as best you can, using a pastry brush and your fingers. Avoid rinsing them if you can, but if you must, then go ahead, briefly, under cold running water. If the morels are very large, cut them either in half or into quarters, lengthwise. If you are using dried morels, place them in a heatproof bowl and pour boiling water over them to cover. Let them sit until tender, generally about 10 minutes, then remove from the water. Strain the hot liquid through cheesecloth to remove any grit, and reserve. You can use this liquid as part of the liquid needed to cook the guinea hen. Set the morels aside.

2. Prepare the guinea hen: Heat the oil and butter in a large heavy-bottomed saucepan over medium-high heat. When the oil is hot and the butter is foaming but not browning, add the guinea hen, season with salt and pepper, and cook until the pieces are browned. Then turn, season, and brown on the other side, about 8 minutes total. Transfer the pieces to a platter and add the onions and shallots to the pan. Cook, stirring often, until they are translucent through and tender, about 5 minutes. As the onions soften, they'll give up some liquid, which will help deglaze some of the caramelization from the bottom of the pan.

3. Return the guinea hen pieces to the pan with any juices that have come from it, nestling it among the onions and shallots. Stir in the wine and the chicken stock or water (with the morel liquid, if you've got it), scraping the bottom of the pan to lift the remaining caramelized bits. Add the bouquet garni and bring the liquids to a boil. Lower the heat so that the liquids are simmering. Cover the pan and cook, turning the guinea hen pieces from time to time until they are cooked through, 30 to 35 minutes.

4. About 10 minutes before the guinea hen pieces are fully cooked, melt the butter for the morels in a large heavy skillet over medium heat. When the butter is foaming, add the morels, season them with salt and pepper, cover, and cook, stirring frequently, until they are tender, about 5 minutes. Add ½ cup (125 ml) of the cooking broth from the guinea hen and let it reduce by about half, then stir in half of the crème fraîche. Remove from the heat.

5. When the guinea hen is cooked, transfer the pieces to a large warmed platter. Reduce the cooking liquid until about ¼ cup (60 ml) remains in the pan. Stir in the morels and their sauce.

6. Whisk the egg yolks into the remaining crème fraîche. Whisk in 2 tablespoons of the liquid from the morels and the guinea hen, then pour the mixture into the pan with the morels, stirring so it is completely incorporated. Cook, stirring and being careful not to let the mixture boil, until the sauce thickens to the texture of heavy cream, 3 to 5 minutes. Adjust the seasonings and pour it over the guinea hen. Garnish with the parsley sprigs and serve.

ASTUCES:

- Use fresh morels if you can find them, though the dried version is a perfect substitute. And the beauty of the dried morel is that when you reconstitute it, there is morel-flavored water to add to your sauce! You'll need to strain it through cheesecloth before adding it to the sauce.
- If you can't find a guinea hen, use a good farm-raised chicken here.
- Why use both olive oil and butter? Because you're after the buttery flavor, and the oil keeps the butter from burning.

BRAISED GUINEA HEN
WITH MOREL CREAM

HAPPY TOASTS WITH CHICKEN
LIVERS, LARDO, AND CAPER SAUCE

Happy Toasts with Chicken Livers, Lardo, and Caper Sauce

LES TOASTS HEUREUSES AUX FOIES DE VOLAILLES ET SAUCE VERTE

This is a lovely and lively plat du jour inspired by a tiny little spot in the 12th arrondissement called Miss Lunch. The Miss of the Miss Lunch is Claude Cabri, who regales her clients every day with imaginative plats du jour that are served only at lunch. Tables spill out onto the sidewalk and there is rarely a spare spot, her dishes are so well loved.

This, she says, is her most frequently requested plat du jour. And I understand why. With one bite, you break into a smile and feel happy. The flavors are so lively, so unexpected, and so much fun!

The trick to this very simple recipe is in the timing. The toast must be hot enough to melt the lardo (or the fat in the guanciale, if that's what you're using), and then the chicken livers must be hot going on top. Once you've got the hang of it, it's an easy main dish, served with a salad on the side, such as A Classic Green Salad (page 265). As Claude says, "Once it's made, you want to wolf it down real fast!" This is wonderful with a light, bright Anjou.

SERVES 6

EQUIPMENT: medium bowl, medium heavy skillet

PREPARATION TIME: 2 hours for marinating the chicken livers; 15 minutes after this

COOKING TIME: 10 minutes max

DIFFICULTY LEVEL: simple

FOR THE CHICKEN LIVERS:

6 tablespoons tamari or soy sauce

One 2-inch (5 cm) piece fresh ginger, peeled and minced (about 1 tablespoon minced)

2 tablespoons dark brown sugar

½ teaspoon curry powder, such as Madras

1 pound (500 g) chicken livers, trimmed

FOR ASSEMBLING THE TOASTS:

1 tablespoon olive oil

12 slices country-style bread that measure about 3½-by-3½ inches (9-by-9 cm)

12 very thin slices lardo (about 0.3 ounce; 10 g each), guanciale, or very fatty prosciutto cut into ½-inch (1.3 cm) strips, crosswise

1 recipe Sauce Verte (page 328)

Fresh flat-leaf parsley sprigs for garnish

1. Marinate the chicken livers: Whisk together the tamari, ginger, brown sugar, and curry powder in a medium bowl. Add the chicken livers, mix, and marinate at room temperature for 2 hours.

2. Just before you are ready to serve the toasts, either preheat the broiler or prepare to toast the bread in a toaster.

3. Drain the chicken livers and discard their marinade.

4. Heat the oil in a medium heavy skillet set over medium-high heat. When the oil is hot, add the chicken livers and cook, stirring and shaking the pan, until they are cooked through, 4 to 5 minutes.

5. Toast the bread while the livers are cooking.

6. To serve, place two hot toasts in the center of each of six heated salad plates. Lay enough slices of lardo crosswise on the toasts to cover them. Top each toast with an equal number of chicken livers, and pour at least 1 tablespoon of Sauce Verte over each toast. Garnish with the parsley sprigs and serve immediately.

ASTUCES:
- The easiest way to serve this is to cut each toast into 2-inch (5 cm) pieces.
- Note that the chicken livers marinate for 2 hours, so plan ahead.
- Tamari is a soy sauce with a richer, deeper flavor than regular soy sauce. If you can't find it, use a good-quality soy sauce.

Chicken in the Pot with Fresh Farm Vegetables

POULE AU POT

Grandmère has been making this dish for centuries and serving it for Sunday lunch; bistro chefs put this on the menu at least once a month, and regular clients flock to take advantage of it; even Michelin-starred chefs deconstruct and reconstruct it over and over again. What all these cooks seem to understand is that the mere whiff of poached chicken and vegetables is comfort for the soul. Make this with a big, fat farm-raised chicken, cook it slowly, and invite your friends and family. Everyone's life and mood will emerge afterward as just that much better than it was before they sat down! Serve this dish in two courses—the broth first and then the chicken and vegetables—along with a lightly chilled Chardonnay.

SERVES 6 TO 8

EQUIPMENT: kitchen twine, large stockpot

PREPARATION TIME: 20 to 30 minutes

COOKING TIME: 2½ hours

DIFFICULTY LEVEL: simple

FOR THE CHICKEN:

One 4- to 4½-pound (2 to 2.25 kg) chicken or stewing hen

Fine sea salt and freshly ground black pepper

2 good-size carrots (about 7 ounces; 210 g each), peeled

2 leeks (about 4 ounces; 125 g each), white and pale green parts only, well rinsed

20 fresh thyme sprigs

1 fresh or dried imported bay leaf

12 ounces (375 g) celery root, trimmed, peeled, and diced

8 cups (2 L) Chicken Stock (page 332)

5 black peppercorns

1 tablespoon coarse sea salt

FOR THE ADDITIONAL VEGETABLES:

12 ounces (375 g) celery root, cut into 2-by-¼-inch (5 cm-by-6 mm) sticks

2 fat leeks or 4 thin leeks, white parts only, well rinsed and cut into 2-inch (5 cm) lengths

2 medium carrots (about 4 ounces; 120 g each), peeled and cut on the bias into ¼-inch- (6 mm) thick slices

10 fresh thyme branches, plus more for garnish

ASTUCE: Note that this dish cooks for 2½ hours, so plan accordingly.

1. Prepare the chicken: Remove the giblets from the bird and reserve them for another purpose. Salt and pepper the cavity and truss the bird. Place it in a large stockpot.

2. Tie the carrots, leeks, thyme sprigs, and the bay leaf into a bundle, using kitchen twine. Add it to the stockpot along with the diced celery root. Add the chicken stock, then enough water to just cover the bird. A small part of the chicken will be sticking above the water, but it will sink

(continued)

below the surface as the vegetables cook. Add the pepper-corns and coarse salt and bring to a boil over high heat. Lower the heat so the liquid is boiling gently, above a simmer but not at a full boil, partially cover, and cook until the chicken is cooked through and the vegetables are tender, about 2 hours, checking the chicken and vegetables for doneness as they cook. The timing for all recipes in this book is checked carefully, but ingredients can cook at different times depending on their size, weight, and freshness.

3. Prepare the additional vegetables: Remove and discard the bundle of vegetables and celery root that cooked with the chicken in the stockpot. Add the fresh celery root, leeks, and carrots to the stockpot holding the chicken, along with the thyme sprigs, pushing them under the liquid. Cook until the vegetables are nearly tender, about 30 minutes. Remove from the heat.

4. Remove the chicken from the stockpot and remove the trussing string from the chicken.

5. Remove the meat from the chicken breast and cut it on the diagonal into 1-inch- (2.5 cm) thick slices. Much of the meat may fall from the rest of the bones of the chicken. Arrange all of the chicken on a warmed platter. Strew the vegetables over the meat, moisten with a bit of the broth, and keep warm.

6. Serve bowls of the broth and then follow with the chicken and vegetables, which you've meanwhile garnished with the herb sprigs.

POULE AU POT AND THE KING

Every dish in France, it seems, has a legend attached to it. One of my favorites is that for Poule au Pot, ascribed to King Henry IV in the 15th century. During a relatively peaceful moment between Catholics and Protestants, he visited the region of Bresse, already noted for its chickens, which had been offered as gifts to royalty since the mid-16th century. He tasted the Bresse chicken and vowed, with pomp and flourish, that not one subject in his kingdom would be without a chicken in his pot, a *poule au pot*. Thus, this luscious dish is credited to him and his reign.

Wine-Braised Chicken with Leeks and Cream

POULET À LA PICARDE

This dish combines wonderful farm-raised chicken with a garden full of leeks, a touch of white wine (which was once produced in Picardie, the region north of Paris, and if global warming continues, will be again), cream, and egg. It's a simple, traditional dish that comes from the farm and uses ingredients that most of us have on hand. Although simple in conception, the result is elegant, making this a dish you can easily serve for a dressy meal. Do include the fried bread dipped in parsley, an old-fashioned and delicious garnish that perfectly punctuates this dish, and be sure not to stint on the butter for cooking the leeks and toasts—it makes all the difference in flavor and crispness. I suggest a lovely white Sancerre here.

SERVES 6

EQUIPMENT: 2 large heavy skillets with lids

PREPARATION TIME: if cutting up the chicken, 25 minutes; if not, about 10 minutes

COOKING TIME: 1 hour 5 minutes

DIFFICULTY LEVEL: simple

---

5 tablespoons (75 g) unsalted butter, at room temperature

4 pounds (2 kg) leeks, just the white parts, cleaned and cut into ¼-inch (6 mm) rounds

Fine sea salt and freshly ground black pepper

One 3½- to 4-pound (1.8 to 2 kg) chicken, cut into 6 serving pieces

2 fresh bay leaves

15 fresh thyme sprigs

1 cup (250 ml) white wine, such as a Sancerre or a sauvignon blanc

2 large egg yolks

1½ tablespoons fresh lemon juice

¾ cup (185 ml) crème fraîche

½ cup (5 g) fresh flat-leaf parsley

Six ¼-inch- (6 mm) thick slices baguette

Fresh flat-leaf parsley sprigs for garnish

1. Melt 3 tablespoons of the butter in a large heavy skillet over medium heat. When the butter is foaming, add the leeks, stir, season with salt and pepper, lower the heat to low, and cook, uncovered, until the leeks are tender and translucent, about 20 minutes.

2. Arrange the chicken atop the leeks, pressing the pieces into the leeks. Season them with salt and pepper. Add the bay leaves and thyme, then pour the wine over all. Increase the heat under the pan to medium-high until the wine begins to boil, then lower the heat to medium, cover the pan, and cook for 20 minutes. Turn the chicken, season with salt and pepper, and continue to cook until the chicken is cooked all the way through, an additional 20 minutes, checking occasionally and stirring the leeks and chicken to be sure they aren't sticking. If they are, simply add more white wine, a few tablespoons at a time.

3. While the chicken is cooking, whisk together the egg yolks, lemon juice, and crème fraîche in a small bowl. Set aside.

4. Mince the parsley leaves and place them in a shallow bowl or plate.

5. Melt the remaining butter in a separate large heavy skillet over medium-high heat. Wait until the butter bubbles, and then add the slices of bread, cooking them until they are golden on one side, about 1 minute. Turn the slices to cook them on the other side until they are golden, less than 1 minute. Remove the bread from the pan and, using tongs to avoid burning your fingers, press one side of each toast into the minced parsley, then let cool on a wire rack.

6. When the chicken is cooked through, whisk 2 tablespoons of the cooking liquid into the egg yolk mixture, then pour the egg yolk mixture over the chicken, stirring it into the chicken and leeks. Cook until the liquid has thickened, less than 5 minutes. Do not let the mixture boil or it will curdle. Garnish with the toasted bread and the parsley sprigs, and serve immediately.

CLEANING AND TRIMMING A LEEK

Leeks are grown deep in the ground, so the lower two-thirds of the vegetable stays creamy white under the soil. Normally, soil doesn't work its way between the layers of the firm, white part, though it can, but it certainly sifts into the base of the green leaves, which need careful cleaning. The tough leaves that emerge from the soil also need cleaning and, often, trimming away because they don't soften in cooking.

- To trim a leek, remove all the tough outer leaves and cut the roots flush with the bottom, so the leek leaves stay intact.
- Trim off the ends of the green part of the leek so that you remove all the tough parts.
- If you want rounds of leek in your dish, trim away all the green leaves and use just the white part, which is firm and tight and impervious to grit.
- If you don't care about the shape, slit the leek from root to top twice, so the leek is cut in fourths lengthwise. Hold the leek under running water, root end toward you, and riffle the leaves so the water goes in among them and washes away any grit caught inside.
- Proceed with the recipe.

Chicken with Walnuts and Lemon, from the Dordogne

POULET AUX NOIX ET CITRON

This is a dish from a farm in the Dordogne, where the walnuts are sweet, fat, and buttery tasting, and they make a perfect complement to poultry. This is the kind of dish that you settle down to with comfort and anticipation, because it's got all the right elements, from cloves of garlic bursting with their sweet flavor to the golden chicken and walnuts and the tang of lemon that lifts the dish out of the ordinary. Serve this with a lovely Chardonnay.

SERVES 4 TO 6

EQUIPMENT: large heavy skillet with a lid, tongs

PREPARATION TIME: 10 minutes if the chicken is in pieces; 20 if not

COOKING TIME: 40 minutes max

DIFFICULTY LEVEL: simple

---

2 tablespoons olive oil

One 3½- to 4-pound (1.8 to 2 kg) chicken, cut into 8 pieces (2 breast pieces, 2 wings with portion of breast attached, 2 legs, 2 thighs), giblets reserved

Sea salt and freshly ground black pepper

2 tablespoons fresh lemon juice

1½ to 2 cups (375 to 500 ml) white wine, such as a sauvignon blanc

12 garlic cloves

1¼ cups (140 g) walnut halves or large pieces

Fresh flat-leaf parsley sprigs for garnish

1. Heat the oil in a large heavy skillet over medium-high heat. When the oil is hot but not smoking, brown the chicken pieces, seasoning them liberally with salt and pepper, until they are golden, about 5 minutes per side, using tongs to turn the chicken pieces.

2. Add the lemon juice, ½ cup (125 ml) of the wine, and the garlic cloves to the skillet. Lower the heat to medium, cover, and cook until the chicken is nearly cooked through, about 15 minutes. Then stir the walnuts into the skillet, along with the giblets, cover, and continue to cook for about 8 minutes. Remove the cover from the skillet and continue to cook, stirring occasionally, until the pan juices have evaporated and the chicken, walnuts, and garlic are golden, 5 to 8 minutes. Be sure to watch the walnuts, for they tend to brown easily. If they are getting too brown at any point in the cooking, remove and return them to the pan just before serving.

3. Transfer the chicken, garlic, and walnuts to a warmed serving platter and deglaze the skillet with the remaining wine, scraping the bottom to loosen any caramelized bits. Begin by adding the smaller amount of wine; if you need more, top it up with the remaining wine and cook until the sauce is reduced by half, about 4 minutes. Then pour the sauce over the chicken, garnish with the parsley sprigs, and serve immediately.

ASTUCE: Garlic turns to a sweet puree when cooked in its skin this way. Use organically produced garlic for this dish if you can, and the freshest possible walnuts.

Pastis and Saffron-Scented Chicken Ragoût

RAGOÛT DE POULET PARFUMÉ AU SAFRAN ET PASTIS

This is a dish from the sunny region of Provence, where saffron, pastis, basil, and the rest of the ingredients are produced with abandon! Like so many plats du jour, this one simply evolved thanks to the Provençale cook who used what she had on hand. Traditionally a summer dish, I serve it throughout autumn, too, while "summer" ingredients are still delicious and French evenings are still long. This is wonderful with a Bandol rosé, which echoes Provençal flavors.

SERVES 6

EQUIPMENT: large stockpot or Dutch oven, large saucepan, medium saucepan

PREPARATION TIME: about 25 minutes

COOKING TIME: 45 minutes, plus time for the chicken to cool

DIFFICULTY LEVEL: simple

FOR THE CHICKEN:

One 3-pound (1.5 kg) chicken, without giblets, trussed

1 quart (1 L) Chicken Stock (page 332)

1 fresh or dried imported bay leaf

1 teaspoon coarse sea salt

FOR THE VEGETABLES:

2 tablespoons (30 g) unsalted butter

1 tablespoon olive oil

1 medium zucchini (about 7 ounces; 210 g), trimmed and cut into ¼-inch (6 mm) dice

3 medium young onions (about 10 ounces; 300 g total), cut into ¼-inch (6 mm) dice

2 small carrots (4 ounces; 120 g total), trimmed, peeled, and cut into ¼-inch (6 mm) dice

1 medium fennel bulb (8 ounces; 250 g), trimmed and cut into ¼-inch (6 mm) dice

1 large or 2 medium tomatoes (15 ounces; 450 g), peeled, seeded, cored, and cut into ¼-inch (6 mm) dice

3 smallish new potatoes (8 ounces; 250 g total), peeled and cut into ¼-inch (6 mm) dice

Coarse sea salt

Freshly ground black pepper

¼ cup (60 ml) pastis

3 cups (750 ml) Chicken Stock (page 332)

Generous pinch of saffron

20 fresh thyme sprigs

2 fresh or dried imported bay leaves

Zest of ½ lemon (for 2 teaspoons minced zest)

FOR GARNISH:

1 cup (10 g) fresh basil leaves

---

1. Prepare the chicken: Place the chicken in a large stockpot, pour in the chicken stock, and add enough water to just cover the chicken. Add the bay leaf and salt and bring to a boil over high heat. Lower the heat so that the liquid is simmering merrily and cook until the meat is cooked through, about 45 minutes. Remove the pan from the heat and let the chicken cool in the stock.

(continued)

2. While the chicken is cooking, prepare all the vegetables: Melt the butter with the oil in a large saucepan over medium heat. Add all the vegetables except the tomato and potatoes, season with salt and pepper, and cook, covered, until the vegetables are nearly tender, stirring them from time to time so they don't stick.

3. Pour the pastis into the vegetables and light it with a match, being careful to tie your hair back and stand away from the flames. Shake the pan occasionally until the flames die down.

4. Add 1 cup (250 ml) of the chicken stock, the tomatoes, and the saffron, thyme, and bay leaves to the vegetables, stir, cover, and cook until the vegetables are tender, about 20 minutes, stirring often so they don't stick.

5. Place the remaining 2 cups (500 ml) of chicken stock and potatoes in a medium saucepan. Bring to a boil over medium-high heat, add a generous pinch of salt, and lower the heat to a merry simmer. Simmer until the potatoes are tender, about 15 minutes.

6. While the vegetables are cooking, remove the skin from the chicken and the meat from the carcass. Cut the meat into 1-inch (2.5 cm) pieces. Reserve any cooking juices.

7. When the potatoes are tender, add them with their cooking juices to the vegetables and stir. Add the chicken with its cooking juices, stir, then add the lemon zest. Bring the stock just to a boil, but not to a full boil. Mince the basil and stir it into the soup. Taste for seasoning and adjust. Serve immediately.

PEELING AND SEEDING TOMATOES

Why peel and seed a tomato? For a dish where silken texture is important, the peel can be tough and it's better to get rid of it.

The typical tomato-peeling method is to cut a cross in the skin of the tomato, right around the base. Then plunge the tomato into boiling water for about 30 seconds. However, before I turn to this method, I try to peel the tomato with a vegetable peeler. Nine times out of ten, it works perfectly, and it preserves the tomato's texture.

To seed a tomato, cut it in half horizontally and shake it, cut side down, over your trash or compost.

Rabbit with Sorrel Cream Sauce

LAPIN À LA CRÈME D'OSEILLE

If I see this dish on a menu, I claim a table immediately, for it is one of my favorite dishes of all time. Rabbit was a novelty to me when I moved to France, on the plate at least. Like many American children, I grew up reading Peter Rabbit, the personification of the bunny. When I arrived in France and had my first taste of rabbit, I broke any tendency to anthropomorphize my food; it was so tender, light, and elegantly flavorful. I teach rabbit dishes in every cooking class, for flavor and for politics. Rabbits leave a light mark on the land. If we could raise more rabbits and take attention away from red meats and pork, we could lower our carbon footprint. As a bonus, rabbit meat is lean and cooks quickly. So here is a recipe to begin your love affair with rabbit on the plate. Serve a gorgeous Sauvignon Blanc with this, and you'll be transported.

SERVES 4 TO 6

EQUIPMENT: kitchen twine, large heavy pan with 3-inch (7.5 cm) sides, slotted spoon

PREPARATION TIME: 20 minutes

COOKING TIME: 35 minutes

DIFFICULTY LEVEL: simple

---

1 tablespoon (15 ml) olive oil (optional)

5 ounces (150 g) slab bacon, rind removed if desired, cut into 1-by-½-inch (2.5-by-1.3 cm) pieces

One 3½-pound (1.8 kg) rabbit, cut into 6 pieces (2 back legs, 2 body pieces, 2 shoulder and front leg pieces), tied with kitchen twine

Fine sea salt and freshly ground black pepper

1 pound (500 g) onions, cut in half and sliced paper thin

1 cup (250 ml) dry white wine, such as a sauvignon blanc

2 fresh or dried imported bay leaves

4 cups (4 ounces; 120 g) loosely packed sorrel leaves, rinsed, patted dry, and stemmed

1 cup (250 ml) crème fraîche or heavy, non-ultrapasteurized cream

1. If your bacon is very lean, you will need to use the olive oil. Heat the oil, if using, in a large heavy pan with 3-inch (7.5 cm) sides over medium-high heat, and add the bacon. Or, with a higher fat bacon, add the bacon directly to the pan over medium-high heat. Sauté until it is just golden on all sides, 3 to 5 minutes. Remove the bacon from the pan with a slotted spoon and set it aside on a plate. Drain all but 1 tablespoon of the fat from the pan.

2. Add as many pieces of the rabbit as will comfortably fit in the pan without being overcrowded. Sprinkle them with salt and pepper and brown until golden, about 5 minutes. Turn, sprinkle with more salt and pepper, and brown the other side, 5 minutes. Repeat until all the pieces are browned. Set the rabbit aside.

3. Add the onions to the pan and cook, stirring, until they are softened, about 8 minutes. Then add the wine to the pan and scrape any browned bits from the bottom. Return the rabbit and the bacon to the pan, along with the bay leaves, pushing the rabbit down among the onions. Bring to a boil, then lower the heat to medium. Cover and simmer until

(continued)

ASTUCES:

- Often in the United States, rabbit is frozen unless you have a local butcher to provide fresh. If you cannot find rabbit, cozy up to a local chef who will know where to find one. Meanwhile, sorrel grows in so many climates and it's an annual plant. So, if you can't find it, I suggest buying seeds to plant in your yard. Otherwise, spinach is a worthy substitute.

- If you're in luck, your rabbit will come with its liver, the way rabbits do in France. If it does, sear the liver, season it, cut it in bite-size pieces, and serve it. You're in for an amazing experience.

- You need to tie the rabbit pieces with kitchen twine so each piece cooks evenly.

the rabbit is tender and nearly cooked through, turning each piece one time, about 20 minutes.

4. While the rabbit is cooking, stack the sorrel leaves atop one another and cut them crosswise into very, very thin strips (chiffonade).

5. Remove the rabbit from the pan, place it on a serving platter. Increase the heat to medium-high, and bring the cooking juices to a boil. Reduce them by two-thirds, until they are almost thick, then stir in the cream. Heat the cream gently, until it is steaming hot. Stir in the sorrel and continue to cook until the sorrel has "melted" into the sauce and turned an olive green color, about 5 minutes. Taste for seasoning.

6. Add the rabbit and any juices it has given up to the cream sauce and stir, turning each piece of rabbit so it is covered with the sauce. Leave the rabbit in the sauce until it is heated through, about 5 minutes, then transfer the rabbit pieces to a warmed platter or shallow bowl. Pour the sauce over it and serve immediately.

THE BASSE-COUR AND THE RABBIT AS POULTRY

When you buy rabbit in France, it is always sold alongside poultry, clearly segregated from the meats.

Why? It goes back to the Middle Ages and even before. The French farm was being built, and it was organized around a central courtyard, the *basse-cour* (farmyard). It was here in the basse-cour where the "little" animals were kept: chickens, geese, ducks, sometimes a pig, and yes, rabbits. These basse-cour denizens were destined for the family table; what wasn't needed there was taken to market and labeled as poultry, hence the rabbit's inclusion with its winged companions.

CHAPTER 3
SEAFOOD

SEAFOOD OF ALL KINDS is dear to the French heart. They not only love it, but they understand it, which is why when you go to a seafood stand at a French farmers' market, the only aroma you smell is that of sea brine. This clean, bright aroma signals fresh, wonderfully flavored seafood.

So that you can get the same quality of seafood, I suggest identifying a great fishmonger in your area. Make sure he or she knows you are picky, that you won't settle for less than pristine. Then you must be flexible: if you don't find the quality you like, change your menu. It's as simple as that, for poor-quality fish is impossible to hide.

For tips on buying seafood, refer to page 16. Here are a couple of websites that will help you in your choices:

Seafood Watch
www.seafoodwatch.org/seafood-recommendations/consumer-guides

Natural Resources Defense Council
www.nrdc.org/stories/smart-seafood-buying-guide

Once you've got what you want, use the recipes in this chapter and share the French love affair with seafood!

THE FRENCH FISHMONGER

It's three a.m. in the small town of Brionne in Normandy. I park my car near the ornate *mairie* (city hall), and emerge into the darkness wondering if I'm in the right place. Everything feels socked in with sleep.

Following distant sounds, I turn a corner, round a bend, and fall into a hive of near-silent, floodlit activity. I've found what I'm looking for: a fishmonger and his crew at work. I've come to spend a day with fishmonger Bruno Richomme to find out what goes on behind the scenes at my weekly farmers' market.

What I witness this chilly middle of the night is like a pantomime of strongmen, hefting boxes and bags of seafood, much of it still pulsing with life. They communicate quietly because this is a residential neighborhood. The business is here because Bruno's home is here, and when he began the business, zoning didn't matter and the scale was small. Now it's one of the biggest fish businesses in the region, and he's built a sort of warehouse to accommodate it. Which means that six out of seven days a week, these men are right here, shifting the tons of seafood that someone else, up even earlier and braving even colder temperatures, has caught and delivered.

After quiet greetings, I dodge the crew and peek into bags holding sea snails and mussels. I lift the lid on Styrofoam boxes to see floppy whole hake, rigid sardines, thick-scaled herring, silvery blue mackerel. Yet another box holds slimy skate wings. Slime is, I learn, a good thing for it indicates freshness.

I recognize the men working here from the farmers' market, and I know them all to be loud wisecrackers. Now they're silent, bent on getting the tons of seafood on the pavement into the waiting vehicles, which will speed away onto country roads to make deliveries and meander toward farmers' markets. Bruno, whose business is called Chez Bulot, has stands at thirteen different markets each week. This is in addition to supplying restaurants, seafood shops, and supermarkets throughout the region.

There isn't a shred of romanticism to this work so far, yet I'm enchanted, as though these silent, working men who've left their warm beds are doing this just for me. In a sense they are, as I'm a loyal customer. Once the men have filled the trucks, I climb into one with Christian Lainé, a wiry, sandy-haired man who has been in the fish business for the past five years. We're going to end up at a market in the town of L'Aigle, but first we've got some deliveries to make.

It will take us a good two hours to get to L'Aigle, and we'll cover about 93 miles (150 kilometers) before we do. First, Christian offloads a dozen Styrofoam boxes of fish at a supermarket called Leclerc. Our next stop is a gorgeous village, where we slide through streets just barely wide enough for the truck and pull up near a church, lit up so it stands above the houses and shops around it. Christian stashes boxes of seafood behind a large garbage can, where he tells me the proprietor will arrive to gather it in about an hour. The morning is cold. What happens when it's hot? "We pack the fish with ice," Christian says. "It's not perfect, but it stays fresh enough."

We stop next at a fish shop, where the proprietor and Christian share a smoke. I realize how much socializing even a seafood delivery man does. "It's part of the job," Christian says. "We want our customers happier than the rest."

Two more stops in two different villages then we strike out for L'Aigle, 37 miles (60 kilometers) away. The roads are empty, the sky still black. Christian keeps up a steady patter about fish, the market, the people.

Before I know it, we've arrived at a small tree-lined square at the back of L'Aigle's main square. "We love this market," Christian says. "They put all the fishmongers together and we have fun stealing customers from one another."

I ponder this economic model as I climb out of the truck. It's that hour just before daylight, when everything is slightly blurry. The fish stand is lit, and under those lights Bruno's team is filling up tables with ice and arranging a briny world on top. The team is small, consisting of Pascal Gosse, Bruno's right-hand man; Beatrice Caron, who has worked for the company for 25 years; and Guillaume Baron, a 16-year-old apprentice. Unlike earlier this morning, there is much laughter and conversation, as colleagues from the various seafood stands shout ferocious insults at each other. If I hadn't lived in France for a long time, I'd think a small civil war was brewing, given the scale of insults. But no, this is life as usual.

We are deep into scallop season, every available hand is busy shucking the pinkish bivalves as fast as they can, and clients are beginning to line up. I know how to shuck scallops, I say, and offer to help. Pascal silently hands me a knife and an apron, and pretty soon I'm slicing off top shells, leaving the sweet, still moving muscle on the bottom shell. Until today I'd thought I was accomplished; I see the error of my ways as I shuck one to everyone else's half dozen.

I discover that scallop boats in the English Channel go out for 45 minutes each day during the season, which begins in November and lasts until early May, if they're lucky enough to have been awarded a license. "Lucky" is the word, because many apply, but not all are accepted; the scallop is a protected resource. The state wants people to enjoy them for generations to come.

Seven thirty is coffee break time, and we all snake through the square around paella and roast chicken stands, clothing, cheese, and butcher trucks to a café where the little *express* are served without being ordered. Paper-wrapped packages of pork pâté and long baguettes come out, too,

and there's mustard on the table, all for breakfast. After a second round of coffee for everyone, it's back to work, where even more early-bird customers await.

Pascal, crumpled cap atop tousled hair, apron enveloping his ample form, turns on, hawking at the top of his lungs as he laughs, jokes, and charms the customers into buying twice what they thought they needed. Meanwhile, Bruno has arrived and is tying on his floor-length apron as he greets customers. I step back to watch this crew ease into their public personas. It's eight thirty a.m., midday for all of them.

The next five hours go by in a blur of customers, most of whom I am introduced to with a story

or a whisper to explain who they are in the vast society of Chez Boulot. It's a familial kind of business, and Bruno knows the back story of almost everyone he sells to.

I meet Marcel, a rakish artist who buys liberally and speaks of his upcoming car trip to Sudan. A shabbily dressed man and woman amble up and are greeted by all at Chez Bulot, then left alone as they peer at everything on offer. Bruno, whose eyes are everywhere as he shucks scallops, makes change, shakes hands, kisses children, asks after the mother-in-law, spies them. He quietly turns to his truck, takes out a large box of yesterdays' mackerel, and sets it on the ground. When the couple makes their way to him, he greets them warmly and discreetly hands over the box. Hands are shaken all around and the couple ambles off.

"He's a potato farmer who lives with his five sisters; they sometimes have a child with them.

We don't dare ask whose it is; they always take our day-old mackerel," Bruno explains. "It's perfectly good, they love it, they bring me potatoes . . ."

He doesn't finish his sentence, interrupted by a woman who wants 10 pounds of scallops, shucked now, so she can run home and freeze them. Others crowd up to the counter to ask about the cod; request their salmon be scaled, filleted, cut into serving pieces; wonder at how long they should cook the snaky-skinned shark; inquire whether the sardines are best grilled or pan-fried. Each question is met with a careful response as the crew satisfies all desires on a makeshift table, with a large bucket of fresh water on the ground for dipping the knife between jobs.

By ten a.m. the stand is choked with customers. Christian has grown silent with concentration, young Guillaume sticks to selling scallops, and Ms. Caron is the busiest with the knife. Bruno is the one customers want and they tend to crowd him. He's generous with his attention to them as he works faster than the rest combined.

The clock strikes noon and the crowd begins to thin. There are still plenty of customers, but the fishmongers are now back to bantering with one another. From start to finish, this job is just what it seems—back-breaking work in conditions most people would hate; a cold, wet service job, filled with slime, flying scales, and the occasional bad-tempered customer. It appears completely compelling as well, given the fond camaraderie. And it is rife with tender vignettes such as the potato farmer and his sister; the little girl who is given a handful of her favorite shrimp, "for your aperitif"; or the father who is in search of affordable lobster to serve at a family celebration. In moments like this, Bruno will take it all in and the price of lobster or shrimp will drop for just a moment. Bruno is in love with seafood, and understands that it is call for celebration, and that celebrations call for it. He wants to give his clients the opportunity to revel in moments of luxury that lobster and shrimp represent.

An hour later the tables are cleaned, the leftovers are carefully packed back into the trucks, which one by one drive away. I get a ride back with Bruno, who talks about this work that consumes his life. "It's full of stories, it's cold, it can drive you crazy with the hours," he says. "But then there's that one small thing, that one little story that brings it all into focus."

We pull up where I met them all at three a.m. It's three p.m. and Bruno's day is far from over as he prepares to shuck pounds more scallops, ready a banquet, order what he needs for tomorrow. He shakes my hand absently as his cell phone rings.

There's more I want to know, but there's no time to ask. I'll catch him tomorrow at my market, where I'll arrive at eight thirty, more than five hours into his workday.

It's all in the life of a fishmonger.

Anchoïade with Seasonal Raw Vegetables

ANCHOÏADE AUX CRUDITÉS

The anchovy has been a vital part of the Provençal economy since time began. Fished by the millions, then preserved in salt or oil, it was shipped throughout the world and made its way to the plate, where it was strewn over salads, tucked between tomatoes, combined with olives, or served in this marvelous "sauce" or dip, *anchoïade*. Served warm, it demands the freshest raw vegetables and excellent country bread.

There is a protocol for eating anchoïade: when you dip a vegetable or piece of bread into the anchoïade, pass it over your anchovy toast and let the excess anchoïade drop onto the toast—this moistens it, and you get all the flavor!

Often anchoïade is a first course, but here, with the anchovy toasts, it becomes a full meal, turned magic when served with any Provençal rosé.

SERVES 4 TO 6

EQUIPMENT: small saucepan

PREPARATION TIME: 15 minutes

COOKING TIME: 5 minutes

DIFFICULTY LEVEL: simple

FOR THE ANCHOÏADE:

40 anchovy fillets, preferably those packed in oil

½ cup (125 ml) olive oil

2 garlic cloves

1 teaspoon best-quality red wine vinegar

Freshly ground black pepper

FOR SERVING:

6 large slices country bread, plus an additional 18 (2-by-1-inch; 5-by-2.5 cm) strips

12 anchovy fillets

4 fennel bulbs (7 ounces; 210 g each), trimmed and cut into ½-inch- (1.3 cm) wide wedges

4 large carrots (7 ounces; 210 g each), trimmed and cut into ½-inch (1.3 cm) lozenges

3 small zucchini (2 ounces; 60 g each), trimmed and cut into ½-inch (1.3 cm) rounds

1 recipe Simple Boiled Potatoes (page 264), without the butter or parsley

1. Prepare the anchoïade: Place the anchovy fillets into a small saucepan and place it over medium heat. Slowly add the oil, breaking up the anchovies as you stir so they form a paste. Add the garlic, then the vinegar. Cook, stirring, just until the mixture is blended, 2 to 3 minutes. The anchovies won't be entirely smooth, and the sauce won't be emulsified—it will be a rough-looking mixture. Keep it warm over very low heat.

2. Toast the large slices of bread either under the broiler or in the toaster. When the bread is toasted, top each with two anchovy fillets, and keep them warm.

3. Arrange the vegetables and the strips of bread on a serving platter.

4. Generously season the anchoïade with pepper. Note that it isn't an emulsified sauce and that the oil rises to the surface.

5. Serve the anchoïade and the platter of bread and vegetables. To eat, dip the vegetables and/or bread into the anchoïade and enjoy with the toasts alongside.

Waterzooi

FISH SOUP FROM FLANDERS

I love the way the name of this wonderful soup slips off the tongue, as easily as the soup itself sits on your palate. The name comes from the Belgian *water* and *zooi*, "to cook or to boil." It is historically a Belgian recipe, reportedly from the city of Ghent, where Philippe Edouard Cauderlier, who wrote the first Belgian cookbook in 1861, included it in his collection. He was considered a "culinary revolutionary" because he objected to the complicated French cuisine in vogue at the time and believed instead in using the finest ingredients to make simple dishes. Waterzooi is a perfect example.

Here I've used white ocean fish, though you can use freshwater fish, too. The soup was originally thickened with bread crumbs instead of egg yolks and cream. If you're short on egg yolks, just use that traditional method instead. Serve a lightly chilled white Sancerre alongside.

SERVES 6

EQUIPMENT: large heavy stockpot, cheesecloth (optional), medium bowl, slotted ladle or spoon

PREPARATION TIME: 25 minutes

COOKING TIME: about 40 minutes

DIFFICULTY LEVEL: simple

FOR THE SOUP:

3 medium carrots (3 ounces; 90 g each), trimmed, peeled, and cut into ½-inch (1.3 cm) rounds

8 cups (2 L) Fish Stock (page 333) or water

Fine sea salt

1 medium onion (5 ounces; 150 g; if using water)

2 whole cloves (if using water)

2 thin lemon rounds (if using water)

1 fresh or dried imported bay leaf

White part of 3 medium leeks (1½ pounds; 750 g), rinsed well, cut into four 2-inch (5 cm) lengths, then each length cut lengthwise into matchsticks

2 medium onions (5 ounces; 150 g each), quartered

3 medium turnips (about 3 ounces; 90 g each), peeled, trimmed, and cut in half, then into ¼-inch- (6 mm) thick slices

6 small waxy potatoes (2 ounces; 60 g each), left whole

1 cup lightly packed (10 g) fresh flat-leaf parsley leaves

2 pounds (1 kg) various kinds of fish, including any cod, haddock, or perch, boned and skinned, rinsed and refrigerated, cut into 3-inch (7.5 cm) pieces

FOR THICKENING BROTH:

2 large egg yolks

1 cup (250 ml) heavy cream or crème fraîche

2 tablespoons fresh lemon juice

Fresh flat-leaf parsley sprigs for garnish

ASTUCE: If you don't have fish stock on hand, make your own using the recipe on page 333. You may also use water; there is a sacrifice of flavor but the waterzooi will still be delicious.

1. Prepare the soup: Place the carrots in a large heavy stock-pot and add the fish stock or water. Add 1 teaspoon of salt and bring the fish stock to a simmer. If you choose to use water, cut an onion in half and place one clove in each half. Then wrap the onion halves and 2 thin rounds of lemon in a cheesecloth and add this to the soup for flavor. (When the soup is cooked, remove the packet and discard the lemon and cloves; keep the two pieces of onion.)

2. Cook until the carrots begin to turn tender, 5 to 8 minutes. Add the bay leaf and remaining vegetables and cook until the vegetables turn tender but not soft, 15 to 20 minutes. To test for doneness, stick a sharp knife gently into each vegetable to test for tenderness.

3. Coarsely chop the parsley leaves.

4. Add the parsley to the soup, stir, then add the fish and cook until the fish is opaque through, 6 to 10 minutes, depending on the thickness of the fish. Gently transfer the fish to a shallow platter.

5. While the fish is cooking, whisk together the egg yolks, cream, and lemon juice in a medium bowl.

6. Whisk about ¼ cup (60 ml) of hot fish stock into the cream mixture, then whisk the cream mixture into the soup and cook, without letting it boil, until it has thickened to the texture of heavy cream. Return the fish with its juices to the soup and continue to cook, stirring gently, just until the fish is heated through—a minute or two. Serve immediately, garnished with parsley sprigs.

Bouillabaisse
MARSEILLAISE FISH SOUP

Bouillabaisse isn't just the culinary flag of Marseille, it's the symbol of all that is best on the French Mediterranean coast. Although it can appear complicated, it was born of simplicity and the local ingredients at hand. Fishermen at the port in Marseille docked, brought their fish up the stone stairs to the wharf, and set up shop for residents eager for their catch. What wasn't sold by midday was turned into this soup, cooked in large solid pots over a blazing fire, and eaten right there at the port. Fishermen let the soup simmer while they repaired their nets, popping their leftover fish in at the last minute. They ate the soup, floating in it rounds of yesterday's bread topped with *rouille*, a sauce made from pepper and eggs. Serve this with a lively white, red, or rosé from Collioure.

SERVES 6 TO 8

EQUIPMENT: large heavy-bottomed saucepan, food processor, baking sheet

PREPARATION TIME: 30 minutes

COOKING TIME: about 50 minutes

DIFFICULTY LEVEL: medium

FOR THE SOUP:

2 tablespoons olive oil

1 medium onion (about 5 ounces; 150 g each), minced

1 small fennel bulb (5 ounces; 150 g), coarsely chopped

8 cups (2 L) Fish Stock (page 333)

Two 3-inch (7.5 cm) strips orange zest

1 cup gently packed (10 g) fresh flat-leaf parsley leaves

Large pinch of saffron

1 tablespoon boiling water

1 teaspoon fresh lemon juice

1 pound (500 g) new potatoes, peeled and cut into ¼-inch- (6 mm) thick slices, plus 1 medium potato, cut in quarters and cooked in the soup

1½ pounds (750 g) tomatoes, cored and coarsely chopped

Sea salt and coarsely ground black pepper

2 pounds (1 kg) fish (a mixture of snapper, rockfish, lingcod, eel, monkfish, sea bream, halibut . . .), bones removed

FOR THE ROUILLE:

1 red bell pepper (8 ounces, 250 g), roasted, skin, seeds and pith removed

3 garlic cloves

1 large egg yolk

6 tablespoons (90 ml) fruity olive oil

Sea salt

FOR THE TOASTS:

1 baguette, cut into ¼-inch (6 mm) rounds

Fresh flat-leaf parsley or fennel sprigs for garnish

1. Prepare the soup: Heat the oil in a large heavy-bottomed saucepan over medium heat. Add the onion and fennel and cook, stirring frequently, until the onion is translucent, about 8 minutes. Add the fish stock, orange zest, and parsley and bring to a boil. Cover, lower the heat so the fish stock is simmering, and cook until the fennel and onion are tender through, about 5 minutes.

- Traditionally, there is no shellfish in bouillabaisse. For the fish, use the best local varieties you can find. Ideally, it will be a mix of monkfish, snapper, rockfish, sea bream, and perhaps a lingcod or halibut. If you can get your hands on some conger eel, use that, too!

- Rouille may or may not have been part of the original recipe, though southern French cooks have been making garlicky versions of mayonnaise since time immemorial. If you finish the rouille with a whisk rather than a food processor, it will be more tender than if made entirely in the processor.

2. Place the saffron in a small dish and cover it with the boiling water and lemon juice. Cover and let steep for 10 minutes.

3. Add the potatoes, tomatoes, and saffron with its steeping liquids to the broth, return to a boil and cook, partially covered, lowering the heat so the broth is simmering merrily, until the potatoes are tender through, about 15 minutes. Season the broth to your taste with salt and black pepper. Remove the quartered potato.

4. Preheat the broiler, if using for the toasts.

5. While the vegetables are cooking, prepare the rouille: Place the red pepper, quartered potato, garlic cloves, egg yolk, and 2 tablespoons (30 ml) of the olive oil in a food processor and puree. Either transfer the mixture to a bowl and whisk in the remaining olive oil to make a rough puree or add the oil while the ingredients are still in the food processor, with the food processor running, and process until all the ingredients form a rough puree, being sure to add the oil slowly so it emulsifies with the other ingredients. Season to taste with salt. Reserve.

6. Make the toasts: Arrange the rounds of baguette on a baking sheet and place under the broiler, about 5 inches (12.5 cm) from the heat source. Toast until golden, turn them over, and toast until golden on the other side. Alternatively, you can toast the bread in a toaster.

7. Add the fish to the soup, beginning with any fish steaks that are thicker than most fillets, which will take longer to cook, gently immersing it in the liquid. Cook until the fish is nearly opaque through, 4 to 5 minutes, then add the remaining fish, gently immersing it as well, and cook until all the fish is opaque through, an additional 3 to 5 minutes.

8. To serve, transfer the fish to a warmed platter, moisten with a bit of the broth, garnish with herbs, then serve.

9. When your guests have finished the fish, ladle the soup into warmed, shallow soup bowls. Serve with the toasts and the rouille on the side, to be floated in the soup.

Fish and the Virgin Sauce of Tomatoes, Shallots, and Fresh Herbs

POISSON, SAUCE VIERGE

Sauce vierge (virgin sauce) has long been in the annals of French cuisine. The original was a frothy blend of butter, lemon juice, salt, and pepper, and it was served over vegetables. Fast-forward to the '70s, when another virgin sauce appeared, this one attributed to Michel Guérard, who changed the course of French cuisine because he focused on light and fresh, and on olive oil instead of butter. Depending on which side of the sauce fence you are on, he got the French feeling guilty about food because he took it from its substantial, buttery, and creamy world into a light, poetic universe. At first, it was almost too light and too poetic—servings were teeny, fat was nearly absent. But Chef Guérard's style was inspiring because of its color and vivid flavor, and we have him to thank for an overall "lightening" of French cuisine. This sauce is a perfect example. Serve this with an Entre-Deux-Mers, not too chilled.

SERVES 6

EQUIPMENT: large bowl, steamer, slotted spatula

PREPARATION TIME: 20 minutes

COOKING TIME: about 5 minutes

DIFFICULTY LEVEL: simple

1½ to 2 pounds (750 to 1 kg) cod or other white fish fillets that are about 1½ inches (4 cm) thick, cut into 6 serving-size pieces

2 tablespoons fresh lemon juice

Fine sea salt and freshly ground black pepper

⅓ cup (80 ml) olive oil

1 medium shallot (⅔ ounce; 20 g), diced

3 medium waxy potatoes (3 ounces; 90 g), sliced very thin (if new potatoes, no need to peel them)

1 cup (10 g) mixed fresh herb leaves, such as basil, parsley, tarragon, or thyme for garnish

1½ pounds (750 g) very ripe tomatoes, peeled if you have thick-skinned tomatoes

1. Remove any bones from the fish, then rinse and refrigerate.

2. Place the lemon juice, salt, and a touch of pepper in a large bowl. Slowly whisk in the olive oil. Fold in the shallot and set aside.

3. Fill a steamer with 3 cups (1.5 L) of water and bring it to a boil over medium-high heat. Oil the basket of the steamer and set the potatoes in the steamer. Season them lightly with salt and pepper, cover the steamer, and steam until the potatoes are nearly tender, about 4 minutes. Set the fish atop the potatoes, season lightly with salt and pepper, and place the basket carefully above the boiling water (so you don't burn yourself). Steam the fish until it is nearly opaque through, 4 to 5 minutes, depending on the thickness of the fillets. When the fish is cooked, carefully transfer it with a slotted spatula to a plate or platter so it can give up its liquid. If the potatoes are cooked through,

(continued)

remove the steamer from the heat and leave the potatoes in the steamer basket for now.

4. To finish the sauce, mince the herbs and whisk them into the lemon mixture. Then fold in the tomatoes. Adjust the seasoning—you'll want to be generous with salt and pepper.

5. To serve, divide the potatoes among six plates, placing them right in the center of the plate. Set a fillet of fish atop the potatoes, then divide the sauce among the plates, pouring it over the fish. Garnish with herb sprigs and serve immediately.

ASTUCES:

- I give a range for the weight of the fish in this recipe because the amount will depend on the appetites of your eaters.
- You may be tempted to skin the tomatoes, but don't because the pieces hold together better with skin intact. This implies a thin-skinned tomato, such as Beef Heart or other heirloom variety. I like to include a couple of green zebra tomatoes, and if I have lovely cherry tomatoes, they go into the mix, too.

Grilled Peppers and Cream with Cod

POIVRONS GRILLÉES À LA CRÈME AU CABILLAUD

The sauce in this recipe is like a sunny vacation: it's so simple and beautiful. It came about one day when I had an excess of peppers and a crowd to feed. I put the peppers on the grill and roasted them until they were black and very soft. While the peppers were roasting, I poached garlic, then blended it with the peppers and a bit of cream and—voilà!—it turns into a plat du jour when served under a beautiful cod fillet.

If you don't have cod at your disposal, serve this sauce with the fish of your choice or alongside a roasted chicken, roasted vegetables, grilled or toasted bread . . . it's a perfect accompaniment to everything. You may even have sauce left over—do not despair. This sauce will disappear as a dip for raw vegetables, with roasted chicken, on toasted bread, and so on. A lovely Côtes Catalanes (or any Grenache/Merlot blend) completes the picture.

SERVES 6; MAKES ABOUT 2 CUPS (500 ML) SAUCE

EQUIPMENT: gas flame (broiler or grill), small saucepan, food processor, large skillet with lid, slotted spatula, linen or cotton towel, tongs, plastic scraper

PREPARATION TIME: practically none

COOKING TIME: 30 minutes

DIFFICULTY LEVEL: simple

FOR THE SAUCE:

5 good-size red bell peppers (about 6 ounces; 180 g each)

5 garlic cloves, unpeeled

Fine sea salt

½ to ¾ cup (125 to 185 ml) heavy cream

FOR THE COD:

1½ pounds (750 kg) cod loin or other thick (about 1½-inch; 4 cm) white fillet, cut into 6 serving pieces, boned if necessary, rinsed and refrigerated

½ teaspoon salt

Freshly ground black pepper

2 fresh or dried imported bay leaves

FOR GARNISH:

Piment d'Espelette or hot paprika

Fleur de sel

6 fresh basil leaves

1. Prepare the sauce: Place the peppers on a gas flame, under the broiler, or over the coals of a grill and grill until the skin is black all over, turning them regularly with tongs. When the peppers are grilled, about 6 minutes per side, depending on the heat you're using, then either put them in a paper bag or in a bowl with a lid and let them cool. When the peppers are cool enough to handle, slip off the skin. Pull out the central core of seeds, then carefully, using a plastic scraper or table knife, scrape out the rest of the seeds. Don't rinse the peppers; you'll rinse away flavor.

(continued)

ASTUCES:

- While I love to braise cod, as suggested here, you may also grill it over low heat on a plancha, bake it in a 400°F (200°C) oven, or gently cook it in butter. The operative word if you cook using any of these methods is tender. Be gentle with the cod, as it is a fragile fish, so no direct broiling or direct grilling!
- Always check fish for bones, and remove any that you find with a tweezer, a fish-bone puller, or a strawberry huller.

2. While the peppers are grilling, place the garlic cloves in a small saucepan, cover them by an inch (2.5 cm) with water, add a generous pinch of salt and a bay leaf, and bring to a boil over medium-high heat. Lower the heat so the water is simmering merrily, cover, and cook until the cloves are soft through, about 25 minutes. Remove from the heat and drain the garlic.

3. When the garlic cloves are cool enough to handle, peel them. Place them, with the cleaned, grilled peppers, in a food processor and puree until smooth. Add the cream, puree, then adjust the seasoning

4. Prepare the cod: Place the cod fillets in a large skillet and add enough water so there is ¼ inch (6 mm) in the pan. Add the salt, black pepper, and remaining bay leaf to the water, then set the cod in the pan. Turn the heat to medium-high, and when the water starts sending up bubbles from the bottom of the pan, lower the heat to medium, cover the pan, and cook until the fish is nearly but not quite opaque through, about 4 minutes, depending on the thickness of the fish. Check the fish for doneness by lifting it with a spatula—it shouldn't flake but should remain in one piece (because the very center won't be fully cooked, which is what you want). Using a slotted spatula, transfer the fish to a large plate or platter to rest while it gives up liquid. It will continue to cook once out of the pan.

5. To serve, pour a thick round of sauce in the center of six warmed dinner plates. Transfer the cod from the plate, using the slotted spatula. Before setting it on the sauce, rest it on a linen or cotton towel to absorb any liquid still on the fish, then set it on the sauce. Season the fish with the piment d'Espelette and fleur de sel, and garnish with a basil leaf. Serve immediately.

Steamed Cod with Melted Leeks and Caper Sauce

CABILLAUD À LA VAPEUR, SUR FONDU DE POIREAUX ET SAUCE VERTE

Anything on a bed of melted leeks ranks high in the French culinary repertoire because the leek is a cornerstone of French gastronomy, a vegetable that lends itself to all manner of perfection. Here, leeks almost literally melt into simple sweetness, as their slightly onion-like flavor softens into the hot, frothing butter. Cod pairs wonderfully with this delicate blend because its flavor is delicate, too. Try a chilled Sauvignon Blanc/Chenin Blanc blend here.

SERVES 6

EQUIPMENT: large heavy skillet, flat steamer (bamboo is ideal)

PREPARATION TIME: 15 minutes; 25 if you're making the Sauce Verte

COOKING TIME: 20 minutes

DIFFICULTY LEVEL: simple

---

1 pound 14 ounces (920 g) fresh cod, lingcod, or flounder fillets that are at least ½ inch (1.3 cm) thick, bones removed

2 tablespoons (30 g) unsalted butter

2 pounds (1 kg) leeks, white part with 1 inch (2.5 cm) of the green part, cleaned and cut into thin rounds

Fine sea salt and freshly ground black pepper

4 fresh or dried imported bay leaves

½ teaspoon curry powder (optional)

1 repice Sauce Verte (page 328)

Fresh flat-leaf parsley sprigs for garnish (optional)

1. Rinse and pat the fish dry and refrigerate until right before you cook it.

2. Heat the butter in a large heavy skillet over medium heat. When it is frothing and melted, add the leeks and stir until they are coated in the butter. Season with salt and pepper, stir, cover, and cook the leeks until they melt and are very tender, checking and stirring them frequently to be sure they don't turn golden, 18 to 20 minutes.

3. While the leeks are cooking, bring 3 cups (750 ml) water to a boil in the bottom half of a steamer. Lay the four bay leaves in the top half of the steamer and set the fish in the steamer over the boiling water. Cover and steam the fish until it is opaque through, 6 to 10 minutes, depending on the thickness of the fish.

4. When the fish is steamed, sprinkle it with the curry powder if desired, then transfer the top of the steamer to a large plate or platter to let the fish give up some of its liquid, for about 5 minutes.

5. Divide the leeks evenly among four plates, making a circle in the center of each plate. Set a piece of fish on top of the leeks, then drizzle each piece of fish with 2 tablespoons of Sauce Verte. Garnish with a parsley sprig if desired and serve immediately.

ASTUCE: Leeks have a soft, rich flavor, and they are one of the few vegetables I cook in butter, because the flavors blend so well.

ASTUCE: When a recipe calls for an onion to be sliced "paper thin," this isn't an exaggeration! Do your best to slice the onion that thin. Here's a tip: Slice down the center of your onion while the peel is on. Peel back the first two layers of the onion. With the onion on the flat side, use your sharp knife blade to cut thin slices, while you hang onto the onion with your opposite hand, keeping your fingers out of the way and eventually using the peel you've turned back as a handle so you get the most you can from your onion.

Smoked Herring and Potato Salad with Mustard Vinaigrette

SALADE DE HARENG FUMÉ ET POMMES DE TERRE À LA VINAIGRETTE DE MOUTARDE

While you'll find this wonderful dish in almost all cafés and bistros, it is usually served as a first course. Here, I turn it into a main course that you can play with, using temperature. If you want a warm-to-hot dish, then mix up the ingredients while the potatoes are hot and serve immediately. If you are fine with room temperature, then add the potatoes to the vinaigrette when they're hot, toss them gently and allow them to cool while they absorb the vinaigrette.

If you can't find smoked herring, use cold-smoked salmon—they're each delicious here! I often serve this salad on a bed of mixed lettuce dressed with lemon juice and olive oil, along with a hard apple cider, dry-style (brut).

SERVES 6 TO 8

EQUIPMENT: large saucepan, large bowl

PREPARATION TIME: 10 minutes

COOKING TIME: 15 minutes

DIFFICULTY LEVEL: simple

---

3 pounds (1.5 kg) waxy potatoes, peeled

2 teaspoons coarse salt

2 tablespoon red wine vinegar

Fine sea salt

2 teaspoons Dijon mustard

3 large shallots (1.5 ounces; 45 g each), sliced paper thin

3 tablespoons neutral oil, such as untoasted peanut oil

1 tablespoon olive oil

Freshly ground black pepper

1 medium red onion (about 4 ounces; 120 g), sliced paper thin

4 fillets smoked herring (about 6.5 ounces; 200 g total), cut into ½-inch (1.3 cm) cubes

½ cup (5 g) fresh flat-leaf parsley leaves

1. Place the potatoes in a large saucepan, cover them by 1 inch (2.5 cm) with water, add 2 teaspoons coarse salt, and bring the water to a boil over medium-high heat. Lower the heat so the water is simmering merrily and cook the potatoes until they are tender through but not overly soft, 15 to 20 minutes. Drain the potatoes.

2. While the potatoes are cooking, make the vinaigrette: Whisk together the vinegar and salt in a large bowl. Whisk in the mustard and the shallots, then slowly whisk in the oils until the vinaigrette is emulsified. Whisk in the pepper to taste.

3. When the potatoes are cool enough to handle, slice them into ½-inch- (1.3 cm) thick rounds and fold them into the vinaigrette. Either let the potatoes cool, or immediately fold in the onion and the herring and let the salad sit while you mince the parsley leaves. Add them to the salad, folding gently, and serve.

Aromatic Mussels with Curry

MOULES AU CURRY

The French have a love affair with mussels. And they prefer those from their own shores, whether they be in Normandy, Brittany, or the Atlantic Coast. I am in complete agreement—French mussels are small, sweet, succulent, and they lend themselves to many different flavors and spices. Here they are combined with curry, which underlines but doesn't dominate the sweetness of the mussels.

Mussels live in a salt water world inside their shell, and when cooked, they release this liquid. Thus, the amount of liquid you end up with in the dish will depend on the freshness of your mussels, for once they are out of the water, they lose much of their liquid. Essentials alongside these tasty morsels are lots of delicious bread and plenty of Muscadet, or hard (brut) apple cider.

SERVES 4 TO 6 AS A FIRST COURSE; SERVES 2 AS A MAIN COURSE

EQUIPMENT: large stockpot or Dutch oven

PREPARATION TIME: 15 minutes

COOKING TIME: 16 minutes

DIFFICULTY LEVEL: simple

---

1 tablespoon (15 g) unsalted butter

1 large onion (7 ounces; 210 g), diced

2 shallots, diced

2 garlic cloves, diced

2 teaspoons curry powder, or to taste

1 teaspoon ground turmeric

Fine sea salt and freshly ground black pepper

½ cup (125 ml) white wine, such as Muscadet

3 pounds (1.5 kg) mussels, debearded (see Astuces)

1 Bouquet Garni (page 338)

1. Melt the butter in a large stockpot over medium heat. When the butter foams, add the onion, shallot, and garlic, then stir and cook until the onion is translucent, about 8 minutes. Sprinkle with the curry powder and turmeric and season with salt and pepper. Cook for a minute or two, stirring, then pour in the wine. Stir, add the mussels and bouquet garni and shake the pot. Increase the heat to medium-high heat, and when the wine begins to boil, lower the heat to medium, cover, and cook until the mussels open, shaking the pot from time to time, 7 to 8 minutes. If the mussels are only open partially, you can continue to cook for another minute.

2. Remove the pot from the heat and turn out the mussels into a warmed serving dish. If there are any mussels that aren't open, remove and discard.

ASTUCES:
- If you look into your pot and see that juices are minimal, simply add more wine.
- Do your best to find mussels with beards (byssus threads), as they will keep their freshness and flavor longer. Wait to debeard your mussels until just before cooking—simply pull the beard, using pliers if the beard is stubborn.

WHY CURRY WITH MUSSELS?

Why are mussels with curry a regional specialty of . . . Brittany?

It has to do with the spice route. In the late 1700s, ships docked in Lorient, on the southern Breton coast, their hold filled with spices. These flavors leaked into the local cuisine, particularly a currylike blend. As the story goes, a deckhand on a spice boat from India met a pharmacist in Lorient, in the early 1800s. A recipe passed between the men for a spice blend from the deckhand's homeland. The pharmacist made and then began to sell the blend, which came to be known as *kari goss*. This fiery mix of spices became part of Breton cuisine, used in the local fish soup *cotriade*, sprinkled on lobster, on the local sea scallops, with mussels.

Kari goss has become a jewel in the Breton culinary crown, though because it is so fiery, a more subdued version of it—curry—is often used in its place. Kari goss is still made and sold by a descendant of that pharmacist who got the recipe from the Indian deckhand. Its story is emblematic of how trade and movement throughout the European continent has had such a big effect on the development of French gastronomy.

If you find yourself in Lorient, visit Parapharmacie Evanescence (Jeunesse Beauté Santé), 11 rue Auguste Nayel, 56100 Lorient, 02 97 21 14 49.

Modern Fish Pot au Feu

POT AU FEU DE POISSON

This pure and elegant dish is inspired by Georges Blanc, a legendary chef whose restaurant, also called Georges Blanc, entered the three-star Michelin pantheon more than four decades ago. He succeeded his mother and grandmother at the stove, and his recipes reflect his respect for tradition, as in this feather-light dish. Here he takes a classic—pot au feu of poached beef and vegetables—and transforms it with fish, which he seasons with a touch of allspice and surrounds with delicately poached vegetables. Serve this with a lovely Picpoul de Pinet from Languedoc, a white that is floral with hints of citrus, to round out a wonderful meal.

SERVES 6

EQUIPMENT: flat steamer (such as a bamboo steamer), slotted spatula

PREPARATION TIME: 25 minutes

COOKING TIME: about 25 minutes

DIFFICULTY LEVEL: simple

Six 1-inch- (2.5 cm) thick fillets of cod, haddock, flounder, or other white fish

8 ounces (250 g) thin, smallish carrots, preferably with the smallest leaves attached, peeled and cut on the diagonal into 3-inch (7.5 cm) lengths

4 small turnips (14 ounces, 420 g total), preferably with the smallest leaves attached, peeled and cut into sixths

Fine sea salt

1 fresh or dried imported bay leaf

6 very small bunch or pearl onions (about ½ ounce; 15 g each), trimmed and left whole

White part from 6 thin leeks, trimmed and cut into 3-inch (7.5 cm) lengths

4 small waxy potatoes (about 2 ounces; 60 g each), peeled and cut lengthwise into sixths

¼ cup (60 g) olive oil, plus a bit more for rubbing on the fish

2 garlic cloves, sliced paper thin

Freshly ground black pepper

¼ to ½ teaspoon ground allspice

1 tablespoon fresh lemon juice

Generous ½ cup (7 g) fresh basil or flat-leaf parsley leaves

Fresh flat-leaf parsley or basil sprigs for garnish

Fleur de sel for garnish

1. Rinse the fish and remove any bones, if necessary. Refrigerate.

2. Place the carrots and turnips in a medium saucepan, cover them by about 2 inches (5 cm) with water, add ½ teaspoon of salt and the bay leaf, and bring the water to a boil over medium-high heat. Lower the heat so the water is simmering, cover, and cook until the vegetables begin to turn tender, 5 minutes. Add the onions, leeks, and potatoes and return the water to a boil. Lower the heat so it is

(continued)

simmering and cook until the vegetables are just tender, about 15 minutes. Depending on the size and freshness of the vegetables, the cooking times may change. What you are after is completely tender, but not soft or mushy, vegetables. Remove from the heat, drain, and keep them warm.

3. Place the olive oil and garlic in a skillet over very low heat and heat until hot to the touch, less than 5 minutes. Do *not* let the mixture boil.

4. Bring 3 cups of water to a boil in the bottom half of a steamer. Lightly rub the fish all over with olive oil, season with salt and pepper, then sprinkle the fish with a light dusting of allspice. Place the fish over the steaming water, cover, and steam until the fish is translucent, 3 to 4 minutes, depending on the fish that you are using. Remove the basket from the steamer and place the steamer on a plate to catch the juices from the cod.

5. Add the lemon juice to the garlic mixture and stir.

6. Coarsely chop the basil or parsley.

7. To serve, using a slotted spatula, transfer a cod fillet to the center of each of six plates. Spoon the vegetables to one side of the fish, sort of wrapping the fish with the vegetables. Pour an equal amount of the garlic mixture over the fish and the vegetables.

8. Sprinkle the chopped basil or parsley over the fish and vegetables, garnish with the herb sprigs and fleur de sel, and serve immediately.

ASTUCES:

- If cod loin is unavailable, lingcod, haddock, sole, or flounder can substitute.
- This dish can be made year-round, though spring into autumn is the best moment, when vegetables are at their sweetest and most flavorful. Do your best to find smaller vegetables, though don't use baby vegetables, as they can be bitter. The very best turnip here is one fresh from the ground (i.e., from your farmers' market). If you cannot find them, you can substitute firm radishes.

Monkfish Confit with Fresh Shell Beans

LOTTE CONFIT, HARICOTS À ÉCOSSAIS

I love substituting fish for meat in a dish that echoes the tradition of lamb with white beans, and the creativity of Chef Sébastien Leroy of restaurant Sauvage in Paris. As he explained it to me, "I always serve lamb with white beans, and one day it occurred to me that I should serve monkfish with white beans." It was a huge success at the restaurant and has become a signature plat du jour there. In this recipe, he poaches monkfish in butter that, he hastens to say, isn't clarified. He simply skims the white foam (whey protein) off the top of the melted butter, then adds the fish to what's left in the pan. You'll find this a brilliant cooking method that gives delicate and delicious results. This is sumptuous, particularly with a white Burgundy.

SERVES 4

EQUIPMENT: medium saucepan

PREPARATION TIME: 10 minutes if you need to remove skin from monkfish

COOKING TIME: 15 minutes

DIFFICULTY LEVEL: simple

---

6 tablespoons (85 g) unsalted butter, melted

1 to 1½ pounds (500 to 750 g) monkfish, cod, flounder, or lingcod

1 recipe Tender White Beans (page 255)

Fresh flat-leaf parsley sprigs for garnish

Fine sea salt and freshly ground black pepper

1. Melt the butter in a medium saucepan over medium heat, then skim away the white foam (whey protein) that floats to the top. Add the fish to the butter and lower the heat to low. Cook, spooning the butter over the fish and turning it carefully two or three times, so that it cooks evenly, until it is opaque through, about 10 minutes.

2. To serve, taste the beans for seasoning, then place them on a warmed platter and lay the fish pieces atop the beans. Drizzle with a generous amount of the butter, then garnish with the herb sprigs, sea salt, and pepper.

ASTUCES:

- When you buy monkfish, look for fish that is firm and bright, and not sitting in a pool of milky liquid, which indicates it's been soaked in phosphates to keep it "fresh." Monkfish, often called poor man's lobster, has two skins, one of which will most likely be removed. The other is more of a membrane, and you'll need to remove it by slipping a sharp knife blade between it and the meat and cutting it away. It isn't difficult to do.

- If you cannot find monkfish, try cod, flounder, or lingcod, all firm white fish. A "light" portion is about 4 ounces (120 g) per person. You can adjust, depending on the appetite of your eaters.

- As for the shell beans, if you can find them fresh, usually in late summer and autumn, you're in luck! If not, use dried white beans, such as Great Northerns.

Sautéed Scallops with Celery Root Puree and Herb Oil

*SAUTÉ DE COQUILLES SAINT JACQUES
À LA PURÉE DE CELERI RAVE ET L'HUILE À AROMATES*

This is a dish I tasted at one of my favorite neighborhood restaurants, Les Botanistes. A family-owned spot, its food is always spectacularly pure and clean-flavored. Once October and scallop season are here, I make this dish, which takes advantage of two of my favorite seasonal ingredients: scallops and celery root.

The quantity of scallops called for here is based on quite large French scallops. If the scallops are small, you may want more per person. This plat du jour is elegant and, with a salad served afterward and a lovely white Burgundy, it makes for a very special meal.

SERVES 6

EQUIPMENT: heavy-bottomed skillet with a lid, food processor, large skillet

PREPARATION TIME: 20 to 30 minutes

COOKING TIME: 25 minutes

DIFFICULTY LEVEL: simple

¼ cup firmly packed fresh flat-leaf parsley or basil leaves

⅓ cup (80 ml) olive oil

1 large celery root (1¾ pounds; 875 g each), peeled and cut into ½-inch (1.3 cm) pieces

Fine sea salt and freshly ground black pepper

3 tablespoons (45 ml) crème fraîche

18 sea scallops, trimmed and rinsed, chilled

Fleur de sel

ASTUCE: Fresh sea scallops are readily available on the East Coast of the United States, and in fine fish markets just about anywhere. When you shop for them, look for firmness. Avoid them if they are bulgy or sitting in cloudy liquid.

1. Mince the herb leaves and mix them with ¼ cup (60 ml) of the oil in a small bowl. Set aside.

2. Place the celery root in a heavy-bottomed skillet over very low heat. Season with fine salt and pepper, add ½ cup (125 ml) of water, cover, and cook until the celery root is tender through, about 20 minutes, checking from time to time to be sure it isn't sticking to the pan. If necessary, add a bit more water during cooking to keep it from sticking.

3. When the celery root is tender through, transfer it to a food processor and puree. Add the crème fraîche, process, adjust the seasoning, and keep it hot over the lowest possible heat on your stove, or in a very low-temperature oven.

4. Heat the remaining 4 teaspoons of oil in a large skillet over medium heat. When it's hot, add the scallops and cook until they are golden on one side, about 3 minutes. Carefully turn the scallops and cook until they are golden on the other side, about 2 minutes. Season them with salt and pepper and remove from the heat.

(continued)

5. To serve, divide the puree among six warmed plates, placing it in the center and shaping it in a disk. Place three scallops atop each disk of puree, then drizzle the herb oil around the scallops and the puree. Season with fleur de sel and serve immediately.

THE FRENCH SOUP TERRINE

When I first moved to France, I was dishless. This was not an unfortunate state to find myself in, since in the early '90s the wonderful institution called *la brocante*, a very French shop offering a combination of antiques and junk, was still in fine fettle. All I had to do was haunt my local shop to stock my cabinets.

My primary need was plates, and I was always on the lookout. I often found them in stacks of at least twenty, and if I liked them and the price was right—usually both were in sync—I would succumb, hauling the stack to the cash register. This was usually a box filled with coins and bills, sitting on an old table among piles of treasures. The owner would look at my plates, then go into a room behind the cash register to emerge with . . . a soup terrine, a sauce dish, a sugar bowl, a smaller covered dish, all in the pattern of my plates. These were thrown in for no extra fee and I realized that stacks of beautiful plates were always accompanied by varied serving dishes, which the owner of the establishment couldn't bear to see separated.

These extra terrines have become especially useful to me while developing recipes for this book. Such plats du jour as Normandy Seafood Stew with Crème Fraîche (page 99), The Ultimate Beef Stew (page 127), Chicken in the Pot (page 52), and Ham Hock, Smoked Sausage, and Vegetable Stew (page 158) are the ideal dishes to serve in colorful soup terrines, and I've had the time of my life pulling mine down and using them.

Most of my terrines are at least 100 years old, some many more. They hearken back to big family meals, the aura of which is part of the warmth of a plat du jour. I hope you have a soup terrine somewhere in your collection. If you don't, make the homey and delicious dishes that suit them anyway, in the spirit of generosity and good cheer they engender.

Normandy Seafood Stew with Crème Fraîche

MARMITE DIEPPOISE

Normandy is the land of seafood and shellfish, cream and butter, intermittent sunshine and world-class blue skies. It is a gently beautiful region, and this gentle touch is reflected in its cuisine. According to local lore, this dish is a recent yet swiftly traditional addition to Norman cuisine, created in 1954 by a certain Georgette Maurice, chef at the Café du Tréport in Dieppe, which is now called La Marmite Dieppoise. Mme. Maurice decided to combine noble fish like turbot and sole with scallops and mussels in a fish fumet, thicken it with egg yolk, lighten it with crème fraîche, and voila! The bouillabaisse of Normandy was born. La Marmite Dieppoise restaurant is on a tiny side street in this coastal town, but as current owner Françoise Toussat says, "The view from here is of what's on the plate!"

This lovely soup/stew is perfect with a Muscadet or Sauvignon Blanc.

SERVES 4 TO 6

EQUIPMENT: large heavy saucepan or stockpot, large saucepan

PREPARATION TIME: 20 minutes

COOKING TIME: 30 minutes

DIFFICULTY LEVEL: simple but requires attention

- 1¾ pounds (860 g) white fish fillets, such as cod, lingcod, flounder, or tilapia
- 1 cup (250 ml) crème fraîche or non-ultra-pasteurized heavy cream
- 2 large egg yolks
- 1½ pounds (750 g) mussels or clams
- 1 cup (250 ml) dry white wine, such as sauvignon blanc, or brut cider

- 2 medium onions (5 ounces; 150 g each), diced
- Several fresh flat-leaf parsley sprigs
- 2 tablespoons (30 g) unsalted butter
- White part of 2 large leeks (9 ounces; 270 g each), cleaned, trimmed and sliced into thin rounds
- 1 fennel bulb, trimmed and diced

- 4 cups (1 L) Fish Stock (page 333)
- 1 Bouquet Garni (page 338)
- 9 ounces (270 g) fresh sea scallops, with coral if possible, or baby squid
- ½ cup (5 g) fresh flat-leaf parsley leaves for garnish
- Zest of ½ lemon, cut into very thin (julienne) strips, for garnish

1. Cut the fish fillet into 2-by-1-inch (5-by-2.5 cm) pieces and refrigerate.

2. Whisk together the crème fraîche and egg yolks in a small bowl, cover, and set aside.

(continued)

3. Remove and discard the beards from the mussels, rinse them well, and transfer them to a large heavy saucepan. Add the wine, half of the diced onions, and the parsley, cover, and bring to a boil over medium-high heat. Cook the mussels just until they open wide, shaking the pan regularly so they cook evenly. When the mussels are cooked, remove them from the heat. Transfer the mussels to a large bowl. Strain and reserve the cooking liquid—there should be about 2 cups (500 ml). If there is not quite that amount, simply add water to make up the difference. When the mussels are cool enough to handle, remove them from the shell, reserving the meats and discarding the shells.

4. Melt the butter in a large saucepan over medium heat and add the remaining onions, leeks, and fennel. Stir and cook until they are translucent and the leeks are beginning to turn tender, about 5 minutes.

5. Add the fish stock, reserved mussel-cooking liquid, and bouquet garni to the pan. Increase the heat underneath the pan to bring the liquid to a simmer. Cook until the vegetables are tender through and the liquid has reduced by about one-third, 20 to 25 minutes. Add the fish and push it gently down into the liquid, then add the scallops. If necessary, to keep the liquid at a simmer, increase the heat under the pan and cook until the seafood is nearly but not quite cooked through, 4 to 5 minutes. Transfer the fish and the scallops to a warm bowl. Remove the bouquet garni from the cooking liquid and discard.

6. Whisk about ½ cup (125 ml) of the hot seafood cooking liquid into the crème fraîche mixture, then stir this mixture back into the seafood cooking liquid in the saucepan. Cook, stirring, until the soup thickens just slightly, being very careful not to let it boil. Return the fish and the scallops to the pan, first draining away any liquid they might have given up. Add the mussels to the soup and cook until all the seafood is heated through, about 5 minutes. Taste for seasoning.

7. Mince the parsley leaves and stir, along with the lemon zest, into the soup. Let cook for an additional 2 to 3 minutes, then serve immediately in warmed, shallow bowls.

ASTUCES:

- When buying fish, beware of a fishy smell in the air. It is a sign of spoiling fish, so be certain that what you are about to buy is bright, with no fishy aroma (ask to smell it—this is perfectly legitimate), and looks appealing.
- As for the mussels, remove their beards right before you plan to cook them, because once they are removed, the mussels die and will spoil quickly.

ASTUCES:

- This recipe is intended to use canned tuna, and I always recommend using albacore, because the albacore doesn't swim with dolphins, so there isn't any bycatch, no trauma to the dolphin population. Make sure you get albacore packed in oil and use the oil in the recipe; it contains omega-3 long-chain fatty acids (good for you), and keeps the fish moist and its flavor intact.
- To desalt capers, simply place them in a bowl, pour warm water over them, and let them sit for about 30 minutes. Then scoop them into a sieve and rinse them, discarding the very salty water. Pat them dry before using. If you're using brined capers, rinse and pat them dry.
- The peppers will keep for 24 hours in the refrigerator.

Tuna-Stuffed Peppers

MINI POIVRONS FARCIES AU THON

From start to finish, this recipe will win you over. The combination of tuna, capers, and garlic stuffed into colorful peppers is as fun to prepare as it is pretty on the plate! Lipstick peppers are perfect for this dish—they take minutes to steam and are easy to stuff. You can either serve them piled on a large platter or in individual servings. However you decide to present this dish, I recommend pairing it with the Parsley, Green Olive, and Almond Salad (page 257) for a perfect combination. Serve this with your favorite non-oaked Chardonnay.

SERVES 4

EQUIPMENT: steamer, food processor, pastry bag (optional)

PREPARATION TIME: about 30 minutes

COOKING TIME: 15 minutes

DIFFICULTY LEVEL: simple

---

16 small (sometimes called lipstick or lunchbox) peppers, rinsed

½ cup (125 ml) olive oil

Two 6-ounce (180 g) cans oil-packed albacore tuna, drained, oil reserved

2 ounces (60 g) capers, preferably those preserved in salt (see Astuces)

1 medium garlic clove

¼ cup fresh flat-leaf parsley leaves for garnish

1. Bring water to a boil in the bottom half of a steamer over high heat. Arrange the peppers in the steamer basket, cover, and cook until the peppers are tender but still hold their shape, about 15 minutes. Remove the peppers from the steamer, and when they're cool enough to handle, slice off the top. Most of the seeds will be attached to the top of the peppers, so discard the top and the seeds. Using a teaspoon, gently scoop out any remaining seeds from the peppers. Don't rinse them to remove seeds—you'll rinse away flavor!

2. While the peppers are steaming, add enough oil to the reserved oil from the tuna to make ½ cup (125 ml) total.

3. Place the capers, garlic, and tuna in a food processor and process just until they are coarsely chopped together. Add the oil mixture to the tuna mixture while the machine is running. Process until you have a homogenous, but still a bit chunky, puree.

4. Using a pastry bag or a small spoon, carefully fill the peppers nearly to bursting, with a bit of the stuffing mounding outside the pepper. Arrange the peppers on a platter or four peppers on each of four plates. Either place the Parsley, Green Olive, and Almond Salad on the plate with the peppers, or serve it separately. If you're not serving the peppers with the salad, garnish the peppers with the parsley leaves. Serve immediately.

CHAPTER 4
BEEF, LAMB, VEAL

MEAT IS AND HAS throughout history been very center-of-the-plate in French cuisine. The French are proud of their meat: the way they produce it and the care they take doing so, their devotion to their traditional meat-based recipes, their constant delight when sitting down to a meat dish at table. There are very specific regional highlights in the French meat selection, such as lamb from the Pyrenees or from the salt marshes around Mont-Saint-Michel, the Charolais beef from Burgundy, and the savored cuts of the Norman cow.

As for dishes, there are favorites, such as Boeuf Bourguignon (The Ultimate Beef Stew), Côtes d'Agneau (Lamb Chops), and Blanquette de Veau (Seasonal Veal Stew). And then there is the ever-popular steak. No matter what cut or recipe, the French go crazy for a delicious steak, seared for a minute, then served with butter and shallots or olives and tomato sauce, or just with salt and pepper.

No matter the meat dish, you'll follow the French way of eating and serving it as delicious plats du jour. With this chapter, welcome to the French world of meat!

HOLY LAMB FROM
MONT-SAINT-MICHEL

From Michel Fautrel's farmhouse in Normandy, one can see across the *pré-salé* (salt marsh) to Mont-Saint-Michel, the monastery dedicated to St. Michael. It was originally built on the promontory that rises in the Mont-Saint-Michel Bay in AD 708, and now it rises massively above the water, its spire reaching to the sky.

It is said that France's best lamb is raised on these salt marshes. Certainly, the animals that graze here are endowed with a magic combination of tender muscle tone from bounding over the rocks and rivulets, and flavor from feeding on the hardy, salt-washed grasses. The result is lamb that is flecked with fat without the thick layer one finds on most lamb, resulting in texture, indescribable tenderness, and an ethereal, distinct flavor.

The reputation of lamb from the salt marshes around Mont-Saint-Michel is nothing new. The brilliant Rouennais writer Pierre Thomas, sieur du Fossé, wrote in 1691: "The seaside grass is like wild thyme, it gives the lamb such a flavor that one is ready to forget about partridge and pheasant, the lamb meat is so delicious."

These pré-salé lambs, which graze around the clock in summer and in the early mornings in winter, are so highly valued they are protected by an Appellation d'Origine, a standard that limits how and where they can be raised, the amount of land each lamb must have for grazing, the quality standard of the barns they go to, and their size. Several hundred farms are entitled to produce these lambs, and are required to let them out on the marsh every single day of their less-than-twelve-month lives.

The tides around Mont-Saint-Michel are the highest in France, rising up to 45 feet (13.5 m) in a matter of hours, sweeping in as far as 9 miles (15 km). "We have major tides once a month, and they last for two days," M. Fautrel told me the day I visited his farm. "We bring the lambs in then, of course, then take them out as soon as the tides recede." We drove down a rutted road to the salt marsh, a broad expanse of hillocky field. "We aren't allowed to fence them in the marsh," M. Fautrel said. "This is a tourist area and the government doesn't want anything to disturb the view."

Although the Fautrel family has leased a portion of the salt marsh for generations, M. Fautrel must reapply for the lease each year. "It's a little unsure," he said, shrugging. "This mayor is in favor of lambs on the meadow; the next one might not be."

We stepped onto the marsh. "I love it here," said M. Fautrel, who has spent his whole life here. "If I couldn't get out here every day, I'm not sure what I'd do."

As it is, his job requires at least a daily visit to the marsh. "Sometimes a lamb will fall in a rivulet or get stick in a bend in one of the streams that runs through the marsh. And tourists bring dogs that love to chase after them. We've got to check them at least once a day," he said.

I kicked a tuft of the tough grass. "That right there is too long for the lambs," M. Fautrel said, smiling. "They want grass moistened with dew, so it isn't too salty, and they won't touch if it if gets too long or too tough."

We returned to the Fautrel farm, where we escaped the biting wind by ducking into a barn that made up one side of a large courtyard. It was warmer inside but still breezy. "The barns have to be open so the difference in temperature isn't so striking to the lambs," M. Fautrel said. "If it were warmer in here, they'd get sick when we let them out."

We walked through the feeding area of the barn, where bunches of dried and faded holly hung from the rafters.

"Those? We hang them up each year before

Christmas," M. Fautrel explained. "It's a superstition, I guess you'd say. We think it keeps illness away from the animals."

We turned into another part of the barn, where his lambs, which he'd just brought in a couple of hours before, were snuggled in clumps. The newest, about the size of lapdogs, huddled against the older lambs to keep warm. The barn was fresh smelling, the straw golden.

"We change the straw every day, and keep the barn clean for them so they're comfortable, and so we meet the standards of the Appellation d'Origine," M. Fautrel said. "But we've always raised our lambs this way, so it doesn't feel like extra work or care."

His reward, aside from contented lambs, is twice the price for their lamb. "I'd raise them this way anyway, but I don't mind the pay."

There are just fourteen farms that produce pré-salé lamb, thus guaranteeing its rarity. And while we may only get the rare taste of Mont-Saint-Michel from time to time, all lamb in France is raised with similar care and pride, and each region produces its own flavorful lamb.

ASTUCE: Although the butter added to the orange juice right before serving isn't obligatory, it adds a velvety richness to the final sauce.

Lamb Chops with Rosemary and Orange Syrup

CÔTES D'AGNEAU AU ROMARIN ET SIROP D'ORANGE

The French love lamb. In fact, many French eat it at least once a week, and the French chef is master of cooking it perfectly, whether it be a shoulder that is braised slowly or these beautiful chops that are cooked until they are *just* crisp and golden on the outside and rare on the inside. Added to that are the flavors of rosemary and orange, which complement each other and intensify the subtle lamb flavor. Be sure to serve with Quinoa with Herbs (page 267) and a rich Coteaux de Languedoc. And once you've mastered the sauce, you'll find yourself using it in all manner of dishes, from freshly steamed fish to grilled duck.

SERVES 4 TO 8, DEPENDING ON APPETITES

EQUIPMENT: medium heavy-bottomed saucepan, large heavy-bottomed skillet

PREPARATION TIME: 5 to 10 minutes

COOKING TIME: 22 minutes max

DIFFICULTY LEVEL: simple

---

1 cup (250 ml) fresh orange juice

1 tablespoon olive oil

8 lamb chops (about 4 ounces; 120 g each), at room temperature

Fine sea salt and freshly ground black pepper

1 heaping tablespoon fresh rosemary leaves

1 tablespoon (15 g) unsalted butter, cut into 4 pieces, chilled

Fleur de sel

Herb sprigs for garnish

1 recipe Quinoa with Herbs (page 267) for serving

1. Place the orange juice in a medium heavy-bottomed saucepan over medium heat. Bring to a lively simmer and reduce until the juice is thickened by about two-thirds, about 10 minutes. Check the juice frequently to be sure it doesn't burn. When the juice has reduced, remove the pan from the heat.

2. Place the olive oil in a large heavy-bottomed skillet over medium heat. When the oil is hot but not smoking, add the lamb chops and sear them on each side, 3 to 4 minutes per side, seasoning each side with salt and pepper. This cooking time for the lamb is short and results in very pink lamb. If you prefer your lamb less rare, simply cook the chops longer on each side.

3. Coarsely chop the rosemary. When the lamb chops are golden, add the rosemary to the pan, stir, and continue to cook for 3 to 4 minutes. Remove the pan from the heat.

4. Return the orange syrup to a gentle boil over medium heat and whisk in the butter, one piece at a time, swirling the pan as you whisk, until the sauce is velvety.

5. To serve, place chops on warmed dinner plates and surround with a drizzle of orange syrup. Season with fleur de sel and garnish with herb sprigs. Serve immediately, with the quinoa alongside.

Roasted Leg of Lamb with Herbs and Mustard

GIGOT D'AGNEAU ROTI AUX AROMATES ET À LA MOUTARDE

Roasted *gigot* (leg) of lamb is one of the most typical plats du jour in France, because it satisfies every possible culinary criteria. It evokes Grandmère and Sunday lunch in the country, home and comfort, and unparalleled delicacy of flavor. The French lamb grower has the know-how to produce the most tender and flavorful lamb on the planet. There is the mythic lamb from Mont-Saint-Michel, the huskier-flavored lamb from the Pyrenees, and the wildflower-fed lamb from the southeastern Alps; that from Provence is flavored with wild thyme, and the lush pastures of Normandy give lamb a noted tenderness. Such lamb abundance makes for wonderful variety on the plate, which is highlighted here. Make this, invite a group, and enjoy! Serve a lovely red from the Loire Valley, such as a Chinon.

SERVES 8 TO 10

EQUIPMENT: large roasting pan, strainer

PREPARATION TIME: 10 minutes; 2 to 12 hours for macerating; 2 hours resting time before cooking

COOKING TIME: 45 to 55 minutes

DIFFICULTY LEVEL: simple

---

1 large garlic clove

2 tablespoons fresh thyme leaves

1 fresh or dried imported bay leaf

One 3½-pound (1.7 kg) leg of lamb

Fine sea salt and freshly ground black pepper

⅓ cup (80 ml) Dijon mustard

6 fresh rosemary sprigs

1 cup (250 ml) water

1. At least 2 hours before you plan to roast the leg of lamb, mince the garlic, thyme, and bay leaf together. Make 10 slits in the lamb that are about ½ inch (1.3 cm) deep and ½ inch (1.3 cm) wide, and evenly divide the minced garlic and herbs among the slits, pushing them right down into the meat. Lightly season the lamb with salt and pepper, then slather it all over with the mustard. Cover and let it macerate at room temperature for 2 hours or in the refrigerator for up to 12 hours.

2. Remove the lamb from the refrigerator at least 2 hours before you plan to roast it, so that the meat can come to room temperature.

3. Preheat the oven to 425°F (220°C).

4. Lay three of the rosemary sprigs in a roasting pan large enough to accommodate the leg of lamb. Set the lamb in the pan and lay the remaining rosemary sprigs over the lamb. Set the pan in the center of the oven and roast until the meat is golden on the outside and the interior temperature registers about 137°F (about 58°C), 45 to 50 minutes; this gives a leg of lamb that offers something

for everyone, from rosy to rare. Remove the lamb from the oven and transfer it to a cutting board, reserving the roasting pan. Let the lamb sit for at least 20 minutes and up to 40 minutes before carving it.

5. Just before carving the leg of lamb, remove and discard the rosemary sprigs from it and from the pan it roasted in. Place the roasting pan over low heat, add the water, and bring to a boil, stirring and scraping up the caramelized juice from the bottom of the pan. Cook until the liquid is reduced by about one-third. Taste for seasoning—if the juices don't have quite enough flavor, continue reducing until their flavor concentrates to your taste, then rectify the seasoning. Strain the sauce and either pour over the leg of lamb once it is carved or serve it alongside.

ASTUCES:
- Note that the seasoned lamb sits at room temperature for 2 hours before cooking, so the garlic and herbs can lend their flavor to the meat. You can also refrigerate it, seasoned, overnight. Remember to remove it from the fridge 2 hours before you plan to cook it.
- Once the lamb is cooked, let it sit for at least 20 minutes before serving, so the meat has time to relax.

Basque Lamb and Sweet Pepper Stew

AGNEAU BRAISÉ AU POIVRONS BASQUE

This rich, simple stew, which is called *chilindrón* in the Basque Country, will win your heart with its color and aroma. It's direct from the verdant region that straddles the southwestern French border with Spain, rich with the flavor of lamb that grazes on mountain pastures. It needs nothing more than a basket full of fresh baguette and a big green salad to follow, such as A Classic Green Salad (page 265). You'll be won over, before you ever put a bite in your mouth, by the color and aroma from this tempting blend.

The ideal wine to accompany this is an Irouléguy from the Basque Country. Barring that, try any blend of Cabernet Franc, Cabernet Sauvignon, and Tannat.

4 TO 6 SERVINGS

EQUIPMENT: large bowl, large saucepan

PREPARATION TIME: about 2 hours 15 minutes, including sitting time for soaking the peppers

COOKING TIME: about 1 hour 30 minutes

DIFFICULTY LEVEL: simple

---

12 ounces (360 g) large red bell peppers (about 2 peppers), cored, seeded, and cut into ½-inch (1.3 cm) pieces

3 cups (750 ml) water, or as needed

1 to 2 tablespoons olive oil

One 3-pound (1.5 kg) leg of lamb, bone removed, cut into 2-inch (5 cm) pieces

Fine sea salt

3 garlic cloves, diced

1 large onion (7 ounces; 210 g), diced

2 medium tomatoes (5 ounces; 150 g each), cored and diced (for ⅔ cup; 160 ml)

1. Place the peppers in a large bowl, cover with the water, or enough to completely cover, and let sit for 2 hours.

2. Heat 1 tablespoon of the olive oil in a large saucepan over medium heat. When the oil is hot but not smoking, add the lamb, season it with salt, and brown it on all sides, 8 to 10 minutes.

3. Remove the lamb from the pot and add the garlic and onion, plus more oil if the pan is dry. Cook, stirring frequently, so the onion doesn't burn, until the onion is tender through, 12 to 15 minutes.

4. Place the lamb back in the pan, along with any juices the meat has given up. Stir, add the tomatoes, the peppers, and the water from the peppers. The lamb should be just covered with water.

5. Increase the heat enough to bring the water to a boil, lower the heat so it simmers, cover, and cook until the lamb is nearly tender, checking and stirring from time to time, about 1 hour. Remove the lid from the pan and continue to cook until the lamb is thoroughly tender and the liquid has reduced into a luscious, rather thick sauce, 30 to 45 more minutes. Adjust the seasoning and serve.

ASTUCES:

- Do note that you need to begin this at least 3 hours before serving it, because the peppers need to soak for 2 hours, which softens their flavor and adds a sweeter dimension to this dish. If you're short on time, you may omit this step.
- You can make this year-round and use canned crushed tomatoes, preferably Muir Glen brand. The weight will be equal.

Saffron-Scented Lamb, Vegetable, and Chickpea Soup, for Couscous

LA SOUPE DE COUSCOUS AU PARFUM DE SAFRAN

This North African soup is really more of a brothy stew, chock-full of delicious vegetables, meat, and chickpeas. Derived from countries with a strong Islamic culture, this dish does not traditionally contain pork but instead chicken, lamb, and beef sausages.

Many people expect couscous soup to be spicy, but it isn't. What's spicy is the hot pepper paste you serve alongside, called harissa. Most people I know, and most restaurants, buy harissa in cans and add freshly minced garlic to it. Put some on the edge of your plate and add it a bit at a time as you eat this wonderful soup. Le Phare du Cap Bon is one of the finest harissas on the market. You can find it online, such as at www.igourmet.com. Serve this with a rich red from the Languedoc, such as one from Domaine de l'Hortus.

8 TO 10 SERVINGS

EQUIPMENT: medium saucepan, heavy saucepan or stockpot

PREPARATION TIME: 30 minutes

COOKING TIME: including cooking the chickpeas, about 2½ hours

DIFFICULTY LEVEL: simple

1⅓ cups (250 g) dried chickpeas

½ teaspoon baking soda

3 tablespoons (45 ml) olive oil

2½ pounds (1.1 kg) lean lamb or cow's shoulder or neck, cut into about ¾-inch (2.25 cm) pieces

5 medium onions (1 pound 6 ounces; 680 g total), diced

2 generous pinches saffron

1 tablespoon coarse sea salt

10 cups (scant 2.3 L) hot water

2 tablespoons (30 g) tomato paste

2 pounds (1 kg) carrots, cut on a slight diagonal into 1-inch (2.5 cm) lengths

1½ pounds (750 g) turnips, peeled, trimmed, and cut into quarters or, if the turnips are large, into 1-inch (2.5 cm) pieces

1½ pounds (750 g) zucchini, rinsed, trimmed, and cut on a slight diagonal into 1½-inch (4 cm) lengths

1½ pounds (750 g) potatoes, peeled and cut into 1½-inch (4 cm) pieces

Fresh cilantro sprigs for garnish (optional)

1 recipe Steamed Couscous (page 317)—essential to serve with this soup

1. Place the chickpeas in a medium saucepan and cover by 2 inches (5 cm) with water. Add the baking soda, stir, and bring the water to a boil. Remove the pan from the heat, cover, and let sit for 1 hour. Drain the chickpeas and cover them with fresh water. Bring to a boil over medium-high heat, lower the heat so the water is boiling gently, and cook until the chickpeas are nearly tender through, about 1 hour.

(continued)

2. Heat the oil in a large heavy stockpot over medium heat. When the oil is hot but not smoking, add the meat and brown it well on all sides, about 9 minutes. Add the onions, stir so they are coated with oil, and cook until they are deep golden, about 10 minutes, then crumble the saffron over the mixture. Season it with the salt, stir, and add 1 cup (250 ml) of the hot water. Stir and cook for 4 to 5 minutes, to blend the ingredients and allow the saffron to soften. Add the tomato paste and the remaining 8 cups (2 L) of hot water, bring to a boil, cover, and lower the heat so the liquid is simmering merrily. Cook until the meat begins to turn tender, about 30 minutes.

3. Add the carrots and drained chickpeas, cover, bring to a boil, lower the heat so the liquid is boiling gently, and cook until the carrots resist slightly when tested with a sharp knife, about 15 minutes. Add all the remaining vegetables and cook until they are tender, about 30 minutes. Check the seasoning and remove from the heat. The soup is ready to serve but will benefit from sitting for an hour or two and being reheated.

4. To serve, transfer the hot soup into a large soup tureen. Garnish it with cilantro sprigs and serve it with the couscous alongside.

ASTUCES:

- Your own cooked chickpeas will be better than anything in a can, and the baking soda tenderizes them as they cook.
- The carrots and the zucchini cook until they are soft. If you want your vegetables a bit more al dente, simply add them later in the cooking time.
- The soup improves once it has sat for an hour or two, or overnight. Reheat it gently before serving. As you make this soup, think ahead so you can start the meat and vegetables while the chickpeas are cooking. This will cut down considerably on the cooking time.

Roast Lamb with Fresh Shell Beans and Garlic

GIGOT AUX HARICOTS ET À L'AIL

This dish is a blend of cooking methods—one from Brittany, where fresh shell beans grow with abandon, and one from Provence, where lambs clamber among the hills and garlic is part of the landscape. The ingredients blend, as do the regional cultures, to make this an exceptionally satisfying plat du jour for a special Sunday when friends and family are together. Serve this with a lovely Côtes du Rhône, from Sablet if you can find it.

SERVES 6

EQUIPMENT: large roasting pan, rack for pan (optional), cutting board that collects juices

PREPARATION TIME: 10 minutes

COOKING TIME: 45 minutes to 1 hour

DIFFICULTY LEVEL: simple

---

15 garlic cloves—1 peeled, 14 unpeeled

1 tablespoon olive oil

One 4- to 5-pound (2 to 2.5 kg) leg of lamb, bone in, excess fat trimmed if desired

Sea salt and freshly ground black pepper

1 recipe Tender White Beans (page 255)

Fresh rosemary or sage sprigs for garnish

ASTUCES:

- Remove the lamb from the refrigerator 2 hours before roasting, so it comes to room temperature. This makes for more even roasting.
- If you cannot find shell beans, use canned cannellini beans

1. Preheat the oven to 400°F (200°C). Mince the peeled garlic clove.

2. Rub the leg of lamb all over with the oil, then rub in the minced garlic. Season with salt and pepper.

3. Place the leg of lamb, fattiest side up, on a rack in a roasting pan. (If you don't have a rack, simply place it in the roasting pan.) Place the pan in the lower third of the oven. Roast the lamb for 30 minutes, then turn it so the fattiest side is down. Add the remaining 14 garlic cloves to the pan, stir so they are coated with fat, and continue to roast the lamb until its internal temperature is 125°F (52°C) for rare lamb, an additional 15 minutes, for a total of 45 minutes. Remove the lamb from the pan and set it on a cutting board that collects juices. Return the pan to the oven so the garlic cloves can continue to cook until they are tender, an additional 15 minutes (for a total of 30 minutes). If you prefer your lamb medium, cook it for 50 to 55 minutes for an internal temperature of 137°F (58°C).

4. When the garlic cloves are cooked, remove the pan from the oven and stir in the white beans.

5. To serve, slice the lamb and transfer it to a warmed serving platter. Spoon the beans and garlic over it, and garnish with the rosemary sprigs.

Oysters and Spiced Lamb Patties

LES HUITRES AUX CAILLETTES D'AGNEAU

This is one of the French versions of surf and turf, gorgeous little patties of fragrant lamb served alongside chilled oysters on the half shell. It comes from the region south of Bordeaux near the Basque Country, where lambs clamber in the hills, and oysters are pulled from the water. While unconventional, it is a delectable combination because the brininess of the oysters and the spiced lamb offer contrasting yet complementary flavor. Red meat and oysters provide a challenge to the wine palate, but you will see that this goes as perfectly with a lightly chilled Sauvignon Blanc, as with a Médoc, which will complement the lamb and, in the end, the oysters, too. Be sure to have bread and unsalted butter on the table for this dish. Oysters are lost without those! To shuck the oysters, refer to page 34.

4 SERVINGS

EQUIPMENT: platter to hold oysters, baking sheet, small skillet, medium heavy skillet

PREPARATION TIME: 15 minutes if the oysters are shucked; 25 if they aren't

COOKING TIME: 20 minutes

DIFFICULTY LEVEL: simple

Seaweed or green lettuce leaves

2 dozen oysters, shells brushed under cold running water, shucked

½ cup (about 2 ounces; 60 g) pine nuts

1 pound (500 g) ground lamb

2 large garlic cloves, minced

½ teaspoon sea salt

¼ teaspoon freshly ground black pepper

¼ cup fresh oregano leaves, or 2 teaspoons dried

¼ to ⅛ teaspoon dried hot pepper flakes

2 lemons, quartered, for garnish

1. Mound a platter with crushed ice and cover it with seaweed or lettuce leaves. Arrange the oysters over the seaweed, balancing them so they don't lose any of their liquid. Cover loosely with aluminum foil and refrigerate. Remove the oysters 10 minutes before serving.

2. Preheat the oven to 300°F (150°C).

3. Place the pine nuts on a dry baking sheet and toast in the oven just until they turn golden, about 8 minutes. Remove them from the oven and let cool. Coarsely chop the nuts.

4. Place the lamb with the nuts, garlic, salt, black pepper, oregano, and pepper flakes in a medium bowl and mix well with your hands until thoroughly blended.

5. Take a teaspoonful of the mixture and cook it in a small skillet over medium-high heat, then taste for seasoning and adjust.

6. Shape the lamb mixture into eight equal-size patties, each about ½ inch (1.3 cm) thick.

ASTUCE: Why brush the oysters? Sometimes their shells are sandy or have loose bits on them and you don't want anything falling into the oyster when you shuck it.

7. Cook the lamb patties in a medium heavy skillet over medium-high heat until golden on the outside and cooked through, about 5 minutes on each side. Drain on paper towels.

8. To serve, place two lamb patties on each of four warmed dinner plates. Garnish each with a lemon quarter and serve the oysters with bread and butter alongside.

ASTUCES:

- You may make this in a single dish—the method is the same; the baking time a bit longer.
- You likely will have leftover mashed potatoes, which reheat perfectly.

Braised Lamb and Vegetable Shepherd's Pie

HACHIS PARMENTIER À L'AGNEAU

Hachis Parmentier is the French version of shepherd's pie, a homey dish originally made with leftover pot au feu. Like so many things, this dish has gone "uptown," and evolved into a smarter version of the original, not made with leftovers but as a featured and favorite plat du jour. It's often made with lamb or duck, and I once tasted a version made with octopus. (I didn't ask for that recipe!)

Like so many comfort foods, this dish originated on the French farm. When the farm cook made hachis Parmentier, she baked it in one dish—I've dressed it up by making individual servings, which gives it a boost of elegance. Serve a rich red with this, ideally one from Cahors.

MAKES 8 SERVINGS

EQUIPMENT: large heavy-bottomed saucepan, large strainer, baking sheet, eight 3½-inch (9 cm) stainless-steel pastry rings, small saucepan

PREPARATION TIME: if shoulder boned, 35 minutes, including making mashed potatoes

COOKING TIME: 2 hours 25 minutes

DIFFICULTY LEVEL: not difficult, but requires patience

One 2-pound (1 kg) lamb shoulder, boned, with bones if possible

1 to 2 tablespoons olive oil

Fine sea salt and freshly ground black pepper

4 medium carrots (3 ounces; 90 g each), peeled and diced

2 medium onions (5 ounces; 150 g each), diced

½ celery stalk, strings removed, diced

10 fresh thyme sprigs

2 fresh or dried imported bay leaves

4 garlic cloves

1 recipe Perfect Mashed Potatoes with Crème Fraîche (page 263)

1. Cut the lamb shoulder into 1-inch (2.5 cm) pieces. Heat the oil in a large heavy-bottomed saucepan over medium-high heat, and when the oil is hot, add the meat, season lightly with salt and pepper, and brown on all sides, 5 to 7 minutes. Remove the lamb from the pan and add the vegetables. Cook, stirring occasionally, until the onions are translucent, about 8 minutes.

2. Preheat the oven to 325°F (163°C).

3. Return the lamb to the pan and stir. Add the thyme, bay leaves, and garlic cloves to the meat and vegetables, along with the shoulder bone(s), and enough water to cover. When the water comes to a boil, remove the pot from the heat, cover, and place it in the center of the oven. Bake until the lamb and the vegetables are very tender, stirring occasionally, for about 2 hours.

4. When the lamb is cooked through and very tender, remove it from the oven. When it is cool enough to handle, go through the pieces of lamb with your fingers, shredding them and removing any bones and herbs.

(continued)

5. Place a strainer over a bowl, and tip the lamb into it to drain, reserving the juices.

6. Increase the oven temperature to 450°F (235°C). Line a baking sheet with parchment paper.

7. Line eight 3½-inch (9 cm) stainless-steel pastry rings with parchment paper. Trim the paper so that it is flush with the edges of the round. Set the rounds on the prepared baking sheet. Place ¾ cup (180 g) of the lamb mixture inside each ring and press on it firmly. Top each round with ½ cup (125 g) of mashed potatoes, pressing it gently into the lamb and smoothing the edges. The potatoes will rise above the edge of the metal rings.

8. Place the baking sheet in the center of the oven. Bake until the potatoes begin to turn golden on top and the meat and potatoes are heated through, about 15 minutes.

9. Heat the reserved lamb juices in a small saucepan over low heat.

10. Remove the baking sheet from the oven. Slide a metal spatula under each ring and transfer to the center of a warmed dinner plate. Carefully remove the rings by pulling up on them. If the parchment paper doesn't come away with the ring, gently remove it. Surround each hachis with sauce, evenly dividing it among the plates. Serve immediately.

ANTOINE-AUGUSTE PARMENTIER AND THE POTATO

Antoine-Auguste Parmentier was a pharmacist in the French army who served in the Seven Years' War between France and Prussia in the 18th century. He was taken prisoner, and his prison diet included potatoes, which in France were only considered good for hogs. In fact, legend says that the French parliament had forbidden the cultivation of potatoes for human consumption, because they were thought to be a possible cause of leprosy.

But Parmentier knew differently and, post-imprisonment, when he returned to France, he tried to get the suspicious French to eat the potato. He realized that if he proposed it as a "medicine" it might take hold, and so he let out the word that the potato was a potential cure for dysentery. The Paris Faculty of Medicine was impressed and declared potatoes edible. Apparently at that point, no one outside the medical profession took real interest in the charms of the potato.

Parmentier persisted, some say to his self-aggrandizement. He hosted all-potato dinners, gave King Louis XVI potato blossoms to wear in his lapel, and with the blessing of the king had the royal gardeners plant potatoes down the center of the Champs-Elysées. During the day, the potatoes were under heavy guard; at night, the guards went home, and the poor and hungry of Paris, and others too, snuck into the potato "fields" to steal the mysterious plants with the misshapen tubers hanging from the roots. Parmentier made sure that rumors abounded on how to prepare the potato, and soon the forbidden vegetable became a staple.

Today if a dish has the word "Parmentier" in its title, you know it includes potatoes.

ASTUCES:

- When you flame anything in the kitchen, make sure your hair is tied back, your sleeves rolled up, and any jewelry tucked away.
- This dish is best made the day before, refrigerated, and reheated the following day. Before you reheat it, you may want to skim off the fat that forms on top of the sauce.

Slow-Cooked Beef and Onion Stew

BOEUF BRAISÉ AUX OIGNONS

This dish is on the menu of so many cafés in winter that it is considered a classic. It's easy to make and oh-so-satisfying to eat. I save it for a chilly, rainy day when I know that I've got big appetites to satisfy. The meat practically melts in the oven, yet it retains a toothsome quality that is so satisfying. And if you've chosen flavorful meat, you'll have a very flavorful dish on your hands. As for the onions, make sure to keep the root end intact, so they will stay together as they cook. Note that white is the chosen wine for this dish, which originates in the north of France. I like to recommend a room-temperature Chardonnay (Burgundy) or a white Sancerre to drink alongside. Serve with bread, of course, or buttered pasta à la française!

SERVES 6 TO 8

EQUIPMENT: large heavy saucepan or flameproof casserole dish, cutting board that collects juices, slotted spoon

PREPARATION TIME: about 25 minutes

COOKING TIME: about 2½ hours

DIFFICULTY LEVEL: simple

---

1 beef top or bottom round roast (3 pounds; 1.5 kg), tied with kitchen twine so it holds together as a piece

9 garlic cloves—5 cloves sliced in half, 4 left whole

6 ounces (180 g) slab bacon, rind removed, cut into 1-by-¼-by-¼ inch (2.5 cm-by-6 mm-by-6 mm) pieces

1 to 2 tablespoons olive oil

¼ cup (60 ml) eau de vie, such as Calvados or Armagnac

1½ to 2 cups (375 to 500 ml) dry white wine, such as Aligoté

1 to 1½ cups (250 to 375 ml) Beef Stock (page 329)

1 large Bouquet Garni (page 338)

Sea salt and freshly ground black pepper

10 small yellow onions (about 2 ounces; 60 g each), peeled but kept whole

Fresh thyme and flat-leaf parsley sprigs for garnish

1. Pat the beef dry. Make 10 deep slits in the beef and insert half a garlic clove into each slit. Set aside.

2. Place the bacon in a large heavy saucepan just large enough to hold the meat, liquids, and onions. Lightly brown the bacon on all sides, adding a bit of oil to the pan if necessary, to keep it from sticking. Transfer the bacon to a small dish, and if there is a great deal of fat in the pan, drain all but about 2 teaspoons.

3. Add the beef and brown it gently on all sides over medium heat, about 7 minutes total. Pour in the eau de vie and

(continued)

apply flame to it, using either a match or a lighter. *Stand back*, as the flames may leap to the ceiling. Shake the pan to roll the meat around in the eau de vie, as the flames gradually die down.

4. When the flames have died down, add the wine and enough stock to bring the liquid about one-third of the way up the meat. Add the bouquet garni and the remaining four garlic cloves. Turn the meat, cover the pan, and bring to a boil. Lower the heat to medium and simmer, basting frequently, for 1 hour. Season the beef with salt and pepper, turn it, cover the pan, and cook, basting, for another 2½ hours.

5. Meanwhile, heat 1 tablespoon of the remaining oil in a medium skillet and brown the onions over medium-high heat for 4 to 5 minutes on all sides, stirring or flipping them in the pan so they turn a golden brown without burning. Remove from the heat.

6. Thirty minutes to 1 hour before the beef is cooked, add the onions and bacon, pushing them under the meat. The cooking time for the onions will vary according to their size. If they are the size of a large marble, they will require about 30 minutes. If they are golf ball–size, they'll take 1 hour.

7. When the beef and onions are tender, transfer the meat to a cutting board that collects juices. Using a slotted spoon, transfer the onions to a warmed serving platter. Discard the bouquet garni. Skim the fat from the surface of the cooking juices (see Astuces), then taste. If they are richly flavored, simply adjust the seasoning as necessary. If the flavor seems thin, bring the juices to a boil and reduce by up to half; you should have at least 2 cups (500 ml) of juices to serve with the beef. Adjust the seasoning.

8. Remove the string from the beef and slice it into ½-inch (1.3 cm) slices. Overlap the slices on the warmed platter, surrounding them with the onions. Arrange some of the onions on top of the meat, drizzle with some of the cooking juices, and garnish the platter with the remaining onions and the herbs. Serve the cooking juices separately.

The Ultimate Beef Stew

BOEUF BOURGUIGNON

According to a poll taken by FranceTV in 2017, if France were a dish, it would be Boeuf Bourguignon. (Otherwise translated, 23 percent of the French say Boeuf Bourguignon is their favorite, most emblematic dish.). This classic stew from Burgundy is traditionally made with the humble cuts of the notable Charolais cattle, which have been raised in the region for centuries, and the simpler wines of Burgundy, such as Passe-Tout-Grains and Côtes d'Auxerre. As this dish cooks an afternoon away, the beef turns tender, melding with the other ingredients to produce a flavorful dish that is ideal for cool temperatures when the fire crackles and you need warmth. This plat du jour is easy—you mostly leave it alone to cook into a flavorful meal. Serve with boiled potatoes or roasted turnips and the same wine you used in the dish, for perfect harmony.

MAKES 4 TO 6 SERVINGS

EQUIPMENT: large nonreactive bowl, large ovenproof stockpot or Dutch oven with lid, skillet, slotted spoon

PREPARATION TIME: 30 minutes

COOKING TIME: 2 hours 40 minutes

DIFFICULTY LEVEL: simple

- 2 pounds (1 kg) beef (see Astuces), cut into 4-by-4-inch (10-by-10 cm) pieces
- 4 cups (1 L) flavorful wine from Burgundy
- 1 fresh thyme sprig
- 2 fresh or dried imported bay leaves
- Freshly ground black pepper
- 1 tablespoon olive oil, plus more if necessary
- 1 medium onion (5 ounces; 150 g), diced
- 4 garlic cloves, diced

- 2 tablespoons unbleached all-purpose flour
- 1 cup (250 ml) Beef Stock (page 329), veal stock, or water
- About 10 ounces (300 g) small carrots, trimmed and cut on the diagonal into ½-inch (1.3 cm) pieces

FOR GARNISH:

- 8 ounces (250 g) lightly smoked slab bacon, rind removed, cut into matchstick pieces
- 2 teaspoons olive oil (optional)

- 10 ounces (300 g) button mushrooms, trimmed, brushed clean, and cut into quarters
- 1 shy tablespoon unsalted butter (optional)
- Sea salt and freshly ground black pepper
- 1 bunch spring or pearl onions (about 7 ounces; 210 g total), trimmed and kept whole (if any approach the size of a golf ball, cut them in half)
- Fresh flat-leaf parsley sprigs

1. Place the meat in a large nonreactive bowl. Add the red wine, herbs, and pepper, mix well, cover, and let sit at room temperature for 2 hours or overnight in the refrigerator.

2. Drain the meat, reserving the marinade. Pat the meat dry.

(continued)

- The French use the upper part of the shank for bourguignon—it's filled with connective tissue that turns tender and rich while slow cooking and gives the dish its special texture. If you cannot find beef shank, try beef chuck roast.
- If you make this in the cool of spring and early summer, you can use fresh, young onions, which lend a special sweetness to the dish.

3. Heat 1 tablespoon of olive oil in a large ovenproof stockpot over medium heat. Add the diced onion and cook, stirring frequently and seasoning lightly with salt and pepper, until it begins to turn translucent and golden on all sides, about 5 minutes. Add the garlic, stir, and continue to cook until the onion and garlic are translucent, 3 to 4 additional minutes. Transfer the onion and garlic to a bowl or plate.

4. Add the meat to the pan, plus more oil if necessary, and brown it on all sides, seasoning it lightly with salt and pepper. Dust it with the flour, turning the meat as you dust, and continue to cook the meat for 2 minutes, turning it and moving it around in the pan. If you need to add a bit more oil, do.

5. Pour the reserved marinade into the pan and stir, scraping up any caramelized bits from the bottom of the stockpot. Add the stock or water and the onions and garlic, then bring to a boil over medium-high heat. Lower the heat under it so the liquids are simmering merrily. Cover and place in the oven to cook for about 2 hours, stirring the meat at regular intervals.

6. After 2 hours, add the carrots, pushing them down into the liquid, and continue to cook until the carrots are tender through, an additional 30 minutes.

7. While the carrots are cooking, prepare the garnishes: Heat a skillet over medium heat and add the bacon (if necessary, add 2 teaspoons of oil to the pan) and cook, stirring often and shaking the pan until the bacon is golden, about 5 minutes. Remove the bacon from the pan with a slotted spoon, transferring it to a waiting dish. Add the mushrooms to the fat in the pan and cook, stirring constantly, until they give up their liquid and are golden on all sides, about 6 minutes. If there isn't enough fat in the pan, then add 1 tablespoon of butter to help them brown. Season them lightly with salt and pepper. Remove the mushrooms from the pan and add the onions. Cook them, stirring often, until they are golden on all sides. Cover and cook until they are nearly tender, about 5 minutes. Season them lightly with salt and pepper. Remove from the heat.

8. Ten minutes before the carrots are cooked, add the bacon, mushrooms, and onions to the boeuf bourguignon in the oven, stirring them into it, and remove the lid.

9. To serve, remove the boeuf bourguignon from the oven and ladle equal amounts of into four to six warmed, shallow bowls. Garnish with parsley sprigs and serve immediately.

Mme. Lambert's Lemon-Scented Seasonal Veal Stew

BLANQUETTE DE VEAU AU CITRON "MME. LAMBERT"

Blanquette de Veau is one of the simplest dishes to prepare, yet so festive and elegant it seems as though it must have taken forever. A standby in the neighborhood cafés of Paris, it is also a comforting dish which has a certain "noblesse," or nobility, and is often reserved for a special Sunday lunch. I think of making it most in the spring because veal is at its best then, and so are the first vegetables that complement this dish, such as small new onions and carrots, fresh thyme with its blossoms, the most tender stalks of celery. If you can find new potatoes to serve alongside (see Buttered New Potatoes with Thyme, Parsley, and Lemon, page 261) that is an added bit of perfection!

This recipe was inspired by Renée Habozit, my Parisian neighbor, who served it to a group on a sunny spring Sunday, and it was so festive and flavorful that everyone asked for more.

This is lovely with a full-flavored white, such as a Saint-Peray, a relatively little-known wine from Ardèche, or a gorgeous white Burgundy.

SERVES 8

EQUIPMENT: large saucepan, fine-mesh sieve, heavy-bottomed sauce-pan or Dutch oven with lid, skillet

PREPARATION TIME: 20 to 25 minutes

COOKING TIME: 2 hours 15 minutes

DIFFICULTY LEVEL: simple

- 2 pounds (1 kg) veal shoulder, cut into 2-inch (5 cm) pieces
- 3 tablespoons all-purpose flour
- 2 tablespoons (30 g) unsalted butter
- 2 tablespoons mild vegetable oil
- Fine sea salt and freshly ground black pepper
- 5 cups (1.2 L) water
- ½ lemon, cut into quarters

- 10 fresh thyme branches
- 2 fresh bay leaves
- 1 large garlic clove
- 5 small carrots (about 8 ounces; 250 g total), trimmed and cut on the diagonal into 2-inch (5 cm) lengths
- 2 celery stalks, kept whole
- White parts of 3 leeks, cut into ½-inch (1.3 cm) rounds
- 18 spring onions (about 0.5 ounce; 15 g each), stems

- and root end trimmed, or 18 pearl onions
- 8 ounces (250 g) button mushrooms, trimmed and cut into sixths
- 2 large egg yolks
- 1 cup (250 ml) crème fraîche
- 3 tablespoons (45 ml) fresh lemon juice
- Fresh flat-leaf parsley or chervil sprigs for garnish

1. Bring about 5 cups (2½ L) of water to a boil in a large saucepan. Add the veal, return to a boil, and boil for 3 minutes. Remove the veal from the water, discard the water, and pat the veal dry on all sides. Roll the veal in the flour. Place the veal in a large sieve and shake it to remove any excess flour.

2. Melt 1 tablespoon of the butter with 1 tablespoon of the oil in a large heavy-bottomed saucepan over medium heat. When the butter froths, add the veal, season with salt and pepper, and brown it on all sides, 8 to 10 minutes. You may need to work in two batches, adding additional butter and oil as you brown the veal.

3. Leave the veal in the pan and pour in enough water just to cover. Bring the water to a boil over medium-high heat, then lower the heat so the water is simmering. Scrape up any browned bits as best you can from the bottom of the pan, then add the lemon, herbs, garlic, carrots, celery, and leeks to the pot. Stir, make sure the water returns to a simmer, then cook, partially covered, stirring from time to time, until the meat is very tender, about 1½ hours.

4. Add the onions to the pan, pushing them under the surface of the water, and continue to cook until the onions are tender, about 20 minutes. Remove from the heat.

5. Just after you've added the onions, melt the remaining oil and butter in a skillet over medium heat. When the butter froths, add the mushrooms and cook them, stirring and shaking the pan, until they are golden and have given off much of their liquid, 6 to 8 minutes. Season them with salt and pepper, give the pan a good shake to blend the seasoning, and remove from the heat.

6. Whisk together the egg yolks, crème fraîche, and lemon juice in a small bowl.

7. Just before serving the veal, whisk ¼ cup (60 ml) of the veal cooking liquid into the crème fraîche mixture until it is combined, then thoroughly stir this mixture into the veal and vegetables. Cook until the mixture thickens slightly, stirring gently and making sure it doesn't boil, 5 to 8 minutes. Stir in the mushrooms and their juices, adjust the seasoning, then serve with a garnish of parsley.

THE LUXURY OF VEAL

Veal is the tender meat of the young cow and a standard on the plat du jour menu. Veal is available in every butcher shop in France, but despite this availability, it is still considered a luxury worthy of a celebration.

It goes into dishes such as the flavorful Seasonal Veal Stew (page 130), which take perfect advantage of the texture of good veal.

Texture, in veal? Yes. Veal has texture when it is raised outdoors in a pasture, where it nips at tender blades of grass and sips mother's milk. Its meat is rosy red and responds perfectly to braising, roasting, even sautéing, giving dishes with full and elegant flavor.

Such veal represents 5 percent of the production in France, and it is labeled "Veau Fermier Lourd Elevé sous la Mère," literally translated as "farm-raised, larger-than-average veal raised under the mother." This method follows tradition, when the male cow was raised outdoors to a certain young age and then butchered, whereas the female was left to grow into a milk and calf producer. The farm cook made the most of the delicately delicious meat from the young animals, including it in her repertoire and turning veal into a common luxury.

Industrially raised veal, on the other hand, is insipid in both flavor and texture, and shrouded with controversy. So it should be, as the conditions in which it is produced are shameful. When I encourage you to eat veal, I intend for you to use that which is humanely raised. Not only is this better from an ethical standpoint, but it is also superior in texture and flavor. In the United States, such veal is labeled "Certified Humane" and it echoes the excellent French veal, raised outdoors "under" its mother.

Butter-Drizzled Seared Steak with Potato Gratin

FILET DE BOEUF GRILLÉ, GRATIN DE POMMES DE TERRE

A classic plat du jour, steak is like a siren call in France. Traditionally, the perfect French steak is seared and nearly raw in the center, seasoned with lots of cracked pepper and a nugget of butter. Alongside creamy potato gratin, it is the ultimate comfort food. Steak is also a celebratory dish for the French—perfect for a birthday lunch or a special meal with friends.

When cooking steak, do as my butcher suggests: heat a dry pan over medium-high heat. When it's hot, add the steak and cook it for one minute per side. You'll have a dark, toasty exterior and a melting interior. If you want the steak cooked more, simply lower the heat to medium and increase the cooking time. Place the butter atop the steak right when you remove it from the pan, and it will melt right into the meat.

For the gratin, resist the temptation to add cheese. When prepared as indicated here, the potatoes melt with the milk and cream into a richly pure and seductive dish. And note just the hint of garlic. If you want more garlic (the gratin doesn't really need it), you could very thinly slice a clove and incorporate it with the potatoes and cream. Serve this delectable combination with a Corbières from Clos de l'Anhel.

SERVES 4 TO 6

EQUIPMENT: mandoline or fine slicing blade on a food processor (for potatoes), medium baking dish, large heavy skillet

PREPARATION TIME: 15 to 20 minutes

BAKING TIME FOR THE GRATIN: 1 hour 10 minutes

COOKING TIME FOR THE STEAK: 3 minutes

DIFFICULTY LEVEL: simple

FOR THE GRATIN:

1 garlic clove

1 cup (250 ml) whole milk

2 cups (500 ml) crème fraîche

Fine sea salt and freshly ground black pepper

Freshly grated nutmeg

2 pounds (1 kg) starchy potatoes, such as russet, peeled and very thinly sliced

FOR THE SEARED STEAK:

Four 6-ounce (180 g) steaks (your choice of steak variety, though I recommend sirloin), trimmed of excess fat (optional)

Sea salt and freshly ground black pepper

FOR GARNISH:

About 3 tablespoons (45 g) unsalted butter, cut into 4 equal-size pieces, at room temperature

Fresh flat-leaf parsley sprigs

(continued)

ASTUCE: The recipe calls for starchy potatoes, which make the most tender and meltingly delicious gratin.

1. Prepare the gratin: Preheat the oven to 375°F (190°C).

2. Cut the garlic clove in half and rub the cut sides firmly all over the interior of a medium baking dish.

3. Whisk together the milk and the crème fraîche in a large bowl. Season generously with salt, pepper, and as you like with nutmeg. Whisk, then add the potatoes and mix them thoroughly (using your hands—the best tool here).

4. Turn the potato mixture into the medium baking dish, making sure to scrape out all of the cream with a rubber spatula.

5. Bake the gratin in the center of the oven for 15 minutes. Stir the potatoes gently, then bake for an additional 20 minutes. Stir the potatoes again, then bake until the gratin is bubbling and golden on top, another 20 to 35 minutes.

6. Remove from the oven and set aside.

7. Prepare the steak: While the gratin is sitting, heat a large heavy skillet (nonstick is fine) over medium-high heat. When it is hot, add the steaks and cook until they are golden on one side, 1 to 1½ minutes. Salt and pepper the steak, turn it, and cook it until it is golden on the other side, 1 to 1½ minutes. Your steak is cooked, French-style. If you want it more cooked, simply increase the cooking time on each side.

8. To serve, place a steak on each of four warmed dinner plates and top each with a piece of butter. Place a generous amount of gratin next to each steak, and garnish with parsley.

Sautéed Tenderloin with Provençale Olives

FILET SAUTÉ AUX OLIVES DE PROVENCE

This combination may seem like it was born from genius. But no, it isn't genius. It's the result of terroir—that of Provence, where the olive is queen and beef is hearty and filled with flavor. Like so many regional dishes, it is born of the simplest of ingredients, which the French cook takes to unimaginable heights. Its sunny flavors are perfect with an elegant Côtes du Rhône. Serve this with a salad, or the Buttered New Potatoes with Thyme, Parsley, and Lemon (page 261).

SERVES 4

EQUIPMENT: nonreactive dish, small saucepan, large skillet

PREPARATION TIME: 10 minutes; 1 to 3 hours macerating time

COOKING TIME: 10 minutes

DIFFICULTY LEVEL: simple

Four 4-ounce (120 g) tenderloin steaks, about ½ inch (1.3 cm) thick

2 tablespoons olive oil

3 fresh or 2 dried imported bay leaves

½ cup (3 ounces; 90 g) black fleshy olives, pitted

Sea salt and freshly ground black pepper

1 cup (250 ml) dry white wine

3 tablespoons tomato paste

ASTUCE: Boiling the olives makes them tender and succulent, and it removes some of the salt, too, which is so good when the olives are served on their own but would be too much here.

1. Rub the steaks all over with 1 tablespoon of the olive oil. Crush two of the bay leaves and sprinkle half of them over the steaks, then turn the steaks and sprinkle with the remaining crushed bay leaves. Place in a nonreactive dish and let sit at room temperature, covered, for at least 1 hour and up to 3 hours in the refrigerator before cooking. If the steaks are refrigerated, bring them to room temperature before cooking by removing them from the refrigerator at least 30 minutes before you plan to cook them.

2. Bring 2 cups (500 ml) of water to a boil in a small saucepan over medium-high heat. Add the olives, return to a boil, drain the olives, and discard the liquid.

3. Heat the remaining tablespoon of oil in a large skillet over medium heat. When the oil is hot but not smoking, add the steaks and brown them on both sides, seasoning generously with salt and pepper, until they are very brown and nearly cooked through, about 5 minutes total. Remove the steaks from the pan, leaving the cooking juices. Add the wine, tomato paste, remaining bay leaf, and olives to the pan, stir, and cook until the liquids are reduced by about two-thirds and slightly thickened, about 5 minutes. Return the steaks and any juices to the pan and cook just until heated through, turning the steaks once so they are coated with the sauce.

4. To serve, arrange the steaks on a warmed, round serving platter. Place the olives in the center and dress the meat with the sauce.

Beef, Onions, Shallots, and Spice Bread Braised in Beer

CARBONNADE DE BOEUF À LA FLAMANDE

This typical Flemish dish is so rich to look at, it almost fills you up before you take a bite. I just love its rough poetry—it's a peasant dish yet laced with the delicate flavors from the *pain d'épices* (spice bread)—cinnamon, some anise, a little orange. And then there is the slight hoppy taste of beer, which identifies it immediately as being a dish from the north of France, near Belgium, where breweries abound and beer is the beverage of choice. Your favorite microbrew will be delicious with Carbonnade, but you can also serve this with a sunny Languedoc, an ideal accompaniment. Serve with Simple Boiled Potatoes (page 264) alongside. And note that while the cooking time is long, it involves just oven and dish, not you!

ABOUT 6 SERVINGS

EQUIPMENT: large, heavy-bottomed, ovenproof stockpot or baking dish; wire rack

PREPARATION TIME: 20 to 30 minutes

COOKING TIME: 2 hours 45 minutes

DIFFICULTY LEVEL: simple

---

1 tablespoon olive oil

1 scant tablespoon untoasted peanut or grapeseed oil

1½ pounds (750 g) beef shoulder, cut into 4-ounce (60 g) pieces

Coarse sea salt and freshly ground black pepper

2 large yellow onions (7 ounces; 210 g each), finely sliced

4 shallots, finely sliced

3 garlic cloves, minced

1 heaping teaspoon light brown sugar

6 tablespoons (90 ml) red wine vinegar

1 tablespoon all-purpose flour

One 8-ounce (250 ml) bottle Belgian beer (or your favorite)

3 cups (750 ml) Beef Stock (page 329) or water

1 Bouquet Garni (page 338)

4 slices Pain d'Épices (page 309) or day-old bread, 3-by-2.5-by-½ inch (7.5-by-6.5-by-1.3 cm)

Fresh flat-leaf parsley sprigs for garnish

1. Heat the oils in a large, heavy-bottomed, ovenproof stockpot or casserole dish over medium-high heat. When the oil is hot but not smoking, brown the meat on all sides, seasoning with salt and pepper, 5 to 6 minutes total.

2. Lower the heat to medium. Remove the meat from the pot and let it drain on a wire rack. Add the onions, shallots, and garlic to the stockpot and stir. Sprinkle with the brown sugar and cook, stirring, until the mixture begins to brown and smell like caramel, 5 to 6 minutes.

3. Preheat the oven to 325°F (160°C).

(continued)

- I make my own Pain d'Épices (page 309) because I prefer its flavor and texture over what is available to purchase, and the leftovers are incredible when toasted.
- Why do I ask for two oils? Because olive oil adds a touch of elegant flavor, and the peanut or grape-seed oil keeps the olive oil from burning!
- This dish improves overnight, so consider making it the day before you plan to serve it and reheating it gently.

4. Deglaze the stockpot by pouring in the vinegar and stirring to scrape up any caramelized bits from the bottom of the pan. Sprinkle the mixture with the flour and stir for at least 2 minutes, so the flour loses its flavor. Add the beer and stock or water and stir. Add the bouquet garni and the slices of pain d'épices to the mixture, pushing them gently into the liquid. Cover the pot and place it in the center of the oven. Cook, stirring it every 15 minutes or so, until the meat is tender, about 2½ hours. Add additional beef stock or water, if necessary, to keep the meat moist.

5. Remove from the oven and rectify the seasonings. Let the dish sit for at least 1 hour, or even overnight, in the refrigerator. If you let it sit overnight, you can easily skim the fat from the Carbonnade before reheating, if desired.

6. Reheat over low heat or in a 325°F (165°C) oven, garnish with parsley, and serve.

MEAT TEMPERATURES

The French like their meat rare (including duck breast), except for the more humble cuts that are marbled with fat and connective tissue. They prefer these cuts slow-cooked, until they melt in your mouth.

The following is a dictionary for the doneness of meat—very handy for a cook using a French recipe for meat or for a diner perusing a French restaurant menu.

- *Très bleu*: just about raw, though it is briefly seared at a high temperature on the exterior; internal temperature is 45°C (113°F)
- *Bleu*: nearly raw, still bright red on the interior and browned on the exterior; internal temperature is 55°C (131°F)
- *Saignant*: rare, the meat is rosy-pink; internal temperature is 60°C (140°F)
- *À point*: medium, the meat is slightly pink on the interior; internal temperature is 65°C (149°F)
- *Bien cuit*: well done, but a French meat-eater might say "ruined," because the meat is brown throughout and there is little moisture; internal temperature is 70°C (158°F)

CHAPTER 5
PORK

AH, FRENCH PORK. It's in a class apart from any other meat, anywhere. First, the French revere the pig because it sustains them and has been a key ingredient for centuries. But also because every part of the animal is edible, from *la barbe à la queue* (literally, "the beard to the tail"). The feet are a delicacy, as are the ears, the cheeks, and the tail. The meat is salted, smoked, eaten fresh. Most gelatin comes from pork, and the head is cooked into a beautiful dish called *fromage de tête* (head cheese), which is a sort of pâté usually served as a first course. The pig is a generous beast and, in the case of French or any pork raised with care and attention, lean and toothsome, ready to be combined with all manner of ingredients. Enjoy these recipes, as they speak to the history—and the tradition—of France!

THE FRENCH PIG

The pig, oh, the pig. It's been a staple on the French table since well before the Romans came to conquer the Gauls. In fact, when the Romans showed up, the Gauls were already artists at preserving the pig. They transformed every little bit of it into something delicious, or something useful around the house. Nothing was wasted, which is why archaeologists find little trace of the animal from antiquity. There was simply nothing left once dinner was done.

Its usefulness didn't end with the Gauls. During Charlemagne's reign, the pig was used as a form of measurement. It lived wild in the forests of the empire, snuffling everything in its path. A brilliant strategist and gourmand, Charlemagne calculated that each pig required about three acres to live, so he would send out his men to count the pigs. If a forest contained 100 animals, he knew that forest was close to 300 acres. This information was useful for his empire, because a forest's owner was taxed according to acreage owned.

Some of those forest pigs migrated to cities, where they served as street cleaners. Not all city residents loved having pigs underfoot, however, and by the 16th century they'd been pretty much banished to the outskirts, where a more organized pig industry was begun. As the wild pigs became gradually domesticated, they evolved into the pig we recognize today, losing their dark, bristly skin and long, razor-sharp teeth.

Today, France produces only 9 percent of Europe's pork, but it might arguably be considered the country that does the most in the kitchen with its gorgeous meat. This makes sense. When one's ancestors—the Gauls—were already making world-class sausages, and braising pork over the coals before the dawn of time, there is a deep trace and an inherited skill in the French culinary memory not just for cooking the pig, but for honoring it, too!

And the French do. They have an entire category of shops devoted to the pig—the charcuterie. Here, the pig is displayed in all its finery, from fat-speckled sausages to chunky, garlic-spiced pâtés, creamy rillettes (pork cooked with herbs in pork fat), coils of deep red blood sausages, paper-thin slices of flavorful ham. And then there is the array of cuts, from thick chops to sinewy shoulders, cheeks, collars, and more. Although an urban charcuterie eschews displaying the head and tail, not so at a countryside farmers' market. There, where good home cooks abound, the head, tail, feet, and the rest are there for all to see, buy, and prepare.

More than one million pigs are produced artisanally (outdoors on the farm) in France each year. Their meat is what makes the reputation of French pork, with its deep flavor and toothsome texture. *Toothsome* doesn't necessarily mean tender, nor does it mean tough. It means tasty/tender/filled with texture. But for the record, French pork needs long, slow cooking to soften and allow the flavor to develop. Even a French pork chop requires time, and any respectable butcher in the land will tell you this as he cuts and trims each chop, carefully wraps it, then holds it hostage while he explains how to cook it. "Cold oven," my butcher always says. "If you're going to cook on top of the stove, slow, slow, slow," he adds. I always agree, because I'm fearful that if I don't, he won't hand over the goods. And most of the time, I do as he suggests.

While I love all the varieties of pork that my butcher has on offer, there is one particular race of pig that wins my heart, as much for its look as for its taste. It's the darling Porc Blanc de l'Ouest from Brittany. Noted in its "characteristics" as friendly and maternal, its ears grow forward, hiding its eyes, giving it a clownish, befuddled sort of look that belies its ability to live and thrive outdoors. And its flavor is unimpeachable. But every region and country has its favorite variety, each for you to discover.

Pork Sausage and Chard Salad

CAILLETTES EN SALADE

This dish is the product of midday hunger, the kind that strikes after a backbreaking morning hefting hay bales, digging postholes, harvesting the white-stemmed chard for market. Historically, this is the dish of the Provençal farmworker, intended to be eaten at noon under the shade of a plane tree, washed down by rough country wine, and followed by a quick nap before taking up the work again. Today, of course, it's a perfect plat du jour, representative of the thrifty and delicious meals that reflect the Provençal landscape and history. Make this and serve it on the salad; if you've got leftovers, send them off as picnic fare or in a lunchbox. Serve this with a 100 percent Carignan wine, such as Temps de Reveurs from Jérôme Maillot.

SERVES 6 TO 8

EQUIPMENT: large pot, small skillet, 2 large (12-by-8-inch; 30-by-20 cm) baking dishes

PREPARATION TIME: 25 minutes

COOKING TIME: 45 to 50 minutes

DIFFICULTY LEVEL: simple

FOR THE SAUSAGES:

Fine sea salt

1 pound (500 g) Swiss chard, well rinsed

1 pound (500 g) unseasoned ground pork

1 medium onion (5 ounces; 150 g), diced

2 garlic cloves, minced

1 tablespoon fresh thyme leaves

Freshly ground black pepper

1 teaspoon sea salt

9 or 10 fresh sage leaves

3 ounces (90 g) caul fat (optional)

FOR THE SALAD:

3 teaspoons balsamic vinegar

1 teaspoon Dijon mustard

Sea salt and freshly ground black pepper

3 tablespoons (45 ml) olive oil

1 tablespoon (15 ml) walnut oil

7 ounces (210 g) salad greens (8 cups, loosely packed), such as red or green oak leaf, or a blend of arugula, oak leaf, romaine, and Lolla Rossa

8 fresh sage leaves for garnish (optional)

1. Prepare the sausages: Preheat the oven to 400°F (205°C).

2. Place 4 quarts (4 L) of water in a large pot, add 2 tablespoons of salt, and bring to a boil. Cook the Swiss chard, in several batches if necessary, until the stems are tender, about 4 minutes. Drain the cooked chard, and when it is cool enough to handle, wrap it in a large tea towel and gently squeeze out as much liquid as possible without turning it to mush. Finely chop the chard.

3. Combine the chopped chard with all the remaining sausage ingredients, except the sage and the caul fat, in a large bowl. Using your hands, blend thoroughly. Pinch off

(continued)

ASTUCES:

- If you cannot find Swiss chard (called either *blettes* or *bettes* in French, with no reference at all to the Swiss!), you may use spinach.
- Caul fat is the thin membrane of fat that covers the internal organs of cows, sheep, and pigs. In France, it is called *crépine* and is often used to wrap sausages like these, which also might be called *crépinettes*. Generally from the pig but sometimes from the cow, it holds the meat together, and while it practically melts away, it leaves a little lacy trace on the exterior of the sausage. It is not indispensable.
- You can assemble the sausages the night before you plan to bake and serve them.

about 1 tablespoon of the mixture and sauté it in a small skillet over medium heat until it is cooked through; taste for seasoning and adjust if necessary.

4. Divide the mixture into 9 or 10 equal-size portions (each about 3 ounces; 90 g). Set a sage leaf atop each sausage, with the inside of the leaf toward the sausage.

5. If you are using caul fat, cut it into roughly 4-inch (10 cm) squares and wrap each sausage firmly in a square. You may need to do a bit of patchwork if the squares don't all quite stretch to cover the sausage. Alternatively, if you have a good-size piece of caul fat, lay it out on a work surface and set the sausage portions on the fat, leaving a 2-inch (5 cm) border of fat around each sausage. Cut around the sausages and proceed with the recipe.

6. Arrange the sausages in two large (12-by-8-inch; 30-by-20 cm) baking dishes, placing them about ¼ inch (6 mm) apart. Bake in the center of the oven for 35 minutes. Turn the sausages over and continue to bake until they are firm (though not rubbery) and cooked through, an additional 10 to 15 minutes.

7. While the sausages are baking, prepare the vinaigrette for the salad: Whisk together the vinegar, mustard, and salt and pepper to taste in a large bowl. Add the oils in a thin stream, whisking constantly until the vinaigrette emulsifies.

8. Remove the sausages from the oven and drain off any excess fat.

9. Tear the greens into large bite-size pieces and add them to the bowl of vinaigrette. Toss the greens with the dressing and divide them among six to eight dinner plates. Top each salad with hot sausage. Garnish with sage leaves, if desired, and serve immediately.

Alsatian Bacon, Onion, and Cream Pizza

FLAMMEKUECHE—TARTE FLAMBÉE

This wonderful dish originated with the bakers of Alsace, the Franco-Germanic region of France. To say it's Franco-German isn't really accurate, except when it comes to the cuisine and perhaps the accent, though the region has been a ping-pong ball between France and Germany at many times during its history.

This dish is a farm tradition, created when the Alsatian baker (who was often a local farmer with a wood-burning bread oven) took a piece of bread dough and rolled it paper thin, slathered it with fromage blanc, sprinkled it with onions and bacon, and put it into the fire before the wood had burned down to coals. The flames licked the tart, slightly burning the edges while the rest of it baked to a creamy tenderness, thus the name *Tarte Flambée* (burnt tart). The farmer's goal was to feed himself and his workers, who would slice the tart, fold the pieces, and eat them dripping hot. Today, this gorgeous dish symbolizes Alsatian cuisine, and it is served like pizza for an appetizer or a whole meal. When properly made, it is still burnt at the edges, and easy to roll or fold so the topping doesn't drip off it. Serve a Riesling or a Pinot Gris with this, and a big green salad, such as A Classic Green Salad (page 265). Make several flammekueches, because all will disappear.

MAKES ONE 10½-INCH (27 CM) TART; SERVES 2 TO 4 HUNGRY PEOPLE!

EQUIPMENT: rolling pin, baking sheet

PREPARATION TIME: 15 minutes max

BAKING TIME: 20 to 25 minutes

DIFFICULTY LEVEL: simple

---

1 medium onion (5 ounces; 150 g), sliced paper thin

½ cup (125 g) Fromage Blanc (page 312)

½ cup (125 ml) crème fraîche

Fine sea salt and freshly ground black pepper

Generous pinch of freshly ground nutmeg

6 ounces (180 g) Tender Bread Dough (page 307)

All-purpose flour for dusting

Semolina for dusting (optional)

6 ounces (180 g) slab bacon, cut into matchstick pieces

1. Preheat the oven to 450°F (230°C).

2. Combine the onion, cheese, crème fraîche, salt, pepper, and nutmeg and let sit for 15 minutes to soften the onion.

3. Roll the dough on a lightly floured surface into a 10½-inch (27 cm) circle and place it on a lightly flour- or semolina-dusted baking sheet.

4. Spread the onion mixture over the dough right to the edge. Sprinkle the bacon evenly over the top.

5. Bake until the dough is crisp and the bacon is browned, about 20 minutes. Serve immediately, dusted with more pepper, if you like.

ASTUCES:

- The secret to the goodness of Tarte Flambée is to roll the bread dough as thinly as you can (try to get the dimension noted in the recipe) and bake in a hot, hot oven!
- If you cannot find or make fromage blanc, you can use crème fraîche.

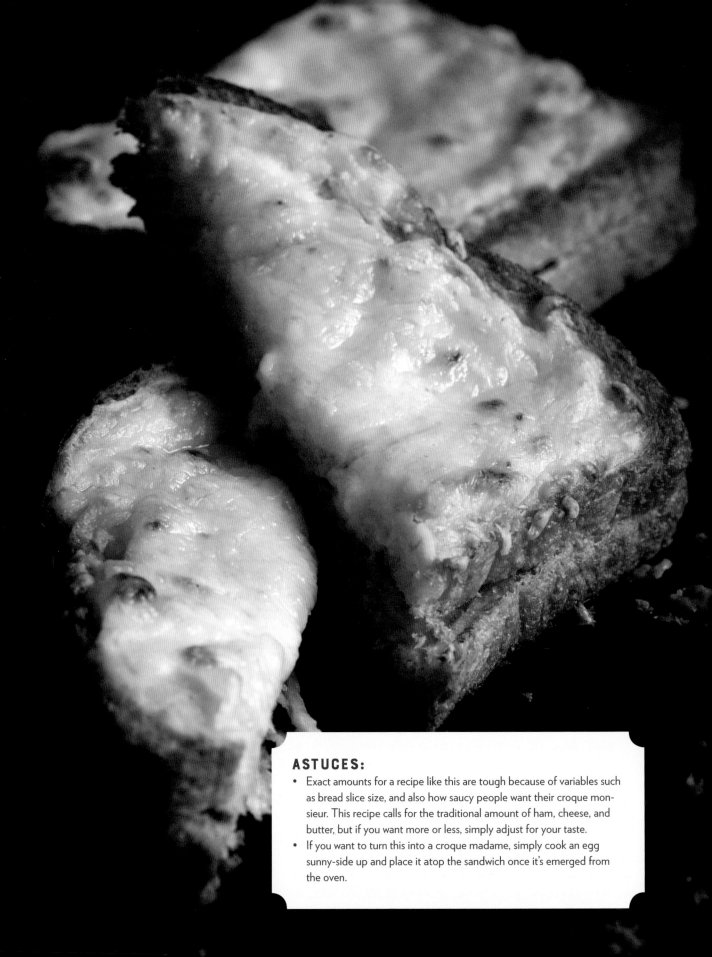

ASTUCES:

- Exact amounts for a recipe like this are tough because of variables such as bread slice size, and also how saucy people want their croque monsieur. This recipe calls for the traditional amount of ham, cheese, and butter, but if you want more or less, simply adjust for your taste.
- If you want to turn this into a croque madame, simply cook an egg sunny-side up and place it atop the sandwich once it's emerged from the oven.

Croque Monsieur

Calling a Croque Monsieur a toasted ham and cheese sandwich hardly does it justice, but that is basically what it is. It is also a *plat du jour incontournable*, which literally translates as "unavoidable daily dish" but actually means "obligatory to make and eat because nothing tastes better." It is a standby at every café and brasserie in the land, and it makes a perfect lunch or early dinner with a green salad alongside, such as A Classic Green Salad (page 265). Today, there are many versions of Croque Monsieur, from one like this that is made with beautifully fresh *pain de mie* (white bread) to those made with rustic sourdough.

Vital to a Croque Monsieur is the quality of the ingredients and keeping the sandwich moist and luscious. The béchamel here takes care of that. In fact, once you've served these, no one will ever again be satisfied with a garden-variety grilled cheese again! Serve with a lightly chilled Sauvignon Blanc.

SERVES 4
EQUIPMENT: baking sheet
PREPARATION TIME: 15 minutes
COOKING TIME: 20 minutes
DIFFICULTY LEVEL: simple

---

3 tablespoons (45 g) unsalted butter, at room temperature

8 slices best-quality sandwich bread (about 5-by-3.5 inches; 12.5-by-9 cm)

5 ounces (150 g) or 4 thin slices best-quality ham (see Astuces)

½ recipe Béchamel (page 326)

3 ounces (90 g) Gruyère, grated

1. Preheat the oven to 450°F (230°C).

2. Butter each slice of bread on one side.

3. Place a piece of ham on four of the buttered slices of bread. Top with another piece of bread, butter side up. Place the sandwiches on a baking sheet, then bake until they are golden at the edges, about 7 minutes.

4. Remove the sandwiches from the oven and place about 3 rounded tablespoons of béchamel atop each sandwich, making sure it evenly covers the top of the sandwich. Top with about 1 tablespoon of grated cheese. Return the baking sheet to the oven and bake until the béchamel is puffed and the cheese is melted and golden in spots, 10 to 12 minutes.

5. Remove from the oven and transfer to a serving platter. Serve immediately, though advise your diners to wait a few minutes before cutting into the Croque Monsieurs, because they will be blistering hot.

Pork, Chicken, and Beer Terrine

POTJEVLEESCH

The literal translation of *potjevleesch* is "little pot of meat." And this "little pot of meat" lives up to the name, except that it isn't very little! A combination of two cuts of pork and chicken, this is actually a gorgeous terrine that is so simple to make. It will impress anyone you serve it to, particularly if you serve it with A Classic Green Salad (page 265), and perhaps a serving of Baptiste's New Potato Fries (page 251). It so typifies the food of the north of France, which is simple, modest, and filled with delicious flavor. Serve this with your favorite amber microbrew, alongside cornichons and Dijon mustard.

SERVES 8 TO 10

EQUIPMENT: large nonreactive bowl, 8-cup (2 L) pâté mold or oven-proof baking dish with a lid

PREPARATION TIME: 40 minutes

COOKING TIME: 3 hours cooking time; 3 to 12 hours cooling/chilling time

DIFFICULTY LEVEL: simple

2 pounds (1 kg) pork shoulder meat, without bone, cut into 1-inch (2.5 cm) pieces

1¾ pounds (875 g) pork loin, cut into 1-inch (2.5 cm) pieces

Four 6-ounce (180 g) skinless chicken breasts, cut into 1-inch (2.5 cm) pieces

2 celery stalks (about 2.5 ounces; 75 g each), strings removed, cut into ½-inch (1.3 cm) pieces

2 medium carrots (3 ounces; 90 g each), trimmed and cut into ¼-inch (6 mm) rounds

5 garlic cloves, halved

10 fresh thyme sprigs

3 fresh or dried imported bay leaves

10 juniper berries

10 black peppercorns

48 ounces (3 pints; 1.5 L) amber beer, preferably microbrew

3 leaves gelatin

Fine sea salt

1. Mix together the meat, vegetables, and herbs in a large nonreactive bowl. Add the beer, stir or mix with your hands, cover, and refrigerate overnight.

2. Drain the meat mixture, reserving the marinade.

3. Place the gelatin leaves in a bowl of cold water, to soften them.

4. Preheat the oven to 300°F (150°C). Line a jelly roll pan with parchment paper and set aside.

5. Remove two-thirds of the carrot rounds from the meat mixture and reserve (if you wish to line the top of the terrine with the carrots).

6. Place one-third of the meat mixture on the bottom of the mold or baking dish. Season generously with salt. Remove a gelatin leaf from the water, squeeze out any excess water, then lay the leaf over the mixture. Repeat twice more with the meat mixture, salt, and gelatin. Arrange the carrot rounds atop the pâté, covering the surface, then pour in as much of the marinade as will fit into the dish—you are likely to use about two-thirds of the marinade.

(continued)

7. Place the lid on the dish, then seal it with aluminum foil. Set the dish on the prepared jelly roll pan and bake until the mixture has reached 180°F (82°C), about 3 hours. Remove it from the oven and let it cool. Set a dish on top of the meat, which will have mounded in the mold, to weigh it down as it cools and ensure that your layers will be nice and tidy. When it has cooled to room temperature, refrigerate it for several hours, preferably overnight.

8. To serve, simply cut slices from the mold and arrange them on a serving platter or cutting board. Note that the slices may not be *perfect*. Trust me, though. No one will mind! Garnish with A Classic Green Salad and serve.

ASTUCE: You can find leaf gelatin in the United States (you can easily get it online, such as at www.modernistpantry.com), and I highly recommend it because it is easy to use and allows for a very gentle solidity.

Belgian Endive and Leek Gratin

LE GRATIN D'ENDIVES ET POIREAUX

The French repertoire is replete with gratins, and the café and bistro menu is as well, for the gratin is a miracle comfort dish. This particular gratin is an example of such comfort food at its best, with the savory combination of leeks and slightly crisp endive, and the wretched excess of both boiled ham and bacon.

You can make this family-style, as indicated here, or make individual portions, whereby the dish suddenly becomes elegant. Simply reduce the cooking time to about 20 minutes for the individual gratins. Serve this as a side dish, or with a big green salad, such as A Classic Green Salad (page 265), and a nice red Gaillac.

SERVES 6

EQUIPMENT: large pot, 2 strainers, medium heavy-bottomed saucepan, large heavy skillet, medium gratin dish

PREPARATION TIME: about 20 minutes, plus 1½ hours draining time

COOKING TIME: 35 minutes

DIFFICULTY LEVEL: simple

---

4 fresh or dried imported bay leaves

2 pounds (1 kg) fresh Belgian endives, trimmed

1½ pounds (750 g) leeks, trimmed, well rinsed to remove the grit, and cut in ½-inch (1.3 cm) rounds

FOR THE MORNAY AND HAM SAUCE:

3 tablespoons (45 g) unsalted butter

¼ cup (35 g) unbleached all-purpose flour

2½ cups (625 ml) whole milk

½ cup (125 ml) non-ultra-pasteurized heavy cream

4 ounces (120 g) Gruyère, grated

Scant ¼ teaspoon freshly grated nutmeg

8 ounces (250 g) ham, trimmed of excess fat and cut into ¼-inch (6 mm) cubes

Fine sea salt

FOR FINISHING THE GRATIN:

6 ounces (180 g) slab bacon, rind removed, cut into 1-by-¼-by-¼-inch (2.5 cm-by-6 mm-by-6 mm) strips

1. Bring a large pot of salted water to a boil over medium-high heat. Add the bay leaves and then the whole endives and cook until the endives are tender through, 10 minutes. Transfer the endives to a strainer set in a bowl or in the sink and let them drain for 1½ hours.

2. Return the water to a boil and add the leeks. Boil just until they soften, about 4 minutes. Transfer the leeks to another strainer set in a bowl or in the sink and let them drain for 1½ hours.

(continued)

- The endives and leeks are blanched, then left to drain for what sounds like a very long time. This is vital to the quality of the dish, for if you don't drain the vegetables, they will give off excess water during cooking, making the dish watery and unappetizing.
- A good-quality, fresh Belgian endive doesn't require much trimming, unless it has been banged about during transport and its outer leaves are bruised. Once it is harvested and cut from its root, the exposed surface turns rusty brown, so you need to trim off the cut surface.

3. Meanwhile, prepare the mornay and ham sauce: Melt the butter in a medium heavy-bottomed saucepan over medium heat. Whisk in the flour and cook until the mixture foams, at least 2 minutes, to cook out the taste of the flour. Whisk in the milk and the cream and cook until the mixture has thickened. Whisk in all but ½ cup of the grated cheese and the nutmeg, and then stir in the ham. Adjust the seasoning and set aside.

4. Preheat the oven to 375°F (190°C).

5. Cook the bacon in a large heavy skillet over medium heat until it is golden all over, about 5 minutes. Remove the bacon from the pan and drain on a paper towel–covered plate.

6. Spread ¼ cup of the sauce on the bottom of a medium gratin dish. Add the endives and the leeks, arranging them evenly and regularly interspersed in the pan. Sprinkle the bacon evenly over them. Pour the remaining sauce over the top of the vegetables, spreading it out evenly, and urging it down among the vegetables. Sprinkle the remaining ¼ cup of grated cheese over the top of the gratin.

7. Bake the gratin in the center of the oven until the gratin is deep golden on top and bubbling, about 25 minutes. Remove from the oven and let cool for about 10 minutes before serving.

Bacon-Braised Lentils with Sausages

LENTILLES BRAISES AU LARD FUMÉ AUX SAUCISSES

Oh, such a heartwarming plat du jour! Lentils have their own marvelous, minerally flavor, and when combined here with the triumvirate of bacon and two types of smoky sausages, they rise to the heights of the sublime. As often on a restaurant menu as they are on a home dinner table, lentils and sausage make for a hearty, simple dish that will please just about everyone.

The key to this dish's goodness is green lentils, preferably from Le Puy, which keep their shape and inimitably pure flavor. As for the sausages, search for the best you can find. They'll need at least 20 minutes of cooking and will add their own flavor to the lentils as they do. Serve this with a Pierre Noires from Jean Maupertuis, if you can find this luscious wine from the Auvergne, which will echo the flinty flavor of the lentils. If you cannot, look for another from the region or a Pinot Noir.

SERVES 6

EQUIPMENT: strainer, large heavy-bottomed saucepan

PREPARATION TIME: 10 scant minutes

COOKING TIME: 42 minutes

DIFFICULTY LEVEL: simple

- 1 pound (500 g) small green lentils, preferably from Le Puy, picked over and rinsed
- 4 ounces (125 g) slab bacon, rind removed, cut into ¼-inch (6 mm) squares
- 1 tablespoon olive oil (optional)
- 1 medium carrot (6 ounce; 180 g), peeled and diced
- 1 rib celery, diced
- 1 small onion (about 3 ounces; 90 g), diced
- 4 cups (1 L) water
- 2 fresh or dried imported bay leaves
- 4 to 5 fresh thyme sprigs
- Fine sea salt and freshly ground black pepper
- 2 smoked sausages (24 to 36 ounces; 720 g to 1.2 kg total), such as kielbasa
- Fresh flat-leaf parsley for garnish

1. Pick through the lentils for any tiny stones that might be there. Place the lentils in a strainer, rinse under cold running water, and set aside to drain.

2. Place the bacon in a large heavy-bottomed saucepan over medium-high heat and brown on all sides, about 5 minutes total. If the bacon is very lean and you need to add the oil, do so once the bacon begins to sizzle. When the bacon is browned, remove it from the pan and add the carrot, celery, and onion. Stir so the bacon fat or oil thoroughly coats the vegetables and cook, stirring frequently, until the onions begin to turn translucent and brown slightly on the edges, 5 to 7 minutes.

3. Add the lentils to the vegetables, stir, then cover with about 3 inches (7.5 cm) of water. Add the bay leaves and thyme and bring the water to a boil. When the water is boiling, reduce the heat to medium so that the water stays at a gentle boil.

(continued)

ASTUCES:

- Check the lentils as they cook, because their cooking time can vary depending on their freshness, with less fresh lentils taking longer to cook than those that are more fresh. The lentils should be tender, but they should hold their shape and not be the least bit mushy.
- Regarding kielbasa, 4 to 6 ounces (120 to 180 g) per person is the ideal amount, but if you want more, simply add more to the pot.

4. Add the whole sausage(s) to the pot and cook for about 20 minutes, at which point they will be cooked through. Remove the sausages from the pot and keep them warm. If necessary, continue cooking the lentils until they are tender but still have plenty of texture, which can take about 10 additional minutes.

5. When the lentils are cooked, taste for seasoning and adjust. Remove the bay leaves and the thyme.

6. To serve, slice the sausages on the bias into thick oval slices. Divide the lentils among six warmed dinner plates. Arrange an equal number of slices alongside the lentils, and garnish with the parsley. Alternatively, place the lentils on a large warmed platter and arrange the sausage slices either atop or around the lentils. Garnish abundantly with parsley and serve immediately.

Golden Potatoes with Bacon, Onions, and Melted Cheese

PELA/TARTIFLETTE

This plat du jour was originally called "Pela," which is the name of the long-handled pan that was used to cook it over coals or in a baker's oven. But today, all you have to do is mention the word "Tartiflette" and sighs of delight fill the air. It evokes the happiest of memories of the ski slopes in the Alps of the Haute-Savoie, as it is the area's signature dish. It is based on the simplest ingredients that every farm in the Savoie had at hand.

The key ingredient is Reblochon, a rich and creamy cheese that is part of the culinary repertoire of the region. An Arbois goes with this perfectly, of course, but if you cannot find one, try a light, non-oaked Chardonnay or even a Chablis! And serve this dish with a big green salad, such as A Classic Green Salad (page 265).

SERVES 6 TO 8

EQUIPMENT: large, heavy, oven-proof skillet; broiler (optional)

PREPARATION TIME: about 15 minutes

COOKING TIME: about 50 minutes

DIFFICULTY LEVEL: simple

---

6 ounces (180 g) smoked slab bacon, rind removed, cut into 1-by-¼-by-¼-inch (2.5 cm-by-6 mm-by-6 mm) strips

2 small onions (3.5 ounce; 105 g each), thinly sliced

2 tablespoons (30 g) unsalted butter

2 pounds (1 kg) potatoes, such as Yukon Gold, peeled and cut into ½-inch (1.25 cm) cubes

Fine sea salt and freshly ground black pepper

1 wheel (1 pound; 500 g) Reblochon or 1 pound (500 g) Raclette, chilled

Fresh flat-leaf parsley sprigs for garnish

1. Preheat the oven to 425°F (220°C).

2. Place the bacon and onions in a large, heavy, ovenproof skillet and cook over medium-high heat, stirring constantly, until the bacon and onion begin to turn dark golden, about 8 minutes. Drain away all but 1 tablespoon of the bacon fat, then add the butter and stir. Add the potatoes and stir so that all the ingredients are thoroughly mixed in the skillet. Season with salt and pepper. Stir and shake the pan until the potatoes begin to brown, then lower the heat to medium, cover, and cook until the potatoes are tender, 15 to 20 minutes, stirring and shaking the pan regularly.

3. While the potatoes are cooking, cut the Reblochon crosswise in half. Slice one half through the center horizontally. Cut the other half into ½-inch (1.3 cm) cubes. If using Raclette, cut half of it into slices, and the remaining cheese into cubes. Return the cheese to the refrigerator.

4. When the potatoes are tender, remove the pan from the heat and fold in the chilled cubes of cheese. Place

(continued)

the remaining Reblochon, cut side down, or the slices of Raclette, atop the potatoes.

5. Bake until the Reblochon is completely melted and golden on top, about 20 minutes. If the cheese isn't golden, turn on the broiler and broil the cheese until it turns golden, 5 to 6 minutes.

6. Remove from the oven, garnish with parsley sprigs, and serve immediately.

THE HISTORY OF REBLOCHON

Reblochon is a cheese with a history shrouded in crime. In the 13th century, milk production was taxed. On the day that the tax was levied, dairy farmers made sure to only partially milk their cows, in what may be one of the first recorded acts of tax evasion. Once the tax inspector left the farm, the farmer went out to relieve the cows of the rest of their milk. This milk, which was doubly rich in cream than that from the previous milking, had to stay invisible, so it was made into small round cheeses that were sold on the sly. Called "reblochon," which comes from the patois "to pinch the udder again," the cheeses were handed to a "sales force" who hid the cheeses in their coats as they clambered down from the mountains and into the towns, where they sold their contraband.

Ham Hock, Smoked Sausage, and Vegetable Stew

LA POTÉE CHAMPENOISE

This lovely stew hearkens to the region of Champagne, with its chalky, rolling plains that rise into the gentle slopes of the Ardennes mountains. The industry there is grapes, of course, which necessitate hours spent outdoors, tending to the vines, while the wind whips through the vineyards and the rain lashes down. What better meal to return to than *potée*, with its hearty blend of pork and fine seasonal vegetables and beans? This stew is rustic yet elegant, like the region, and the Sauce Gribiche (page 327), along with a golden shower of hard-cooked eggs, adds cheer and tang. Serve this with a lovely Coteaux Champenois, or even Champagne, if you like!

SERVES 6 TO 8

EQUIPMENT: medium saucepan, large stockpot, kitchen twine, fine-mesh stainless-steel sieve

PREPARATION TIME: 1 hour for soaking the beans, then 20 to 25 minutes

COOKING TIME: 2 hours

DIFFICULTY LEVEL: simple, but it takes some time to cook

1½ cups (270 g) dried white beans, such as navy beans

2 pounds (1 kg) russet potatoes, cut into 1½-inch (4 cm) chunks

10 fresh thyme sprigs

2 fresh or dried imported bay leaves

2½ pounds (1.3 kg) fresh ham hock

10 black peppercorns

½ teaspoon fine sea salt

4 small turnips (2 ounces; 60 g total), trimmed, cut into quarters

4 medium carrots (3 ounces; 90 g total), peeled and cut diagonally into thin slices

4 leeks, white part and 1 inch (2.5 cm) of green, trimmed, well rinsed, and cut into ½-inch (1.3 cm) chunks

6 smoked sausages, such as kielbasa

Freshly ground black pepper

1 large Savoy cabbage (about 2½ pounds; 1.25 kg), trimmed, cored, and cut into 2-inch- (5 cm) thick wedges

3 hard-cooked eggs for garnish

Sauce Gribiche (page 327) for garnish

1. Place the beans in a medium saucepan and cover with water. Bring to a boil over high heat, remove from the heat, and let sit for 1 hour. Drain the beans and set aside.

2. Peel the potatoes and place them in a bowl of water to cover.

3. Tie the thyme and bay leaves together with kitchen twine. Place the ham hock in a large stockpot with the herb bundle, peppercorns, and salt and cover with 1 inch (2.5 cm) water. Cover and bring to a boil over high heat.

(continued)

4. Lower the heat to medium and cook at a rolling simmer for 30 minutes. Add the beans and cook for an additional 30 minutes.

5. Add the turnips, carrots, leeks, and sausages to the pot. Cover and bring to a boil. Lower the heat to medium and cook at a rolling boil, partially covered, until the vegetables are tender, about 30 minutes. Taste for seasoning, adding salt and pepper if necessary.

6. Add the potatoes and cabbage to the pot, pushing the vegetables down into the liquid. Cover and bring to a boil. Then lower the heat and cook, uncovered, until the cabbage is tender but still has some crispness and deep green color, and the potatoes are tender through, about 30 minutes. Adjust the seasoning.

7. Just before serving, press the hard-cooked eggs through a sieve into a small serving bowl, using either a wood pestle or a stainless-steel spoon or fork, to prevent the eggs from developing a metallic flavor.

8. Ladle just the broth into warmed soup bowls and serve. When everyone has finished their soup, transfer the vegetables, ham hock, and sausages to a large warmed platter and serve with the Sauce Gribiche and the hard-cooked eggs alongside.

Peppers and Tomatoes with Poached Egg, Basque-Style

PIPÉRADE A L'OEUF POCHÉ

This summer dish is a festival of peppers and tomatoes seasoned with an onion, some garlic and, perhaps most important, air-cured ham. In the Basque Country, it would be ham from the Kintoa race of pig, which feeds on ferns, gorse, hazelnuts, chestnuts, and more, resulting in a complex-flavored, tender meat. The ham is cured in the mercurial Basque wind from the south, called the Foehn, which can be exceedingly hot at one moment, and exceedingly cool and dry at others. Combined with the pig's varied diet, this gives the Kintoa ham its special flavor.

The Kintoa ham is the pride of the Basque farmer; *pipérade*, the pride of the Basque cook since the 16th century, when the pepper and the tomato both arrived in the Pyrenees from the New World and were put to simmer in large cauldrons over a wood fire. Once the sauce was made, eggs were poached in it, chicken was simmered in it, fish was bathed with it. Nothing has changed, and when you visit the Basque country, pipérade is on every menu.

Try this once, and it will become a summer staple. Serve with an Irouléguy, the hearty red from the Basque Country, or another rich and hearty red of your choice.

SERVES 4 TO 6

EQUIPMENT: large heavy skillet, saucepan

PREPARATION TIME: 30 minutes

COOKING TIME: 1 hour 17 minutes (plus or minus)

DIFFICULTY LEVEL: simple

---

1 tablespoon olive oil

1 large onion (7 ounces; 210 g), thinly sliced

6 large sweet Italian peppers (can use Anaheim or Cubanelle), cored, seeded, and cut crosswise into very thin slices

2 garlic cloves, minced

Fine sea salt

4 ounces (125 g) very thinly sliced air-cured ham, such as jambon de Bayonne or Parma ham

4 pounds (2 kg) tomatoes, peeled, cored, seeded, and coarsely chopped

Piment d'Espelette or hot paprika

4 to 6 large eggs

Fleur de sel for garnish (optional)

Fresh basil leaves or flat-leaf parsley sprigs for garnish

1. Place the oil and the onion slices in a large heavy skillet over medium heat and cook, stirring occasionally, until the onion softens and begins to turn translucent, about 5 minutes. Add the peppers and garlic, season lightly with salt, and cook, stirring occasionally, until the peppers have softened but aren't completely limp, 5 to 7 minutes.

(continued)

2. While the peppers are cooking, cut the ham into thin strips.

3. Stir the ham into the peppers. Then add the tomatoes. Increase the heat, if necessary, to bring the mixture to a boil, then lower it to a steady simmer. Season lightly with salt and piment d'Espelette, cover, and cook until the ingredients have formed a soupy mixture and are tender, about 1 hour, stirring from time to time to be sure nothing is sticking to the bottom of the pan. Adjust the seasoning to your taste.

4. Break the eggs, one by one, into the mixture, cover, and cook until they are just set, 3 to 5 minutes. To serve, use a large shallow spoon to scoop around each egg, grabbing some tomatoes and peppers as you do, and set it delicately in the center of a shallow soup bowl. Once all the eggs are out, scoop out more tomato mixture and surround the eggs with it. Garnish each plate with fleur de sel, if desired, and the basil sprigs. Serve immediately.

ASTUCES:

- You can make this sauce without the eggs and serve it with any number of other things—roast chicken, steamed fish, garlic-rubbed toast, or all by itself!
- Pipérade freezes well, so make it in summer to brighten your winter meals!

Seared Pork Fillet with Mashed Potatoes and Jerusalem Artichokes

LE FILET DE PORC À LA PURÉE DE TOPINAMBOURS

This plat du jour is inspired by a sweet little restaurant in the 7th arrondissement of Paris, Les Botanistes, where chef and owner Jean-Baptiste Gay can be spied through a little window into the kitchen, working quietly, with calm efficiency. His wife, Virginie, is in the dining room, where she directs traffic at this bustling spot. The food here is always delicious, always seasonal, always comfortingly simple, with a bright, imaginative touch. Like the restaurant, this recipe speaks of conviviality and deep, rich flavor. Try a wonderful Saint-Aubin from Domaine de Montille with this. It will be the perfect pairing!

SERVES 6

EQUIPMENT: medium saucepan, large heavy skillet

PREPARATION TIME: 10 minutes

COOKING TIME: 35 minutes max

DIFFICULTY LEVEL: super simple

FOR THE MASHED VEGETABLES:

1 pound (500 g) starchy potatoes, peeled and cut into large chunks

8 ounces (250 g) Jerusalem artichokes, peeled and cut into ½-inch- (1.3 cm) thick slices

Coarse sea salt

1 fresh or dried imported bay leaf

4 to 6 tablespoons (60 to 90 g) unsalted butter, cut into 4 pieces

Fine sea salt and freshly ground black pepper

FOR THE PORK:

1 tablespoon olive oil

1 pound (500 g) pork fillet, sliced on the diagonal into ½-inch- (1.3 cm) thick slices

Fine sea salt and freshly ground black pepper

1 tablespoon balsamic vinegar

2 garlic cloves, minced

Fresh flat-leaf parsley sprigs or other herb for garnish

1. Prepare the vegetables: Place the potatoes and Jerusalem artichokes in a medium saucepan. Cover with 1 inch (2.5 cm) of water, add ½ teaspoon of coarse salt and the bay leaf, and bring the water to a boil over medium-high heat.

2. Lower the heat to medium so the water is boiling merrily, partially cover, and cook until the vegetables are tender, about 25 minutes. Remove from the heat. Drain, reserving the cooking liquid. Remove and discard the bay leaf. Add the butter to the vegetables and, using a fork or a potato

(continued)

ASTUCE: Jerusalem artichokes are often called sunchokes, and are available at specialty vegetable shops, both brick and mortar and virtual.

masher, mash the mixture into a rough puree. If the puree is slightly dry, add cooking liquid to loosen it up to your taste. Taste for seasoning. Keep the vegetables hot.

3. Prepare the pork: Heat the oil in a large heavy skillet over medium-high heat. When the oil is hot but not smoking, add the pork slices and cook until they turn golden, 3 to 4 minutes. Season the pork with salt and pepper, turn, and cook the slices until they are golden, about 3 minutes. Add the vinegar and shake the pan, lower the heat to medium, and add the garlic. Turn the pork slices and cook, shaking the pan, until the garlic just begins to turn golden and is very fragrant, and the pork is just slightly pink in the center, 1 to 2 additional minutes.

4. To serve, place the puree to the side of the center of six warm dinner plates. Place two or three slices of the pork next to the puree. Drizzle the pork with any pan juices, garnish with herbs, and serve immediately.

Roast Pork with Bacon, Comté, Onions, and Mushrooms

ROTI DE PORC JURASSIEN

I love to make this dish, because it's kind of like putting together a puzzle. You have to slide ham and cheese into slits of the pork loin, then wrap and tie it together, and it all ends up being the most delicious and hearty of dishes, evoking the lovely mountains east of Dijon, in the Jura where it originated. It is made of that region's finest ingredients, designed for the hardworking people who climb the mountains, milk the cows, make the delicate liqueurs, and smoke the gorgeous hams that are an integral part of the region's cuisine. Despite its rusticity, this dish is elegant, absolutely appropriate for a celebration, a white tablecloth event. You'll be happy while you're making it, and very proud to serve it, along with a white wine from the Jura, such as an Arbois.

SERVES 6 TO 8

EQUIPMENT: kitchen twine, roasting pan that is at least 14½ by 10 inches (37 by 25 cm), large skillet

PREPARATION TIME: about 20 minutes

COOKING TIME: 1 hour 15 minutes

DIFFICULTY LEVEL: medium

One 2-pound (1 kg) pork loin

10 very thin slices smoked air-cured ham (about 4 ounces; 120 g total)

10 very thin slices Comté (about 10 ounces; 300 g total)

10 thin slices non- or lightly smoked slab bacon (about 3 ounces; 90 g total)

3 large onions (6 ounces; 180 g each), diced

½ cup (125 ml) dry white wine, such as a sauvignon blanc

½ to 1 cup (125 to 250 ml) water

2 fresh or dried imported bay leaves

1 tablespoon (15 g) unsalted butter

2 teaspoons olive oil

1½ pounds (750 g) mushrooms, cleaned and cut into quarters

Fresh flat-leaf parsley sprigs for garnish

1. Preheat the oven to 375°F (190°C).

2. Make 10 cuts in the pork loin, at equal distance to one another (roughly every ¼ inch; 6 mm), cutting down about three-quarters of the thickness of the pork roast, to leave the roast intact. Insert a slice of smoked ham and a slice of cheese into each slit. You may need to slightly fold the ham to tuck it into the slit. Trim the cheese slices so they're flush.

(continued)

3. With kitchen twine, tie the roast together lengthwise, using at least two lengths of twine, so the cheese and ham are firmly held in the roast.

4. Lay the bacon atop the roast, overlapping the slices slightly so they completely cover the top of the roast. Tie a piece of kitchen twine around each slice of bacon, to keep it in place.

5. Place the prepared pork loin in a roasting pan that is large enough to hold it.

6. Strew the diced onions around the pork loin and pour the wine and half of the water over all. Add the bay leaves to the liquids and place the roast on the rack in the center of the oven. Bake, checking the pork and basting it every 20 minutes or so (check to be sure there is just enough liquid around the pork so the onions don't burn), until the pork and onions are dark golden and the interior temperature of the roast is about 145°F (63°C), about 1 hour 15 minutes.

7. While the pork bakes, melt the butter and oil in a large skillet over medium heat. Add the mushrooms and cook, shaking and stirring frequently, until the mushrooms give up their liquid and begin to turn golden and cook through, about 6 minutes. Remove from the heat.

8. When the pork is cooked, transfer it to a cutting board to rest.

9. Add the mushrooms to the onions in the roasting pan, stir so they are mixed, and return to the oven for about 15 minutes, while the pork rests, so the mushrooms can heat back up and the onions can turn golden.

10. To serve, slice the pork into six to eight slices. If you like, cut the slices in half crosswise and place one slightly overlapping the other. Surround the pork with the onions and mushrooms and any cooking juices that remain in the pan. Garnish with a sprig of parsley and serve immediately.

Cabbage with Pork Stuffing

CHOU FARCI

Cabbage is a plat du jour mainstay, a generous vegetable that cooks to a tender sweetness. There are many versions of stuffed cabbage, and the mere mention creates a polemic, for each cook is wedded to his or her version. This is my favorite, because it's so simple to assemble and so luscious and flavorful that it makes you feel like you're wrapped in a huge, flavorful comforter.

This dish takes time to assemble, but it's worth every minute, as you'll note by the light in your guests' eyes as they taste its sumptuous flavor. Serve this as a homey or a dressed-up plat du jour. I recommend a fine Burgundy here—you'll see, it will be perfect!

SERVES 6 TO 8

EQUIPMENT: large stockpot, several wire cooling racks and cotton towels, small skillet, large heavy-bottomed Dutch oven or ovenproof baking dish

PREPARATION TIME: 30 to 40 minutes

COOKING TIME: 1 hour 45 minutes

DIFFICULTY LEVEL: simple

---

1 Savoy cabbage (about 3 pounds; 1.5 kg), leaves separated from the central stalk, any very thick ribs removed

Coarse sea salt

FOR THE STUFFING:

12 ounces (360 g) ground pork

1 bunch fresh flat-leaf parsley

1 bunch fresh chives

1 medium onion (5 ounces; 150 g), minced

2 shallots, minced

2 garlic cloves, minced

1 bunch Swiss chard, green leaves only (for 8 ounces; 250 g leaves), chopped finely

1 scant teaspoon (5 g) fine sea salt

Freshly ground black pepper

½ teaspoon freshly grated nutmeg

1 generous tablespoon unsalted butter

1 tablespoon olive oil

FOR THE REMAINING CABBAGE:

1 scant tablespoon unsalted butter

Fine sea salt and freshly ground black pepper

1. Fill a large stockpot with salted water—use about 1 tablespoon of coarse sea salt per gallon (4 L) of water—and bring to a boil. Line several wire racks with cotton towels.

2. When the water is boiling, add several cabbage leaves and cook them just until the water returns to a boil and the leaves are soft but not overcooked, 4 to 5 minutes. Remove the leaves and lay them in one layer on the cotton towels. Return the water to a boil and repeat until all of the leaves are cooked.

(continued)

ASTUCES:

- You don't need to plunge the cabbage leaves into ice water once they've been blanched, because they will hold their shape, and for this dish, their color doesn't matter.
- Make sure to taste-test the stuffing by cooking a tiny portion; you'll be glad you did when your dish is perfectly seasoned.
- Any cooked leaves that have torn beyond recognition can be chopped for the final garnish.

3. Prepare the stuffing: Place the ground pork in a medium bowl.

4. Mince the parsley and the chives.

5. Add the herbs to the pork along with the onion, shallots, garlic, Swiss chard, salt, several grinds of black pepper, and the nutmeg, and mix together.

6. To test the seasoning of the stuffing, pinch off a very small piece, cook it in a small skillet, and taste. Adjust seasonings accordingly.

7. Preheat the oven to 400°F (200°C).

8. Melt the butter and oil in a large heavy-bottomed Dutch oven or other ovenproof dish.

9. When the butter is hot, remove the pan from the heat and line the bottom of the pan with cabbage leaves, in an overlapping layer. They'll sizzle; this is good. Spread the cabbage with a layer of stuffing, and continue to layer the cabbage and stuffing, finishing with cabbage leaves. More than likely, you will have leftover cabbage leaves.

10. Cover the cabbage with a sheet of parchment paper, pressing it on and around the cabbage. Cover the pan and place it in the center of the oven to cook for about 1½ hours. Remove the cover and parchment paper and leave the cabbage in the oven for 15 minutes, so it browns lightly on top.

11. While the cabbage is cooking, dice the remaining cabbage leaves.

12. Remove the stuffed cabbage from the oven and let it sit for about 10 minutes.

13. Cook the remaining cabbage: Melt the butter in a large skillet over medium-high heat. Add the diced cabbage and cook, stirring, just until it is heated through, about 4 minutes. Season with salt and pepper, toss a couple more times, and remove from the heat.

14. Carefully flip the stuffed cabbage out onto a serving plate. Surround it with the sautéed cabbage and serve, cut into wedges as you would for a cake.

CHAPTER 6
VEGETABLES

THE FRENCH ARE BLESSED in many ways, not the least in the quality of produce at their disposal and the ease with which they can get it. Every town and village, every arrondissement in large cities, has a market where at least one local grower, and often many, offers their wares. Even grocery stores and supermarkets put local produce on their shelves, because France is a small agricultural country with abundance everywhere you look.

But the French aren't the only ones to have fine-quality vegetables at their fingertips. Now, in so many countries, including the United States, farmers' markets proliferate because the notion of farm-to-table and buying seasonal and local has taken hold. This means increasingly better tasting produce is available to the consumer.

The French array of vegetables and vegetable dishes isn't exotic—in fact, the French palate is quite conservative and the choice of typical vegetables relatively limited if you compare it with the United States. But in France, produce is all freshly harvested and excellent, its journey from farm to shop or market short. And that's what makes it so flavorful. Combine that with the innate French culinary expertise of "less is more" in letting the flavor of the vegetable shine through, and you have the key to incredibly flavorful French vegetable dishes, which you will find in this chapter.

Although vegetables have starring roles in the dishes of this chapter, they aren't necessarily vegetarian, but they can be if you omit the meat. Enjoy these vegetable-based dishes, and adapt as you will.

Apple Cider–Braised Artichoke Hearts

ARTICHAUTS RENNAISES

Something about the artichoke is exciting. It could be its reputation as an aphrodisiac, or its inherent natural beauty, but most likely it is the promise of so much fun and flavor on the plate. Its nutty leaves are delicious dipped in melted butter, its heart sublime prepared in a number of ways.

Here the heart of the artichoke is braised in apple cider with vegetables and slices of pork, to make one of the most popular dishes of Brittany, known for its apple cider and the capital of French artichoke production. The dish's home is the city of Rennes, where you will find it everywhere, served as a plat du jour.

I grew up eating the artichoke leaf by leaf, with its heart the ultimate reward, but in general the French eschew the leaves and go straight for the heart. Of course they do; they're lovers, not fighters! As French as I've become, I save the leaves after snapping them off, steam them, and melt butter. They make a perfect appetizer!

Serve this during the spring or the autumn, when artichokes are at their best and the temperatures are cool. It's hearty and delicious, simple to prepare, and you'll have guests clamoring for more. I recommend hard apple cider, or a Loire Valley white alongside. Vegetarians note that this recipe has pork in it, which you can omit.

SERVES 6

EQUIPMENT: stainless-steel spoon, small saucepan, kitchen twine, large heavy-bottomed Dutch oven or saucepan, slotted spoon

PREPARATION TIME: 20 to 40 minutes, depending on whether you are preparing the artichokes

COOKING TIME: 1 hour

DIFFICULTY LEVEL: medium, if you're preparing the artichokes

1 lemon, cut in half (optional)

6 large whole artichokes, or enough frozen artichoke hearts to give 2 pounds (1 kg)

11 ounces (330 g) salt pork (see Astuces), desalted and thinly sliced, or lightly smoked bacon

15 fresh thyme branches

2 fresh or dried imported bay leaves

10 fresh flat-leaf parsley sprigs, plus several more for garnish

6 tablespoons (90 g) unsalted butter

3 medium onions (5 ounces; 150 g each), diced

3 medium carrots (3 ounces; 90 g each), peeled, trimmed, and diced

1 cup (250 ml) hard apple cider or Muscadet

1½ cups (375 ml) Chicken Stock (page 332) or water

4 whole cloves

Fine sea salt and coarsely ground black pepper

(continued)

1. If preparing the artichokes, squeeze both lemon halves into a medium bowl of cool water.

2. Break off the stem of each artichoke, so it pulls out some of the stringy fibers from the heart. Trim any remaining stalk flush with the bottom and remove the tougher outer leaves of the artichoke. Trim off all the green from the heart and, angling the knife blade toward the center of the interior of the heart, cut away the "choke" and discard. Scrape away whatever remains with a stainless steel spoon. Cut the artichoke hearts into quarters and place them in the lemon water.

3. Bring a small saucepan of water to a boil. If using the salt pork, add it to the water, return the water to a boil, and let the salt pork boil for 3 to 4 minutes, to remove as much salt as possible. Remove the salt pork from the pan, pat it dry, and when it is cool enough to handle, slice it into thin slices. This step isn't necessary if you use bacon.

4. Tie the thyme, bay leaves, and parsley together with kitchen twine.

5. Melt the butter in a large heavy-bottomed Dutch oven over medium heat. When the butter is foaming, add the onions and carrots and cook, stirring regularly, until the onions are tender through, about 10 minutes. Transfer the vegetables from the pan to a waiting bowl or dish, using a slotted spoon.

6. Line the bottom of the Dutch oven with the slices of salt pork. Spread the vegetables evenly over the salt pork. Arrange the artichoke hearts over the vegetables, then add the herbs, cider, stock or water, and the cloves. Season with salt and pepper, remembering if you've used salt pork, not to oversalt.

7. Cover the Dutch oven and bring the liquid to a boil over medium-high heat. Lower the heat until the liquid is simmering merrily, cover, and cook until the artichokes and all the vegetables are very tender, 30 to 45 minutes. Test the artichoke hearts regularly, and when they are tender but offer a tiny bit of resistance, they are ready.

8. Remove the herbs and cloves from the pot, garnish with the herb sprigs, and serve.

APPROACHING THE ARTICHOKE

If you've had the good fortune to visit Brittany in the spring through the autumn, you've no doubt walked by a sea mist–bathed field of artichokes, their huge, green, leafy globes reaching for the sun. The Breton artichoke is considered the best in the land—perhaps the best in the world. The primary and most abundant variety is the Camus, which is large (each one weighs about a pound), round, and pale green.

The artichoke is a majestic plant, with its silvery green leaves and its bulbous, leafy fruit that symbolizes hope and love. It can be grown from seed, to emerge into a plant whose long taproot reaches deep into the soil, one reason the plant thrives in Brittany, where the soil is rich and loose. Breton artichoke growers counsel letting an artichoke ripen for at least three days after harvest, to get the most flavor from it. At that stage, an artichoke will still be soft green. If its leaves are striated with brown and look dry and shriveled, stay away.

Artichokes are gorgeous on the plant from start to finish, when the choke erupts from the center of the bulb as an intensely vibrant, violet-colored flower. Should you be tempted to plant artichokes, be patient. The first year will offer a humble harvest. After that, you can expect 6 to 10 globes per plant.

A quick note on baby artichokes—they're not babies at all, but fully mature artichokes that grow lower down on the stem than their larger brethren.

REVEALING THE HEART:

- Cut a lemon in half and set it on your work surface.
- Begin by cutting the stalk flush with the bottom of the artichoke. Then tear off all the leaves, reserving them if you plan to steam them for an appetizer. Once you are down to the pale

yellow leaves in the center of the artichoke, get your sharp chef's knife and cut the leaves off at their base, at the very top of the heart. This leaves you with the beautiful heart full of the *foin* (choke). Before you begin to remove this, trim off all the dark green from the heart, so you have just the tender meat. Rub the outside of the heart with the lemon half.

- Use a 2½-inch- (6.5 cm) bladed knife and put the blade into the artichoke heart angled slightly down toward its center—you are going to cut around the heart and under the choke to remove as much as you can. Do this carefully, using a sawing motion; you won't remove all the choke, but most of it. Use a stainless-steel spoon to scrape out what remains—a silver spoon will turn the artichoke black. Trim the heart of any shaggy pieces so you have a nice round. Rub it all over with the lemon, and then proceed to your recipe.

Braised Spring Vegetables with Crispy Air-Cured Ham

JARDINIÈRE DE LEGUMES AU JAMBON SECHÉ

A *jardinière* is a "planter full" of vegetables, a spring ritual, a celebration of the new season, when vegetables are at their best, because every French cook knows that late spring is a perfect moment in the life of vegetables. Peas, carrots, potatoes, and onions are brand new, filled with tender, sweet flavor, the juiciest and most flavorful they will be all year. And this includes lettuce, which here is kept whole but carefully rinsed, then set atop the rest of the vegetables to melt gently into them. The slices of air-cured ham, baked to a crisp, give it a delicious crunch. I serve this with a Sauvignon Blanc from the Loire Valley.

SERVES 4

EQUIPMENT: large heavy-bottomed saucepan or Dutch oven with lid, baking sheet

PREPARATION TIME: 15 to 20 minutes

COOKING TIME: about 45 minutes

DIFFICULTY LEVEL: simple

---

2 tablespoons (30 g) unsalted butter

1 pound (500 g) new carrots, peeled and cut into thin rounds

1 pound (500 g) new potatoes, washed

10 ounces (300 g) new spring onions, trimmed and thinly sliced

3 shallots, cut in half lengthwise, then into thin half-moons

1 cup (250 ml) water

Fine sea salt and freshly ground black pepper

4 pounds (2 kg) fresh peas in their pods, shelled (for 4 cups; 600 g shelled peas)

1 head butter lettuce (about 1 pound; 500 g), leaves separated, heart left intact, rinsed

4 thin slices (about 2 ounces; 60 g) air-cured ham, such as prosciutto

Fresh flat-leaf parsley sprigs for garnish

ASTUCE: You may use frozen peas here, if you like.

1. Preheat the oven to 425°F (210°C).

2. Melt the butter in a large heavy saucepan over medium heat. Add the carrots, potatoes, onions, and shallots, stirring so they are coated with the butter. Season lightly with salt. Cover and cook, stirring occasionally, until the carrots are softened but still have plenty of texture, about 8 minutes.

3. Stir in the water, season with salt and pepper, and continue to cook, covered, until the carrots are nearly tender, an additional 8 minutes. Add the peas and stir. Then lay

(continued)

the lettuce heart and leaves over the vegetables. Cover and cook until the lettuce leaves are wilted and the peas are done to your liking (I like them bright green and just cooked through to a juicy tenderness), 10 to 15 minutes.

4. Meanwhile, place the ham slices on a baking sheet and slip them into the oven to bake until the ham is darkened and almost completely crisp, 8 to 10 minutes. Remove from the oven, transfer to a cutting board, and cut across or horizontally into ½-inch (1.3 cm) slices.

5. When the vegetables are cooked, adjust the seasonings. Divide them among six to eight warmed plates. Garnish with the ham slices and parsley, and serve.

"Bathed" Bread—Vegetable Sandwich from Nice

PAN BAGNAT—LE SANDWICH NIÇOIS

Anyone who has ever been to Nice has most likely had the iconic *pan bagnat*, this gorgeous, sunny sandwich whose beginnings are very humble. *Pan bagnat* means, in Provençal dialect, "bathed bread," referring to the traditional Niçois cooks' habit of sprinkling stale bread with water to refresh it, then adding it to a bowlful of tomatoes seasoned with salt. The salt encourages the tomatoes to give off their juice, while the bread happily soaks it all up. As time passed, the pan bagnat became more elaborate, as an increasing variety of vegetables were added; it became less humble and more structured, too, until it turned into the lovely plat du jour it is today.

How does a sandwich rank as a plat du jour? Simple. You make and place this in the center of the plate, pour a glass of rosé, pull out your chair, and sit down to one of the best and most full meals of your life!

SERVES 6

EQUIPMENT: bread knife

PREPARATION TIME: about 2½ hours if you're making the buns; about 20 minutes if the buns are already made

BAKING TIME: 20 to 30 minutes

DIFFICULTY LEVEL: simple

---

1 recipe Tender Bread Dough (page 307), baked into 6 buns, or 6 large best-quality hamburger buns

About ¾ cup (185 ml) olive oil

2 tablespoons best-quality red wine vinegar

3 garlic cloves, sliced very thin

6 medium tomatoes (about 4 ounces; 120 g each), sliced into ½-inch (1.3 cm) slices

2 red bell peppers, seeded, pith removed, sliced very thin (for 12 slices)

12 radishes, trimmed, rinsed and thinly sliced lengthwise

Fine sea salt and freshly ground black pepper

6 small new onions (about .5 ounce; 15 g), trimmed and diced

⅔ cup (about 72) fava beans (frozen and thawed, or fresh in season)

6 small artichoke hearts (about 3.5 ounces; 105 g), fresh or canned

12 anchovy fillets, or one 12-ounce (360 g) can oil-packed tuna

6 large eggs, hard-cooked

12 black olives, pitted

12 large fresh basil leaves

Fresh basil sprigs for garnish

1. Cut the buns in half horizontally. Pull out most of the crumb from the center of each half, leaving the crumb around the edges. This way, you make room for the ingredients.

(continued)

- I suggest making homemade bread for the pan bagnat. This way, you get the oversize, bun-shaped bread.
- If you're going to use canned tuna, make sure it is albacore, packed in oil. Albacore tuna don't swim with dolphins the way other species of tuna do, so there is no bycatch; tuna packed in oil retains its wonderful texture, while that packed in water can be very dry.

2. Drizzle each cut side of the buns with about 2 teaspoons of the olive oil, and then with about 1 teaspoon of the vinegar.

3. Strew an equal number of garlic slices on the lower half of the buns, then top with tomato slices and an equal number of bell pepper and radish slices. Season with salt and pepper, and top with an equal amount of diced onion and fava beans, sprinkling them evenly with salt and black pepper.

4. Very thinly slice the artichoke hearts and lay an equal number of slices on top of the ingredients already in the sandwich. Crisscross each sandwich with two anchovy fillets or sprinkle each with an equal amount of tuna, and an equal number of egg rounds and olives. Lay two basil leaves on top. You've now got a colorful, architecturally perfect sandwich nearly ready to eat.

5. Drizzle each sandwich with an equal amount of the additional oil, place the top half of each bun on top, and press down firmly to press the ingredients into the bun. Delicately put the sandwich on a plate and garnish each plate with a sprig of basil. Serve immediately.

THE "RULES" FOR PAN BAGNAT

As so often happens in France, when a dish reaches icon status, a group forms to protect it. This is the case with pan bagnat. It spawned La Commune Libre du Pan Bagnat (The Free Municipality of Pan Bagnat), a group devoted to the purity of this sandwich. La Commune is strict about what a pan bagnat can—and cannot—include. Its charter states that any ingredient can be left out of the approved list of ingredients, but *nothing* can be added that isn't on the list, if the sandwich is to be called pan bagnat. This is the result of a heresy noted by traditionalists, which is the addition of lettuce to a pan bagnat. "There are some who call the pan bagnat a vegetable sandwich," bemoaned a member of La Commune, "because it includes lettuce. No pan bagnat *ever* includes lettuce."

The recipe I offer for pan bagnat (page 182) respects the traditional list of ingredients (which follows), to create a gorgeous sandwich that becomes an entire meal. You may be tempted to add lettuce, but *don't*. You'll be going against La Commune, and we all know the results when that happens! (Hint: The French Revolution . . .)

OFFICIAL LIST OF PAN BAGNAT INGREDIENTS:

- Bread
- Tomatoes
- Radishes
- Scallions (preferred, but small spring onions tolerated)
- Bell pepper
- Tuna or anchovies
- Hard-cooked egg
- Olive oil
- Salt and pepper
- Fava beans
- Small artichokes
- Vinegar (tolerated)

Baked Pasta with Caramelized Tomatoes

PÂTES AUX TOMATES CARAMELISÉES

There is almost always a pasta dish on the daily menu in a French café or bistro because the French simply adore pasta; a contradictory love because their bread is so delicious and their relationship with their Italian neighbors is so fraught. Nevertheless, the French turn their talent to pasta dishes like this one, with its caramelized tomatoes, ends up being slightly sweet, slightly tart, totally delectable. It is a perfect dish for late tomato season, when the temperatures demand something hearty yet bright. Serve this with a Buzet or Sancerre Rouge.

SERVES 4 TO 6
EQUIPMENT: large pot, large skillet
PREPARATION TIME: 10 minutes
COOKING TIME: 20 minutes
DIFFICULTY LEVEL: simple

Coarse sea salt

5 good-size slightly underripe tomatoes, cored

¼ cup (60 ml) olive oil

3 garlic cloves, halved

1 cup (10 g) fresh flat-leaf parsley leaves

Sea salt and freshly ground black pepper

10 ounces (300 g) dried pasta, such as fettuccine

1 cup (about 60 g) finely grated Parmigiano-Reggiano

Fresh flat-leaf parsley sprigs for garnish

1. Fill a large pot with 4 quarts (4 L) of water, add 2 tablespoons of salt, and bring to a boil.

2. Cut the tomatoes in half horizontally.

3. Heat the oil in a large skillet over medium-high heat. When it is hot but not smoking (when small ripples move over its surface), add the tomatoes, cut side up. Cook, shifting them slightly in the pan to prevent scorching, until their skins are slightly bubbled on the bottom and have golden spots on them, about 4 minutes. Turn the tomatoes over and continue to cook until the cut side is golden, about 6 minutes, shaking the pan two or three times to move the tomatoes around so they don't burn.

4. While the tomatoes are cooking, finely mince the garlic and parsley together.

5. Turn the tomatoes again, so the cut side is up. Working around the tomatoes, scrape up any browned bits from the bottom of the skillet. Sprinkle the tomatoes with the garlic and parsley, and season them generously with salt and pepper. Lower the heat to medium and cover the skillet. Cook the tomatoes until they are tender through and the garlic is tender, about 10 minutes, shaking the pan occasionally to prevent the tomatoes from sticking. The juice from the tomatoes will turn a deep caramel color but shouldn't burn.

(continued)

6. While the tomatoes finish cooking, add the pasta to the boiling water, stir, and cook just until al dente, 7 to 10 minutes. Drain, reserving 1 cup (250 ml) of the pasta cooking liquid. Return the pasta to the pot, pour half of the reserved cooking liquid over it, and toss so the pasta is thoroughly moistened.

7. Arrange the tomatoes around the edges of a large warmed platter. Deglaze the skillet over medium-high heat with the remaining pasta cooking liquid, scraping up any browned bits, and reduce the liquid by about two-thirds, so it is slightly thickened. Pour that over the pasta as well. Toss so the liquid is well blended with the pasta. Transfer the pasta to the center of the serving platter, so it is surrounded with the tomatoes. Sprinkle generously with Parmigiano-Reggiano and garnish with parsley sprigs. Serve any remaining cheese alongside.

ASTUCES:

- Pasta cooking liquid is ideal to moisten and thicken a sauce because of the starch it contains.
- If you cannot find round tomatoes, use plum tomatoes here.
- If you don't have fettuccine, use your favorite pasta shape. I recommend Benedetto Cavalieri, Latini, or Rustichella pasta brands.
- *Al dente* means "to the tooth," or pasta cooked so that it is still slightly hard at the very center, the ideal firmness for pasta.

Belgian Endive and Chicken Soup

SOUPE À L'ENDIVE ET BOUILLON DE POULE

Endives are known as *chicons* in the north of France, a region that is called Nord-Pas-de-Calais, where they are the economic staple to both the region's economy and its cuisine. They are braised, steamed, fried, baked, and turned into soups, like this one, which make an entire meal along with bread and a salad to follow.

The endive is a winter vegetable, and so this is a winter soup. Because the endive has a split personality, I sometimes serve a raw endive salad to precede it. Crunchy with a sweet and slightly bitter flavor, the salad is a perfect introduction to the endive's other personality. I recommend Chenin Blanc with this or, as they might do in the north, a microbrew.

SERVES 6 TO 8

EQUIPMENT: large heavy-bottomed saucepan or stockpot

PREPARATION TIME: 20 minutes

COOKING TIME: about 25 minutes

DIFFICULTY LEVEL: simple

1½ pounds (750 g) Belgian endive

2 tablespoons (30 g) unsalted butter

1 large onion (7 ounces; 210 g), thinly sliced

2 quarts (2 L) Chicken Stock (page 332)

4 medium carrots (6 ounces; 180 g each), peeled and grated

Sea salt and freshly ground black pepper

1 tablespoon fresh thyme leaves

2 cups (300 g) cooked chicken meat, cut in bite-size pieces

Crème fraîche for serving (optional)

1. Strip away any outside endive leaves that are discolored. Trim the stem, then slice the endive crosswise into ¼-inch (6 mm) rounds.

2. Melt the butter in a large heavy-bottomed saucepan over medium-high heat. Add the onion and cook, stirring occasionally, until it begins to turn translucent, about 5 minutes.

3. Add the chicken stock to the onion, stir, and bring to a boil. Lower the heat to medium and add the carrots. Cook, covered, until the carrots are tender, about 10 minutes.

4. Stir in the endive and cook until it is just tender, about 10 minutes. Season to taste with salt and pepper. Add the thyme and the chicken, if desired. Stir and adjust the seasoning. Continue to heat until the soup is steaming. Serve with crème fraîche alongside, for dolloping into the soup, if desired.

ASTUCES:

- Cut endive at the last minute because it quickly turns orange where it is cut and looks unpleasant.
- Grated carrot cooks quickly and gives a sprightly look to the soup.

FRENCH—NOT BELGIAN—ENDIVES

We attribute the endive to Belgium where, it is said, it was an accidental discovery nearly 200 years ago. Then a Belgian farmer went to dig up a chicory root and found a lovely, white, torpedo-shaped vegetable hidden under the soil, growing up and out of the root. He squeezed it gently in his hand and it resisted, giving off some moisture and a faint nutty aroma. He pulled off a leaf and tasted it and was struck with its wealth of crunch and flavor, and so began to cultivate this unknown vegetable. He was successful and so were the neighbors who followed his example, all the way from Belgium to the north of France, which is now the home of the endive. There, field after field of this gorgeous winter vegetable is grown, in soil warmed by water pipes that stabilize the endive's growth.

The endive, or chicon as it is called in the north, is a curious vegetable, planted in the fall and sequestered under the soil, so no light touches it. This results in its ivory color, which is tinted yellow on the ruffled edge of its leaves. There is also a variety of endive with leaves edged by a beautiful burgundy color. Harvested in the dead of winter, all *endives de terre* (endives grown in soil) are the pride of the northern farmer.

Endives are so popular in France—it is the sixth most popular vegetable, consumed by the French to the tune of nearly 12 pounds per capita—that many are now produced hydroponically or grown in water. These are a pale version of the chicons that are grown in soil.

Endives grown *en pleine terre* are the *summum* of the endive—rich in flavor, firm of texture, offering the crunch and juice of a fresh vegetable in a season where that is rare. *Vive l'endive!*

Tomato, Olive, and Anchovy Tart of Nice

PISSALADIÈRE

Pissaladière, the traditional tomato, olive, and anchovy tart of Nice, is found everywhere along the Côte d'Azur, sold by the piece in pastry shops, on the street, and in cafés and bistros. It has made its way north, too, and is often served as a plat du jour in cafés, along with a green salad. Its heady blend of ingredients makes it a delicious and satisfying dish. Once you make and taste this, you'll be transported to the Mediterranean and will simply luxuriate in the rich, savory flavors. Serve this with a Côtes de Provence, either red, white, or rosé.

MAKES ONE 9½-INCH (24 CM) TART; SERVES 4 TO 6

EQUIPMENT: removable-bottom tart pan, baking sheet, large heavy skillet

PREPARATION TIME: 20 to 25 minutes

BAKING TIME: 52 minutes total

DIFFICULTY LEVEL: simple

---

1 recipe Tender Tart Pastry (page 314)

2 pounds (1 kg) onions, thinly sliced

3 tablespoons olive oil

Sea salt and freshly ground black pepper

3 slightly underripe tomatoes, cored and cut into thin slices

18 anchovy fillets

20 cured black olives, with pits

1. To prebake the pastry, roll it out to fit a 9½-inch (24 cm) removable-bottom tart pan. There will be pastry overlapping the tart pan. Trim it, then crimp the edges. Reserve any excess pastry for another use. Chill the pastry for 1 hour.

2. Preheat the oven to 425°F (220°C).

3. To bake the pastry, pierce it all over with the tip of a sharp knife, line it with aluminum foil and pastry weights, set it on a baking sheet, and bake in the center of the oven until the edges are golden, about 12 minutes. Remove the pastry from the oven, remove the weights, and return the pastry to the oven. Bake until the bottom is a pale golden, about 5 additional minutes. Remove from the oven and set aside.

4. Place the onions and oil in a large heavy skillet over medium heat. Toss so the onions are coated with the oil and cook, covered, stirring occasionally, until the onions are completely tender and sweet, about 40 minutes. Season with salt and pepper.

5. Transfer the onions to the prebaked shell, spreading them evenly across the bottom.

(continued)

ASTUCES:

- The ideal anchovy for pissaladière is that from the tiny fishing port of Collioure on the Mediterranean coast of France. You can find it in the United States in both brick-and-mortar and virtual specialty shops.
- Small Niçoise olives are perfect here, but if you cannot find them, use the finest brined black olives you can find. Why include the pits? It's a question of quality here in France—an olive worth the name always has a pit in it, and the French cook doesn't take the time to remove it. If you leave the pits in the olives, warn your guests.
- I offer the recipe here made with tart pastry. You can make it with bread dough, too. Refer to the recipe for Tender Bread Dough (page 307).

6. Arrange the tomato slices in slightly overlapping concentric circles over the onions. Arrange the anchovy fillets atop the tomatoes, making nine crosses with them. Evenly distribute the olives on the top, pressing them gently into the other tart ingredients so they don't roll off. Carefully place the baking sheet in the center of the oven and bake until the tart is heated through and slightly golden on top and the tomatoes are tender, 35 to 40 minutes.

7. Remove the tart from the oven and remove the sides of the pan. Let the tart cool for about 10 minutes before serving. Remind diners that the olives in the tart have pits in them.

THE STORY OF PISSALADIÈRE

The pissaladière is either the best first course or one of the most magnificent plats du jour that the Côte d'Azur has given to the world.

It has a multicultural history. First thought to hail from Genoa, where it was called *piscialandrea* after a famed Italian naval officer, Andrea Doria, it gradually made its way to Nice, where the first mention of pissaladière was made in the 19th century. The Niçoise name comes from a blend of tiny anchovies and sardines, *poutine*, that, when salted and pureed, was called *pissalat*. Pissalat was spread atop bread dough, covered with onions, garnished with olives, and baked in a hot oven to emerge bubbling and fragrant. Today pissalat is hard to come by, since the fishery for baby anchovies and sardines is strictly limited, so anchovy fillets have become the substitute. And when you use top-quality anchovies, what a substitute they are! Because the French love their food to look as beautiful as it tastes, the anchovy fillets are always arranged crossed atop the pissaladière, as in the recipe above. Another major difference in the pissaladière of yesteryear and today is the use of pastry as a base instead of the more traditional bread dough. Both are made today, and both can be found in restaurants, cafés, and bistros along the Côte d'Azur and beyond.

Colorful Eggplant and Tomato Tart

TARTE D'ÉTÉ

Putting together this vivid tart, so emblematic of the perfect summer plat du jour, is a bit like completing a simple puzzle. You need just the right number of slices of each vegetable—though you can cheat with half slices if that's all you've got—to make it look extraordinarily pretty. It is simple to make even though it takes some time to arrange it all just right. I like to make it with both red and gold tomatoes, and you can throw in a green one, too. This way, it jumps off the plate with all the color! It is garnished with a basil puree, which is referred to as *pistou* in French. Note there is no cheese in it. Serve this with a rosé from the Languedoc.

SERVES 4 TO 6

EQUIPMENT: sieve, 12-inch (30 cm) removable-bottom tart pan, baking sheet, food processor

PREPARATION TIME: 45 minutes

COOKING TIME: 50 minutes

DIFFICULTY LEVEL: medium

FOR THE TART:

3 medium eggplant (1½ pounds; 750 g total), rinsed

3 medium ripe tomatoes (7 ounces; 210 g each), cored

1 medium zucchini (about 9 ounces; 270 g), trimmed

1 recipe Tender Tart Pastry (page 314)

2 garlic cloves, coarsely chopped

Fine sea salt

Piment d'Espelette or hot paprika

2 tablespoons olive oil

FOR THE BASIL AND ALMOND PISTOU:

1 bunch basil (for 3 cups [30 g] gently packed leaves)

2 tablespoons raw almonds

Generous pinch of sea salt

½ cup (125 ml) olive oil

1. Either preheat the oven or light up the gas grill to about 400°F (200°C).

2. Pierce the eggplant all over with a skewer, then place them right on the oven rack or gas grill and roast them, turning often, until they are soft inside, 45 minutes to 1 hour. Remove from the oven or grill. When the eggplant is cool enough to handle, cut them in half lengthwise, scoop out all the flesh, and place it in a sieve set over a bowl to drain. Press on it from time to time to remove the excess liquid. You won't remove all the liquid, but you want any excess gone.

3. While the eggplant is grilling and draining, very thinly slice the tomatoes and zucchini.

4. Roll out the pastry to fit a 12-inch (30 cm) removable-bottom tart pan and line the pan with the pastry, leaving the edges of the pastry falling outside the pan.

5. Place the eggplant and garlic in a food processor and puree. Season with salt and piment d'Espelette to taste. Spread the puree on the bottom of the pastry.

6. Top the eggplant with overlapping and alternating rounds of tomato and zucchini, fitting them all into the tart pan.

(continued)

If you have a couple of excess rounds of vegetables, try to pack them into the center.

7. Crimp the edges of the pastry and reserve the trimmings for another use.

8. Drizzle the tart with the oil, season with salt, and place on a parchment-lined baking sheet. Bake in the center of the oven until the pastry and the vegetables are golden, about 50 minutes, checking the tart occasionally to be sure the vegetables or the edges of the pastry aren't getting too dark. If they are, simply lay a piece of parchment paper lightly over the tart so it is protected while it finishes baking.

9. While the tart is baking, prepare the pistou. Place the basil leaves and almonds in a food processor and process until minced. Add a generous pinch of salt, process, then add the oil while the food processor is on. Adjust the seasoning.

10. When the tart is baked, remove it from the oven and let it cool slightly. Remove the tart ring, then transfer the tart to a serving plate or platter. Drizzle with a generous amount of pistou and serve the remaining pistou on the side.

ASTUCES:
- Be sure to prick the eggplant before roasting; otherwise, they are likely to explode in the heat of the oven.
- If you're using an outdoor gas grill to roast the eggplant, you can also bake the tart on it. Just double up on your baking sheets and turn off the middle burner so the exterior two burners are providing the heat, which avoids burning the tart on the bottom.
- By leaving the edges of the pastry over the rim of the tart pan, you can fill the tart to the brim easily, then crimp the pastry once the tart is filled.
- When baking a tart, always set the tart pan on a parchment-covered baking sheet, to catch any juices that overflow.

Provençale Vegetable Soup with Basil

SOUPE AU PISTOU

I love this Provencal soup, with its colors of late summer and autumn, and the rich flavors that these seasonal vegetables give. As in Provence's neighbor, Italy, where soups are based on water, pistou too is made with water and not stock, which makes it fresh and lively. Serve this with plenty of fresh and crisp-crusted bread, and follow it with a selection of goat cheeses, as though you were sitting in the garden, overlooking the vineyards of Provence! I recommend serving a rosé along with this soup, as befits its nature.

SERVES 6

EQUIPMENT: large saucepan, mortar and pestle or food processor

PREPARATION TIME: 25 to 30 minutes

COOKING TIME: 31 minutes

DIFFICULTY LEVEL: simple

FOR THE SOUP:

1 small celery root (7 ounces; 210 g), peeled and cut into ¼-inch (6 mm) dice

1 medium carrot (3 ounce; 90 g), peeled, trimmed, and cut into ¼-inch (6 mm) cubes

2 small waxy potatoes (about 2 ounces; 60 g each), such as a Yukon Gold, peeled and cut into ¼-inch (6 mm) cubes

Coarse sea salt

1 large zucchini (about 3 ounces; 90 g), trimmed and cut into ¼-inch (6 mm) cubes

1 cup (150 g) fresh coco blanc, Jacob's Cattle, or other shell beans (or dried beans, cooked until tender, to make 1 cup)

2 ounces (60 g) angel hair pasta, broken into ½-inch (1.3 cm) lengths, to give ½ cup broken pasta pieces

Freshly ground black pepper

FOR THE PISTOU:

3 large garlic cloves

¼ teaspoon fine sea salt

4 cups gently packed (40 g) fresh basil leaves

⅔ cup (160 ml) extra virgin olive oil

FOR SERVING:

½ cup (30 g) finely grated Parmigiano-Reggiano

1. Place the celery root, carrot, and potatoes in a large saucepan. Add 8 cups (2 L) of water and ½ teaspoon salt, bring to a boil, and cook, covered, until the carrots are nearly tender through, about 12 minutes. Add the zucchini and the fresh beans (if using) and cook until tender, about 15 minutes. (If using cooked dried beans, add them after the zucchini has cooked for 12 minutes.) Add the angel hair pasta and cook until it is al dente, 3 to 4 minutes. Season to taste with pepper, then remove the pot from the heat.

2. While the soup is cooking, prepare the pistou: Crush the garlic cloves and salt with a mortar and pestle until they are a rough paste. Add the basil leaves and crush them

with the mortar and pestle until they mix with the garlic into a rough paste. Slowly add the oil to the mixture until you have a thick, deep green sauce. Alternatively, you can make the pistou in a food processor, following the same order of ingredients.

3. To serve, divide the soup among six warmed shallow soup bowls. Serve the soup with the pistou and the cheese alongside.

ASTUCES:

- The recipe calls for the vegetables to be cut into tiny dice, important because tiny pieces are so pretty, and they allow more flavor to emerge.
- Note that pistou and pesto are different. There is neither cheese nor any nuts in the pistou mixture.
- If you have very big basil eaters to enjoy this, go ahead and make a double portion of the pistou. Any leftover can be frozen in ice cube trays for a later date.
- This is a very traditional blend of vegetables for a soupe au pistou. Use the seasonal vegetables you find at your market.

Potimarron (Kuri) Squash Soup with Bacon

SOUPE AU POTIMARRON AU BACON

Potimarron squash comes around at the end of August or beginning of September. Round, vivid orange, and hard as a rock, when cooked it turns mouth-meltingly sweet. The name is a combination of *potiron* and *marron* (pumpkin and chestnut), which reflects the flavors in this one vegetable. Its flesh is tender and smooth once cooked and pureed, and it needs no peeling as the skin melts right along with the flesh.

The addition of star anise goes back in French history to the spice route. Star anise arrived at the port of Marseille and meandered its way through the southwest, almost the only place in France where it is a traditional seasoning.

This soup, though delicate in flavor, is filling. If you want to turn this into a vegetarian dish, simply omit the bacon. Try a full-bodied red with this, such as wine from Cahors.

SERVES 4 TO 6

EQUIPMENT: small heavy skillet, medium saucepan, immersion blender or food processor

PREPARATION TIME: 10 minutes max

COOKING TIME: 25 minutes

DIFFICULTY LEVEL: simple

---

5 ounces (150 g) slab bacon, rind removed, cut into 1-by-¼-by-¼-inch (2.5 cm-by-6 mm-by-6 mm) pieces, or as near to that as you can get—the pieces shouldn't be too big

1 medium onion (5 ounces; 150 g), diced

1½ pounds (750 g) kuri squash, cut into small cubes (see Astuces)

1 mounded teaspoon coarse sea salt

2 star anise

Sea salt and freshly ground black pepper

1. Place the bacon in a small heavy skillet over medium-high heat. When it begins to sizzle, lower the heat to medium and sauté until the bacon is golden on all sides and cooked through, 6 to 8 minutes. If the bacon sticks, you may need to add a bit of oil to the pan; otherwise, it will brown in its own fat. Transfer the bacon to a paper towel–lined dish, if it is very fatty, and set aside.

2. Melt the butter in a medium saucepan over medium heat, add the onion, and cook, stirring, until the onion is translucent, about 8 minutes. Add the squash, stir, and cover it by 3 inches (7.5 cm) with filtered water. Add the coarse salt and star anise and bring to a boil over medium-high heat. Lower the heat, cover, and cook until the squash is tender through, about 25 minutes.

3. Remove the star anise and puree the soup, then season it to taste with salt and pepper. To serve, divide the soup evenly among four to six bowls, depending on if it is a first or main course. Sprinkle equal amounts of bacon over it and serve.

ASTUCE: If you use other squash for this recipe—kombucha, butternut, acorn—you will need to peel away their tough skin before cooking .

Crisp Confit Tomato Tarts with Olives

CROUSTILLANT DE TOMATES CONFITES AUX OLIVES

These pretty tarts make an impressive plat du jour, delicious for a cool day in summer or early fall, when tomatoes offer their fullness of flavor. The tomatoes bake to an unparalleled sweetness as they absorb the delicate flavors of the fresh herbs. The pastry is crisp, and when you combine that with the texture of the tomatoes, add a touch of goat cheese, and sprinkle in some olives, you've got a meal made for the stars. Serve a green salad alongside, such as A Classic Green Salad (page 265), and pour a lovely Rully from Burgundy to complete this meal.

SERVES 4 TO 8 (HUNGRY PEOPLE WILL EAT TWO!)

EQUIPMENT: nonreactive baking dish, 2 baking sheets

PREPARATION TIME: 20 minutes

COOKING TIME: 1 hour 20 minutes max

DIFFICULTY LEVEL: simple

---

8 medium tomatoes (4 ounces; 120 g), medium ripe, cored and sliced into ½-inch- (1.3 cm) thick slices

3 tablespoons (45 ml) olive oil

Fine sea salt and freshly ground black pepper

5 small fresh rosemary stalks

10 fresh thyme branches

2 fresh summer savory or oregano branches

2 recipes Tender Tart Pastry (page 314)

¾ cup (135 g) fresh goat cheese

24 small black olives, pitted and coarsely chopped

8 fresh basil sprigs for garnish (optional)

1. Preheat the oven to 350°F (175°C).

2. Arrange the tomato slices in a single layer on the bottom of a nonreactive baking dish. Drizzle about 1½ tablespoons of the oil over the tomatoes, sprinkle generously with salt and pepper, and lay the rosemary, thyme, and oregano on top.

3. Bake the tomatoes in the bottom third of the oven until they are slightly golden on top, about 1 hour. Remove from the oven and let cool for at least 10 minutes before proceeding.

4. While the tomatoes are baking, roll out the pastry to ⅛-inch (3 mm) thick. Working quickly, cut out eight 5-inch (12.5 cm) circles from the pastry, transfer them to baking sheets, and chill for 30 minutes to 1 hour.

5. Increase the oven temperature to 425°F (220°C).

6. Remove the pastry circles from the refrigerator and prick the bottoms several times with a fork. Set a sheet of parchment on top of the pastry, then set a baking sheet on top of the parchment and bake the pastry for 12 minutes. Remove the baking sheet and the parchment and continue to bake until the pastry is golden, about 8 more minutes. Remove from the oven and let cool on wire racks.

(continued)

7. Assemble the tarts by arranging three tomato slices, overlapping slightly, in the center of each of the pastry rounds. Spoon an equal amount of goat cheese on top of the tomatoes, then sprinkle an equal amount of olives over the top of each. Let sit for about 30 minutes. Just before serving, drizzle each tart with an equal amount of the remaining olive oil, garnish with a basil leaf, and serve.

ASTUCES:

- Medium-ripe tomatoes are easier to cut into thick slices than are fully ripe tomatoes; they also offer some welcome acid.
- Bake the tomatoes early in the morning while the day is still cool, or even the day before. They do not need—and won't benefit from—refrigeration.
- It is important to let the tarts sit before serving, so the pastry and tomatoes can meld. The tarts should be just slightly warmer than room temperature when you serve them.

King Henry IV's Garlic and Potato Soup from Agen

TOURIN BLANCHI OU SOUPE À L'AIL D'HENRI IV

This soup, a favorite of Henry IV, is a staple in the southwest of France near the town of Agen, where garlic flourishes. Never a wealthy region, its cuisine was simple and poor, like this dish made of potatoes and garlic and dressed up with eggs and toasted bread. Nothing simpler, nothing better! Typically, the toasted bread was put in the bottom of the bowl and the soup was poured over it. I prefer to serve the toast alongside the soup, but you will follow your own instincts on this!

You really need nothing more with this than a bottle of Buzet, the satisfying and sunny red wine from Lot-et-Garonne, of which Agen is the county seat.

SERVES 6

EQUIPMENT: kitchen twine, heavy-bottomed stockpot, potato masher

PREPARATION TIME: 10 minutes

COOKING TIME: about 40 minutes

DIFFICULTY LEVEL: simple

FOR THE SOUP:

20 fresh thyme sprigs

1 fresh or dried imported bay leaf

2 tablespoons olive oil

6 very large garlic cloves (about 2 ounces; 60 g total)

1 large onion (6 ounces; 180 g), diced

1 large shallot (about 2 ounces; 60 g), diced

2 quarts (2 L) Beef Stock (page 329) or water

2 pounds (1 kg) starchy potatoes (such as russet), peeled and cut into cubes

½ teaspoon fine sea salt

Several grinds of black pepper

FOR THE TOASTS:

6 slices country bread

1 garlic clove

FOR SERVING:

1 cup (10 g) loosely packed fresh flat-leaf parsley leaves

6 large eggs

1. Tie the thyme sprigs and bay leaf together with kitchen twine.

2. Heat the olive oil in a heavy-bottomed stockpot over medium-high heat and add the garlic cloves. Cook, stirring, until they are golden on the outside, about 4 minutes. Lower the heat to medium and add the onion and shallot. Cook, stirring, until the onion begins to turn translucent, about 5 minutes.

3. Add the stock or water, potatoes, and thyme bundle and bring the liquid to a boil. Add the salt and pepper and

(continued)

ASTUCES:

- This recipe calls for six very large (and pungent) garlic cloves—you'll need at least that many, and double if your cloves aren't large. Don't worry, though. The long cooking will transform them into something sweet and lovely, and despite Henry IV's aroma, you won't suffer the same.
- You don't need to worry about the green germ of the garlic here, as it, too, will melt in the cooking.
- When you eat this soup, use the toast to pierce the egg yolk and dip the toast into it! *Miam.*

cook until the potatoes and garlic are completely tender through, about 30 minutes. Adjust the seasoning.

4. Prepare the toasts: Toast the bread in a toaster, and when it is golden, rub each piece with the garlic clove. Set aside.

5. Using a potato masher or a fork, transform the soup into a rough puree. Return the soup to the heat and bring it nearly to a boil.

6. Mince the parsley and stir it into the soup.

7. Break the eggs into the soup and cook without stirring until the whites are firm and the yolks are still soft, about 6 minutes. You'll need to drizzle some of the potato mixture over the eggs, to encourage them to cook.

8. To serve, using a large ladle, ladle out the soup with an egg in it and place it gently into a shallow soup bowl. Ladle any remaining soup around the eggs. Garnish each serving with a parsley sprig and set a piece of toast in the soup bowl.

KING HENRY IV AND HIS GARLIC

Fleurette, Henry IV's first mistress, said to him, "Sire, it's lucky you are the king because if you weren't, no one could stand to be near you because you smell like a dead bird." This, because Henry IV loved to, and often did, eat garlic, a habit he was nearly born with; it is said that his grandfather, Henri d'Albret, rubbed his little infant lips with a garlic clove. No doubt to keep away vampires.

Later, the king-to-be was fed the foods of the Béarn, in southwest France, which included this gorgeously simple and delicious soup. He was astonished for it combined his favorite dish—a garlic omelet—with toasted bread rubbed with garlic. When you eat this, you'll love it as much as Henry IV did.

Zucchini Soup with Ginger and Mint

SOUPE AUX COURGETTES AU GINGEMBRE ET À LA MENTHE

This is a magical summer soup, and an elegant way to use up zucchini that have gotten just a little too large in the summer sun. You don't want to use *huge* zucchini, but midsize, too-big-for-sautéing versions. Delicately seasoned, this soup will astound with its beguiling flavor. You can serve it warm, as indicated here, or chilled. If you decide to serve it chilled, you may need to increase the seasoning slightly, but go easy as subtlety is the name of this soup's game. Turn this soup into a plat du jour with a big green salad alongside, such as A Classic Green Salad (page 265), and serve it with a lovely, chilled Chenin Blanc.

SERVES 6

EQUIPMENT: medium saucepan, slotted spoon, food processor

PREPARATION TIME: 10 minutes

COOKING TIME: about 30 minutes

DIFFICULTY LEVEL: simple

---

2 pounds (1 kg) zucchini, rinsed and trimmed

Coarse sea salt

1½ cups (375 ml) heavy cream

1 teaspoon curry powder, preferably Madras

2 teaspoons grated fresh ginger (from a 2-inch; 5 cm piece)

Fine sea salt and freshly ground black pepper

7 large fresh mint leaves

1. Cut the zucchini in half lengthwise. If there are any seeds, remove them. Coarsely chop the zucchini. Place it in a medium saucepan and cover by 1 inch (2.5 cm) with water. Add the coarse salt and bring to a boil. Lower the heat so the water is simmering and cook until the zucchini is tender, 25 to 30 minutes.

2. Remove the zucchini from the pan, using a slotted spoon, and transfer it to a food processor. Reserve the cooking liquid. Puree the zucchini, then add the cream, curry powder, and ginger, and puree until thoroughly combined. If the soup is thicker than you like it, add up to ½ cup (125 ml) of the reserved cooking liquid. Taste for seasoning, then return the soup to the saucepan in which the zucchini cooked, and heat until it is just about, but not quite, boiling. Don't boil it!

3. While the soup is heating, scissor cut (chiffonade) the mint leaves.

4. Taste the soup for seasoning, then divide it among six warmed soup bowls. Garnish each with mint and serve immediately.

ASTUCES:

- If your zucchini has *very* tough skin, you'll want to remove it, so use slightly more than 2 pounds (1 kg) of zucchini to make up for the weight of the peel.
- To peel ginger, use the edge of a teaspoon to scrape away the skin—this is much more efficient than a knife!
- If you serve the soup chilled, you may want to add additional cream or chicken broth, or if you've saved the zucchini cooking liquid, use that to loosen it, as it thickens when it is chilled.

CHAPTER 7
SALADS

I'LL ALWAYS REMEMBER the first time I ordered a *salade composée* (main-dish salad) at a French café. Intrigued by all the offerings, from a *Salade Nordique* with smoked salmon and shrimp, to a *Salade Landaise* heaped with thin-sliced ham and foie gras, I settled for a standard *Salade Frisée aux Lardons* (curly endive with bacon). And I've never looked back. Since that day, serving hot things on a perfectly dressed green salad has been one of my favorite plats du jour, a meal on a plate offering both warmth and freshness. Enjoy the *salades composées* in this chapter and let them nourish your imagination to make up many others, using your own combination of favorite ingredients.

Curly Endive Salad with Hot Bacon and Goat Cheese

SALADE FRISÉE AUX LARDONS ET CHÈVRE

There is no salad more classic nor more delicious than *frisée aux lardons et chèvre*, perhaps the most popular in the French retinue of composed salads that are served as plats du jour. This is certainly one of my favorites, because it offers everything—crunchy, fresh, salty, nourishing. Since frisée—curly endive—is a winter green and goat cheese is best in winter, this is a winter dish, to be eaten in a cozy environment, accompanied by a lightly chilled Sancerre Blanc.

SERVES 6

EQUIPMENT: large heatproof salad bowl, baking sheet, large heavy skillet

PREPARATION TIME: 15 minutes max

COOKING TIME: 10 minutes

DIFFICULTY LEVEL: simple

FOR THE GREENS:

- 11 ounces (330 g) curly endive (about 12 cups, loosely packed) or escarole, rinsed, patted dry, and torn into small pieces
- 1 large shallot (2 ounces; 70 g), cut into paper-thin rounds
- 1 garlic clove, cut into tiny dice

FOR THE TOASTS:

- 12 small slices baguette or other fresh crusty bread
- 1 garlic clove
- 3 small goat cheeses (3.5 ounces; 105 g each), such as Crottin de Chavignol, each cut into 2 horizontal rounds, or six 1-inch (2.5 cm) rounds of goat cheese

FOR SERVING:

- 8 ounces (250 g) slab bacon, rind removed, cut into 1-by-¼-by-¼-inch (2.5 cm-by-6 mm-by-6 mm) pieces
- 3 tablespoons (45 ml) olive oil, if needed
- 3 tablespoons (45 ml) best-quality red wine vinegar
- Freshly ground black pepper
- Sea salt (optional)

1. Preheat the broiler.

2. Prepare the greens: Place the curly endive, shallot, and garlic in a large heatproof salad bowl, and toss to mix.

3. Prepare the toasts: Place the bread slices on a baking sheet and toast them on one side about 3 inches (7.5 cm) from the heat element for about 2 minutes. Remove from the broiler and rub on both sides with the whole garlic clove. Place one round of cheese on the untoasted side of six toasted bread slices and place them, along with the remaining pieces of bread, untoasted side up, under the broiler. Broil until the cheese is golden and bubbling and the bread is toasted, 2 to 3 minutes.

(continued)

4. Place the bacon in a large heavy skillet over medium-high heat and cook, stirring frequently, just until it is golden, about 5 minutes. Depending upon how much fat is rendered from the bacon, add up to 3 tablespoons oil because you want 4 tablespoons (60 ml) total of fat. Add the vinegar, standing back as it gives off steam. Stir, scraping up all the browned bits from the bottom of the pan, then pour over the salad. Toss thoroughly, seasoning generously with pepper and salt if necessary, and toss again.

5. Divide the salad among six warmed salad plates. Place a cheese-topped toast atop each salad, and one piece of plain toast on the side of the plate. Serve immediately.

ASTUCES:

- French bacon, and some American brands, are notably lean, so your bacon may need oil for cooking. Have oil at the ready if you need it. If you don't and wind up with more than 4 tablespoons in the pan, simply drain any excess.
- Note that I ask you to cut the garlic into tiny dice rather than mince it. This is because the "bite" of a piece of garlic is necessary, and if it's minced, it tends to disappear into the salad.

Melted Escarole and Bacon on a Bed of Crushed Potatoes

FONDU DE SCAROLE ET LARDONS SUR LIT DE POMMES DE TERRE

In France, escarole is the biggest lettuce that exists, sometimes so large it fills an entire shopping basket. But you may wonder, "Cooked escarole?" Yes! It turns into a lushly tender green when it's melted like this. Topped with bacon and served on potatoes, it makes a perfect main dish for winter, when escarole is at the market. Escarole's interior leaves are creamy white, protected from the light by the huge green leaves on its exterior. Try this with a soft yet hearty Merlot from Languedoc, Reserve Denois recommended.

SERVES 4 TO 6

EQUIPMENT: large saucepan or Dutch oven with lid, large skillet with 2-inch (5 cm) sides, tongs

PREPARATION TIME: 15 minutes

COOKING TIME: 25 minutes

DIFFICULTY LEVEL: simple

- **2 pounds (1 kg) russet potatoes, peeled and cut into quarters**
- **1 tablespoon coarse sea salt**
- **6 ounces (180 g) slab bacon, rind removed, cut into 1-by-¼-by-¼ inch (2.5 cm-by-6 mm-by-6 mm) pieces**
- **2 large shallots (2 ounces; 70 g each), minced**
- **1 large garlic clove, diced**
- **1 tablespoon olive oil, if needed**
- **1 pound (500 g) escarole (about 16 cups leaves), rinsed, patted dry, and torn into large bite-size pieces**
- **2 tablespoons sherry vinegar**
- **Fine sea salt and freshly ground black pepper**

1. Place the potatoes in a large saucepan and add enough water to cover them by 2 inches (5 cm). Add the salt, cover, and bring to a boil over medium-high heat. Cook, partially covered, until the potatoes are tender through, about 20 minutes. Drain and keep warm.

2. While the potatoes are cooking, sauté the bacon over medium-high heat in a large skillet. When the bacon has begun to brown and has rendered some of its fat, add the shallots and garlic and cook, stirring constantly, until the shallots are translucent, about 10 minutes. If the bacon is very lean and doesn't give up enough fat, add the olive oil and stir so it coats all the ingredients. Lower the heat to medium to keep the shallots and garlic from browning too much.

3. Add the escarole and cook, turning it frequently with tongs, until it is mostly limp but still slightly crisp and the green parts have turned a very dark green, 10 to 15 minutes. (You may need to add the escarole in several batches. When the first batch has softened and reduced in volume, add the second batch and continue until all the escarole is in the pan.)

(continued)

4. When the escarole is cooked, drizzle the vinegar over it and toss to incorporate. Then season to taste with salt and plenty of black pepper.

5. To serve, place the potatoes in one warmed serving bowl, the escarole mixture in another. To eat, place some warm potatoes on your plate, crush them gently with a fork, and top with the escarole mixture. Enjoy!

ASTUCES:
- There is some waste, because those outer leaves can be so tough and bitter. Once you've discarded them, you are left with a tasty green.
- The amount of escarole is impressive, so add it to the pan bit by bit, as the leaves in the pan reduce in the heat and make room.

Cabbage Salad with Tuna Lardons

SALADE DE CHOU AUX LARDONS DE THON

Lardons are those savory bits of bacon in the French repertoire that are strewn over everything from salad to soup, eggs to bread dough. Here, tuna plays the role of bacon in the seasoning of this wonderfully crisp, satisfying cabbage salad. Serve this often in the winter, when cabbage is at its best, along with a red Sancerre, which enhances the light meatiness of the tuna, and the cabbage, too. And remember, lots of crusty baguette here! Serve an Anjou here, lightly chilled.

SERVES 4 TO 6
EQUIPMENT: large heavy skillet
PREPARATION TIME: 20 minutes
COOKING TIME: 10 minutes
DIFFICULTY LEVEL: simple

---

7 tablespoons (105 ml) walnut oil

1 garlic clove, minced

6 ounces (180 g) fresh bluefin or albacore tuna, cut into 1-by-½-by-¼-inch (2.5 cm-by-6 mm-by-6 mm) pieces

2 shallots, cut into paper-thin slices

½ small Savoy cabbage (about 18 ounces; 540 g), halved, cored, and very thinly sliced

⅓ cup (75 ml) best-quality red wine vinegar

Sea salt and freshly ground black pepper

½ small red cabbage (about 9 ounces; 270 g), halved, cored, and thinly sliced

½ cup (80 g) walnuts, coarsely chopped

1. Heat 3 tablespoons (45 ml) of the walnut oil in a large heavy skillet over medium heat. Add the garlic and stir until it begins to turn translucent, just a minute or two, then add the tuna and sauté, stirring constantly, until golden on all sides, about 4 minutes. Transfer the tuna and garlic to a paper towel–lined plate to drain. Set aside.

2. Add 2 more tablespoons of the walnut oil to the skillet. Add one-third of the shallots and cook, stirring, until just slightly translucent, about 1 minute. Add the green cabbage and toss to coat with the oil. Add half of the vinegar and cook, stirring constantly, until the cabbage is slightly wilted, 2 to 3 minutes. Season with salt and pepper to taste. Remove the green cabbage and arrange it around the outside edge of a warm serving platter. Keep the cabbage warm.

3. Add the remaining 2 tablespoons walnut oil to the skillet. Add half of the remaining shallots to the oil and cook until just translucent, about 1 minute. Add the red cabbage and toss in the oil. Add the remaining vinegar and cook, stirring constantly, until the cabbage is slightly wilted, 2 to 3 minutes. Season with the salt and pepper to taste. Remove the cabbage from the skillet and mound it in the center of the serving platter. Sprinkle the remaining shallots and walnuts over the cabbage. Scatter the tuna on top. Serve immediately.

ASTUCES:

- Albacore, skipjack, and yellowfin tuna are the ideal species to eat, in reference to environmental and health issues.
- I call for Savoy cabbage here because it is so sweet and delicious, and the ubiquitous cabbage of France. But we also have a spring cabbage called *chou nouveau* (new cabbage), and it is even sweeter and more tender than Savoy. Look for it at your farmers' market, where it might be called caraflex, conehead, or arrowhead cabbage.
- This is a rare time when walnut oil is used in cooking, the way the walnut oil producers do in the Dordogne. Go easy, for it can burn quickly. Leblanc brand is the best-quality walnut oil you can find. It is available from virtual and brick-and-mortar shops.

Winter Greens with Hazelnut Vinaigrette

SALADE D'HIVER À LA VINAIGRETTE DE NOISETTES

Two things I love about winter are the abundance of bitter greens at the farmers' market and the number of salads as plat du jour on menus. This recipe veers from the traditional in that hazelnuts—rather than more typical walnuts—are combined with Roquefort to give this hearty salad heft and turn it into a full meal. Don't be concerned by the word *bitter* here in reference to the greens—their natural sweetness, brought on by the cold, is a counterpoint, set off even more by the salty Roquefort and the rich flavor of hazelnuts. Enjoy a white Gaillac here.

SERVES 6

EQUIPMENT: medium bowl, large bowl

PREPARATION TIME: 10 minutes

COOKING TIME: 8 minutes to toast the hazelnuts

DIFFICULTY LEVEL: simple

FOR THE VINAIGRETTE:

1 tablespoon sherry vinegar

1 tablespoon balsamic vinegar

½ teaspoon fine sea salt

Freshly ground black pepper

1 small egg yolk (optional)

1 shallot, sliced paper thin

2 tablespoons hazelnut oil, Leblanc brand preferred

2 tablespoons olive oil

¼ cup (40 g) hazelnuts, lightly toasted and finely ground

FOR THE SALAD:

10 cups (260 g) bitter greens (see Astuces), washed and torn into small pieces

2 Belgian endives, trimmed and cut lengthwise into thin slices

6 ounces (180 g) Roquefort, at room temperature

Freshly ground black pepper

1. Prepare the vinaigrette: Whisk together the vinegars, salt, pepper to taste, and egg yolk (if using) in a medium bowl. Whisk in the sliced shallot, then slowly add the oils, whisking constantly, until the mixture is emulsified. Whisk in the ground hazelnuts, which will further thicken the vinaigrette.

2. Prepare the salad: Place the greens and endive in a large bowl. Add the vinaigrette and toss thoroughly until all the leaves are coated. Evenly divide the salad among six salad plates. Crumble equal amounts of the Roquefort over each salad, then season generously with black pepper. Serve immediately.

ASTUCES:

- Bitter greens include radicchio, dandelion greens, escarole, and curly endive.
- When buying Roquefort, look for either Carles or Gabriel Coulet, the last two artisanal Roqueforts. If you cannot find Roquefort, Maytag blue makes a wonderful substitute!
- The vinaigrette contains a raw egg yolk. If you prefer, you may omit it from the recipe.
- Use a small spice grinder for the hazelnuts, and add a pinch of salt before you begin grinding them, which will prevent them from turning oily.

Dandelion, Apple, and Bacon Salad

SALADE DE PISSENLITS AUX POMMES ET AUX LARDONS

This salad speaks of Normandy, where dandelion greens are a specialty, the quality of its eggs are unparalleled, and apples are its main crop. This salad combines all these ingredients into one dish, an ultimate Norman plat du jour, offering a gustatory tour of the region. The combination of fats in this salad—bacon, butter, oil—gives it depth, while the tartness of the apples makes it weightless. I serve two eggs per person for a truly satisfying plat du jour, but do as your appetite suggests. Serve a hard apple or pear cider along with this dish.

SERVES 4

EQUIPMENT: large saucepan, cotton tea towel, slotted spoon, large heatproof bowl, large heavy skillet, medium heavy skillet, medium skillet, scissors

PREPARATION TIME: 10 to 15 minutes

COOKING TIME: 15 minutes

DIFFICULTY LEVEL: simple

FOR THE POACHED EGGS:

⅓ cup (80 ml) distilled white vinegar

4 to 8 large eggs

FOR THE SALAD:

7 ounces (210 g) dandelion greens (8 cups loosely packed), white stems trimmed, well rinsed, and patted dry, torn into bite-size pieces

7 ounces (210 g) slab bacon, rind removed, cut into 1-by-½-by-¼-inch (2.5 cm-by-1.3 cm-by-6 mm) pieces

2 tablespoons olive oil, if needed

1 tablespoon (15 g) unsalted butter

1 large apple (about 7 ounces; 210 g), such as a Boskoop or Cox's Orange Pippin, peeled and cored and cut into 16 thin wedges

1 garlic clove, diced

2 tablespoons best-quality red wine vinegar

Fleur de sel and freshly ground black pepper

1. Poach the eggs: Pour water to a depth of about 6 inches (15 cm) into a large saucepan, add the vinegar, and bring the liquids to a rolling boil over medium-high heat. Fill a large bowl with hot water and set it near the stove. Line a dinner plate or small platter with a cotton tea towel.

2. Break one of the eggs into a small bowl. Slide the egg into the water where the bubbles emerge from the bottom of the pan—there will be several places in the pan where this happens, and each spot gets its egg, so repeat the process. Lower the heat if the water is boiling too violently and poach the eggs just until the whites are set, about 3 minutes. Very carefully, using a slotted spoon, remove the eggs, dip them in the bowl of hot water, then set them on the prepared plate. Repeat until all of the eggs are poached. If you're not going to use the eggs immediately, prepare a bowl of warm, lightly salted water. Slip the eggs into this water, where they will stay warm for up to 20 minutes without cooking further.

3. Prepare the salad: Place the dandelion greens in a large heatproof bowl.

4. Place the bacon in a medium heavy skillet over medium-high heat and brown on all sides, stirring frequently, until

(continued)

it is thoroughly golden, about 7 minutes. If the bacon is dry, as French bacon will be, add the tablespoon of oil to the pan.

5. While the bacon is browning, melt the butter in a separate medium skillet over medium heat until it is foaming and hot. Don't let it brown. Add the apple wedges and sauté until slightly golden and nearly soft through, 3 to 5 minutes. Remove the pan from the heat, leaving the apples in it so they stay warm.

6. When the bacon is golden, drain off all but 3 tablespoons of fat. Add the garlic and cook, stirring, just until it begins to turn golden on the edges, about 1 minute. Then stir in the vinegar, scraping any browned bits from the bottom of the pan. Some of the vinegar will evaporate, creating a cloud of stinging steam, so stand back as you do this.

7. Pour the bacon and its cooking juices over the dandelion greens and toss thoroughly until all the ingredients are thoroughly combined. Add the apples to the salad, along with any juices they've given up, and toss very carefully. Taste the salad and adjust the seasoning, including adding additional vinegar to your taste, if necessary.

8. Divide the salad among four warmed plates. Trim the eggs of any messy white, then place one or two atop each salad, patting the egg dry before doing so, if necessary. Season with fleur de sel and a shower of freshly ground pepper and serve

ASTUCES:

- Why add so much vinegar to the poaching water? Because vinegar makes the white wrap around the egg yolk, so the poached egg is presentable. I suggest dipping the poached eggs in warm water to remove any trace of vinegar flavor.
- If you want to keep the eggs warm for longer than a few minutes, you don't need to rinse them, but can slip them into a bowl of warm, lightly salted water, where they'll keep without further cooking.
- I call for typical Norman apples—either the Boskoop or the Cox's Orange Pippin, which are both tart and perfumed. If you can't find either, then try Pink Lady, Honeycrisp, or a good, fresh Jonagold.

Salade Niçoise

Salade niçoise. How we all love this blend of potatoes, green beans, lettuce, tomatoes, tuna, and . . . wait, stop! Do not ever tell any self-respecting inhabitant of Nice that you like Salade Niçoise with potatoes, green beans, or even lettuce. This will make you an outcast, a poor, sad excuse for a human being. Why? Because a true Salade Niçoise is a blend of seasonal vegetables that every Niçoise had at hand long, long ago. That selection did not include potatoes and green beans. Those ingredients were added by Auguste Escoffier, who came from the other side of Provence, where these vegetables were introduced sometime after the 17th century. Even tomatoes are a relatively recent addition, but, perhaps with some reluctance, the Niçoise find them acceptable.

There are a few other "rules" to Salade Niçoise. A true Salade Niçoise doesn't have any cooked ingredients but the eggs—it is the assemblage of fresh ingredients dressed only with olive oil, salt, and pepper. In addition, the olives must have their pits, and while anchovies are traditional, canned tuna is acceptable even to a purist. But the two are never added to the same salad—two fish would simply be too much.

Try this version of Salade Niçoise and you'll forever want to save your green beans and potatoes for some other dish. This makes a meal, along with bread and a chilled rosé from Cassis.

SERVES 6

EQUIPMENT: colander, small saucepan, large salad bowl

PREPARATION TIME: 25 minutes

COOKING TIME: 10 minutes to boil the eggs

DIFFICULTY LEVEL: simple

- 1 pound (500 g) cherry tomatoes, trimmed and cut in half, lengthwise
- 1 cucumber (about 12 ounces; 360 g), peeled and thinly sliced
- Fine sea salt
- 2 pounds (1 kg) fava beans in their husks, shucked (frozen fava beans work perfectly here; you'll need about 1½ cups' worth)
- 12 anchovy fillets, or 8 ounces (250 g) canned oil-packed albacore tuna
- 1 cup gently packed (10 g) fresh basil leaves
- 1 garlic clove, cut in half
- One 4-ounce (120 g) green pepper, such as Cubanelle or Shishito, trimmed and cut into thin rounds
- 4 small round spring onions or 8 scallions (8 ounces; 250 g),
- cut in half lengthwise and sliced very thinly
- ½ cup black olives (3 ounces; 90 g), such as Niçoise, with pits
- About ¼ cup (60 ml) olive oil
- 3 large eggs, hard-cooked and cut into quarters
- Freshly ground black pepper
- Basil leaves for garnish

(continued)

ASTUCES:

- Small artichokes peeled of their leaves are often included in a Salade Niçoise. If you can find them, make sure that once the leaves and choke are removed, you rub the artichoke with a lemon, to keep it from turning black. Just before serving the salad, thinly slice the artichoke and toss it with the rest of the ingredients.
- If you cannot find fresh fava beans, use frozen. They benefit from a quick plunge into boiling water—see instructions. If you can't find either fresh or frozen favas, simply omit them from the salad.

1. Place the tomatoes and cucumber slices in a colander set over a large bowl. Salt them with an even shower of salt (about 1 teaspoon), shake the colander so all the vegetables are evenly salted, and reserve while you prepare the rest of the salad.

2. Bring a small saucepan filled with lightly salted water to a boil over medium-high heat. When the water is at a rolling boil, add the shucked fava beans, let boil for 2 minutes, then remove the fava beans from the water, leaving the hot water in the saucepan. Carefully make a slit in the outer skin of each fava bean and squeeze or take out the tender green been inside. Discard the skins. If the outer skin doesn't easily cut and peel off, return the fava beans to the hot water for a minute or two. (If using frozen favas, they're already peeled but will benefit from a quick plunge into boiling water, literally less than a minute. Drain and use them in the salad.)

3. Cut the anchovy fillets into large dice. If using canned tuna instead, crumble it into bite-size or smaller pieces. If using fresh, seared tuna, slice it thinly.

4. Tear the largest basil leaves into bite-size pieces. Reserve several sprigs of smaller leaves for garnish.

5. To serve the salad, rub a large salad bowl with the garlic clove. Place all the ingredients, except the tuna (if using) and eggs, in the bowl.

6. Mince the basil leaves and add to the bowl. Pour the olive oil over the salad and toss very gently, so all the ingredients are coated with oil. Taste for seasoning. Garnish the salad with the crumbled or sliced tuna (if using), the eggs, and the reserved basil sprigs and serve immediately.

TRADITIONAL INGREDIENTS FOR A SALADE NIÇOISE

Tomatoes, hard-cooked eggs, anchovies, or tuna (not both fish at once!), cebettes (spring onions or scallions), black olives, basil leaves. In season, you can add fava beans, tiny artichokes, celery hearts, or small green peppers (not spicy).

CHAPTER 8
EGGS

THE FRENCH ARE CRAZY ABOUT EGGS, in every form and fashion. After all, they invented the soufflé and the quiche, and they still make and serve them all the time. The French cook is the one who offers hard-cooked eggs bathed in homemade mayonnaise as though it were the crown jewels, and who has raised the making of an omelet to high art. And it's easy to understand why, because eggs in France are something special, as is any egg produced anywhere, as long it's from a chicken that gets to run around and eat yummy things. Towns all over the country are offering two chickens to each inhabitant in an effort to reduce compostable waste in landfills, as a chicken eats nearly its own weight in produce trimmings, and the result of that is even *better*-tasting eggs, for even better and more wonderful egg dishes. Stroll through this chapter and you'll want to make every single recipe in it, with the most marvelous eggs you can find.

THE FRENCH AND EGGS

The French are in love with eggs. In fact, they reportedly consume 230 per capita per year. And the French cook knows exactly what to do with the egg, from the simple soft-cooked version to the fried egg served atop a croque madame.

Why this love affair? Like nearly everything in France, it goes back to the farm, where so many either grew up or spent their vacations, usually under the auspices of Grandmère and Grandpère.

Grandmère had chickens, and collecting their eggs was a daily treasure hunt for the grandchildren. Grandmère would mark the day's take with the date so she could rotate the eggs. She would use the most fresh for uncooked preparations, such as mayonnaise, while she let the others age slightly before cooking, knowing from experience that a several-day-old egg gives a fluffier, lighter result when cooked. She then went on to prepare eggs in every possible way, passing along their deliciousness and her belief that the egg is a perfect symbol of nature's bounty.

Little has changed to the French eye or palate. Topping the list of favorite ways to prepare the French egg is, surprisingly, over easy. Called *oeuf sur le plat*, it is served on its own, nestled near sautéed potatoes and a green salad, or *à cheval* (on horseback), which typically refers to a fried egg atop a freshly sautéed steak.

In France, the egg is typically a lunch or dinner food. Tradition holds that the thought of an egg for breakfast would send a French person fleeing from the room. This is changing, though, as the French discover brunch. Today, 15 percent of the French population eat eggs in the morning. They also consume them for dessert, where the egg is the basis of clafoutis, crème brûlée, chocolate mousse, sweet soufflés, and so much more.

Of the 16 billion eggs produced in France (Europe's top score), an increasing number are referred to as "alternative" eggs, which includes free range (*plein air*), organic (*bio*), and the diminutive quail egg (*oeuf de caille*), which combined account for 38 percent of France's egg production.

The label "plein air" indicates that chicken is let outside at least once each day to exercise, as opposed to "free range," which by FDA definition means simply that a chicken has "access" to the outdoors, even if it never gets there.

Eggs aren't refrigerated in France, even at the supermarket, which follows tradition but is backed up by science. Studies reveal that an egg produces its own protective film more readily at room temperature than in the refrigerator, and that eggs which are subject to constantly changing temperatures—in the door of a refrigerator that is constantly opened and closed, for instance—develop condensation on the shell which can foster salmonella. The egg absorbs aromas through its permeable shells, too, so those in the refrigerator deteriorate in flavor quality more quickly than those at room temperature, and their shells are much harder to remove when the egg is hard-cooked. Finally, a cold egg doesn't blend easily with other ingredients, and should be at room temperature before being used.

The ideal way for a cook to store an egg, so it will always be ready to use is either in its carton at room temperature, or in an egg stand made for the purpose. And egg aficionados suggest storing the egg upside down, so the yolk stays in the center of the egg.

Zucchini Quiche

QUICHE AUX COURGETTES

Zucchini, oh zucchini! What does the French chef do with it when she or he has a plat du jour to serve? Wraps it in custard, nestles it in gorgeous pastry, and serves it as a quiche, of course! You may even want to make two, depending on how many guests you have, because everyone will want a second piece. You can use medium zucchini in this quiche, those that are slightly too large to sauté, steam, or serve in a salad, because they'll soften and melt into the custard. If you happen to have leftovers, this is wonderful at room temperature, and it will keep overnight. Serve this with A Classic Green Salad (page 265), and a light red, such as a Gamay.

SERVES 4 TO 6

EQUIPMENT: one 10½-inch (27 cm) glass or metal pie plate, baking sheet, medium bowl

PREPARATION TIME: 15 minutes

COOKING TIME: up to 45 minutes; 10 minutes cooling time

DIFFICULTY LEVEL: simple

---

1 recipe Tender Tart Pastry (see page 314)

6 large eggs

⅔ cup (160 ml) heavy cream or crème fraîche

1 cup (250 ml) milk (preferably whole)

Fine sea salt and freshly grated black pepper

½ cup (5 g) lightly packed fresh basil leaves

1 generous ounce (35 g) Parmigiano-Reggiano, grated finely (for ½ cup grated)

2 cups (300 g) grated zucchini (from 3 medium zucchini)

1 garlic clove, sliced crosswise very thinly

1. Roll out the pastry to fit a 10½-inch (26 cm) glass or metal pie plate. Crimp the edges, poke the bottom with a fork or the tip of a sharp knife, and place the pastry in the freezer for 30 minutes or in the refrigerator for at least 1 hour.

2. Preheat the oven to 425°F (220°C).

3. Line the pastry with aluminum foil and pastry weights, place on a baking sheet, and bake in the bottom third of the oven until the pastry is golden at the edges, about 15 minutes. Remove from the oven and remove the aluminum foil and pastry weights. Return the pastry to the oven to bake until the bottom is golden, an additional 5 minutes. Remove from the oven and set aside.

4. Whisk together the eggs, cream, and milk in a medium bowl until thoroughly blended. Season with the salt and pepper.

5. Mince the basil and add it to the egg mixture along with the cheese and grated zucchini, and stir until all the ingredients are well mixed.

6. Sprinkle the sliced garlic evenly over the pastry, then turn the egg mixture into the pastry. Carefully put the quiche,

(continued)

along with its baking sheet, on the center rack of the oven and bake until the filling is golden and completely baked through, 30 to 40 minutes. To test for doneness, shake the quiche—if it is solid without a pool of uncooked filling in the center, it is done. You may also stick a sharp knife blade into the center of the filling, and if it comes out clean, the quiche is baked through.

7. Remove the quiche from the oven and show it to your guests while it's at its best, as it will deflate. Wait for it to cool for about 10 minutes, then serve.

ASTUCES:
- If all you have is a removable-bottom pie plate, use it, but make sure that you save a little pastry so that if the pastry shrinks during baking and there are small holes, you can patch them.
- Chilling the pastry makes the butter cold so that when the pastry bakes, the butter melts, leaving distinct air spaces in the pastry and making it flaky and crisp.
- If you don't have pastry weights, use rice or dried beans. You can reuse them.

Country Omelet with Wild Mushrooms and Potatoes

OMELETTE CAMPAGNARDE AUX CÈPES ET POMMES DE TERRE

This is a famed plat du jour inspired by the equally famed and classically Parisian café, Le Select, in the city's Montparnasse neighborhood. Le Select has been and still is a place where writers, actors, and musicians congregate. Its team of maître d'hôtel and waiters dressed in long, starched white aprons is out of central casting, as is their warm welcome to every customer.

Le Select offers traditional plats du jour on its menu, and my favorite is this earthy, savory omelet, which is filled with cèpes, or porcini as the Italians call them, and potato. When Le Select's owner, Jacques Viguier, called the chef over to give me this recipe, I noted there was no garlic in it, unusual for a dish that contains cèpes. *"Mais non, mais non! Le saveur est dans les cèpes!"* ("No, no, the flavor is in the cèpes!") he said, and he is right. This dish is a symphony of simplicity, a house special, and it is luscious with a lightly chilled white Burgundy and plenty of fresh baguette. With every bite, you'll be transported to Montparnasse!

SERVES 4

EQUIPMENT: large nonstick skillet

PREPARATION TIME: 10 minutes max

COOKING TIME: 5 to 7 minutes

DIFFICULTY LEVEL: simple

---

1 generous tablespoon unsalted butter

2 teaspoons olive oil

2 waxy potatoes (5 ounces; 150 g total weight), such as Yukon Gold, cut into ¼-inch (6 mm) squares

8 ounces cèpes or shiitake mushrooms, trimmed and cut into thin slices

6 large eggs

Fine sea salt and freshly ground pepper

1. Heat the butter and oil in a large nonstick skillet over medium heat. Add the potatoes and cook, stirring, until they are golden on all sides, about 7 minutes. Add the mushrooms and shake the pan so they are mixed with the potatoes, cover, and cook until the mushrooms are golden and tender, 6 to 7 minutes, shaking the pan at least once during the cooking time.

2. While the mushrooms are cooking, whisk the eggs in a bowl with the salt and pepper just until they are blended and beginning to foam.

3. Pour the eggs over the vegetables and cook, using a spatula to pull them back from the edges of the pan and tipping the uncooked eggs in the center out toward the edge of the pan. When the omelet is evenly set on the bottom but there is still some uncooked egg on top, about 5 minutes, it is cooked according to French standards.

(continued)

If you want to make an omelet that is cooked all the way through, cover the pan with a lid and continue to cook it until it is done to your liking, an additional minute or two.

4. Turn out the omelet onto a warmed serving platter by letting one-third of it hit the platter, then flipping the other half on it, to create a folded omelet.

Egg Flowers with Kuri Squash

FLEUR D'OEUF SUR LIT DE POTIMARRON

When you make and serve these eggs, everyone's eyes will light up, they're so beautiful and flavorful. I don't believe in using plastic wrap in the kitchen *except* to prepare these eggs, which are a play on poached eggs, only cooked in the tightly twisted plastic so they emerge from it looking like happy chrysanthemums. It's fun, and the result is simply worth it. Serve this in autumn and winter when it's cold and the skies are gray. The flavors in this dish are lively and exciting, and they bring the sun inside to your plate. Serve this with a Riesling.

SERVES 4

EQUIPMENT: large heavy saucepan, food processor, plastic wrap, pastry brush, kitchen twine, medium saucepan, tea towel, kitchen scissors

PREPARATION TIME: 20 minutes

COOKING TIME: 35 minutes

DIFFICULTY LEVEL: medium

FOR THE SQUASH:

1 small round kuri squash (about 3 pounds; 1½ kg), washed, seeds and pith removed

1 star anise

1-inch (2.5 cm) fresh ginger, peeled and thinly sliced

1 generous pinch Cumin Salt (page 337)

Fine sea salt and freshly ground black pepper

FOR THE VINAIGRETTE:

1 tablespoon apple cider vinegar

Pinch of fine sea salt

Generous pinch of piment d'Espelette or hot paprika

3 tablespoons (45 ml) olive oil

½ cup (4 g) fresh cilantro or tarragon leaves

FOR THE EGGS:

1 teaspoon olive oil

4 large eggs

¾ teaspoon pine nut or extra virgin olive oil

Fine sea salt

FOR GARNISH:

Cumin Salt (page 337)

ASTUCES:

- If someone can help you make the eggs, it's easier—one to twist the plastic and one to tie it *tight*.
- To peel ginger, simply scrape the skin off with the edge of a spoon.

1. Prepare the squash: Place the squash in a large heavy saucepan and cover it with 2 inches (5 cm) of water. Add the star anise, ginger, and cumin salt. Bring the water to a boil over medium-high heat, lower the heat so the water is boiling gently, partially cover, and cook until the squash is tender through, about 30 minutes. Check occasionally and add additional water if necessary. When the squash is tender, remove the star anise and transfer the squash and ginger to a food processor. Reserve the cooking liquid. Puree the squash, and season to taste with salt and pepper. Return the squash to the pan and keep the puree warm.

(continued)

2. While the squash is cooking, prepare the vinaigrette: Whisk together the vinegar, salt, and piment d'Espelette in a small bowl. Slowly whisk in the extra virgin olive oil until the mixture is thoroughly combined. Mince the cilantro leaves and whisk into the vinaigrette. Season to taste.

3. Line a small bowl with a double thickness of plastic wrap, leaving plenty of plastic wrap to hang over the edges of the bowl. Oil the plastic wrap with a pastry brush dipped in the olive oil. Break one egg into the lined bowl. Add one-quarter of the pine nut or extra virgin olive oil and a bit of salt. Bring the edges of the plastic wrap up and around the egg and twist it so it tightly encloses the egg. Tie it tightly (tightly!) with kitchen twine.

4. To cook the eggs, fill a medium saucepan three-fourths full of water and bring it to a boil over medium-high heat. Add the eggs in their plastic wrap, making sure the wrap hangs over the side of the pan, and cook them until they solidify, but the yolk remains soft inside, about 4½ minutes. Remove the eggs from the pan and set them on a tea towel. Wait 2 to 3 minutes, then use scissors to cut the plastic film right under the kitchen twine.

5. If the squash puree is dry, stir in enough cooking liquid to make it the consistency you want, then adjust the seasonings.

6. To serve, evenly divide the squash among four warmed plates, flattening it slightly in the center of the plate. Place an egg in the center. Drizzle the egg with an equal amount of the vinaigrette, drizzling some of the vinaigrette over the squash as well. Repeat with the remaining squash and eggs, and serve immediately.

Buckwheat Galette with Egg, Cheese, and Ham

GALETTE COMPLÈTE

In Brittany, the galette is cooked on a blistering skillet, called a *billig*. Traditionally, these sat over the coals; today they are mostly electric, but other than that, not much has changed. Clarified butter is slathered on the skillet, the batter still cooks to a lacey turn, and fillings are manifold. What was once the dish of survival has become something so special and satisfying that I can't imagine eating anything else after hiking the Sentier des Douaniers. And I'm not alone—any Breton crêperie worth its salt offers standing room only. With a *bolée* (bowlful) of hard cider, a galette makes a full and complete meal, an unforgettable plat du jour.

Serve this with A Classic Green Salad (page 265) and hard apple cider or a microbrew.

SERVES 4 TO 6

EQUIPMENT: flat nonstick skillet, pastry brush

PREPARATION TIME: 10 minutes

COOKING TIME: about 2 minutes per galette; 10 minutes

DIFFICULTY LEVEL: simple to medium (once you've got the technique, it's very simple!)

1 recipe Buckwheat Galettes (page 322; see step 1 below before preparing)

4 to 6 thin slices boiled ham

½ to ¾ cup (35 to 53 g) grated Gruyère

4 to 6 large eggs

3 to 4 tablespoons (45 to 60 g) lightly salted butter, melted

ASTUCES:

- Buckwheat flour has no fat in it, so it keeps almost forever.
- To make these, use a flat nonstick pan if you've got one, or a cast-iron skillet that is well seasoned.
- The ideal is for diners to sit near the galette maker, so that the galettes can be enjoyed hot from the skillet.
- Although this is my favorite galette, you can use your imagination for the filling.

1. Make your first perfect galette (see page 322). While it is on its second side, lay one slice of ham in the center, top with about 2 tablespoons of cheese, and break the egg right on top of the cheese, right in the center of the galette. Fold the edges of the galette up to the egg yolk on four sides, then paint the galette with melted butter, using a pastry brush.

2. Serve the galettes as you make them, which means you've got to have your guests nearby.

OF BRIGANDS, ARTICHOKES, AND GALETTES

Back when brigands approached the Breton shores (many say they still do!), customs agents patrolled the trails that ring the region, high above the waves, so they could spot suspicious activity. Today, these trails , which are called the "Sentier des Douaniers" or custom agent's trails, are maintained for hikers. Walking them is a little like walking on top of the world, for the waves crash and spit far below, and the English Channel seems as vast as any ocean. On the land side are small fields of sleep-inducing artichokes or ivory cauliflower in their purple dresses, the two major vegetable contributions of the Breton farmer. Centuries ago, when the customs officials were at their busiest, buckwheat thrived in these fields, becoming a player in the economy of the region and a mainstay of Breton cuisine. The buckwheat groats, called *sarrasin*, were ground into a dark flour that was mixed with wheat flour, water, and egg to form a thin batter. This was poured onto a blistering skillet, where it cooked into a crisp and lacy galette, which was filled with everything from eggs to seafood, to a thin layer of lard and a generous shower of ground black pepper.

Poached Eggs on Carrot Puree with Red Wine Sauce and Bacon

OEUFS EN MEURETTE AU BERNARD LOISEAU

Traditionally, you wouldn't have *oeufs en meurette* unless you'd already eaten boeuf bourguignon. Why? Because anyone who makes boeuf bourguignon knows there is ample sauce left over. The thrifty Burgundian solution was to heat up the sauce the day after and poach eggs in it. What does *meurette* mean? Red wine sauce, nothing more.

I borrowed the idea for this version of the dish from Chef Bernard Loiseau, who was the top chef in Burgundy for a very long time. A creative, exacting perfectionist, his food has stayed in my memory, and this dish, which I tasted eons ago, is no exception. This is a beautiful version of oeufs en meurette, and you don't even have to make the boeuf bourguignon the day before to enjoy it. I like to serve this with lovely Burgundy (of course!) and a basketful of toasts alongside.

SERVES 4

EQUIPMENT: 2 medium heavy saucepans, food processor, large heavy skillet, large saucepan, slotted spoon or ladle, kitchen scissors

PREPARATION TIME: 20 minutes

COOKING TIME: about 45 minutes

DIFFICULTY LEVEL: medium (which becomes simple once you've mastered the poaching)

FOR THE RED WINE SAUCE:

2 tablespoons (30 g) unsalted butter

1 small onion (2 ounces; 60 g), diced

1 shallot, diced

2 cups (500 ml) lovely red wine, ideally a Pinot Noir (Burgundy or other)

1 fresh or dried imported bay leaf

¼ teaspoon unsweetened cocoa powder

½ teaspoon granulated sugar

FOR THE CARROT PUREE:

4 medium carrots (12 ounces; 360 g total), trimmed and diced

1 teaspoon fine sea salt

1 large garlic clove, diced

2 tablespoons (30 g) unsalted butter

FOR THE BACON:

4 ounces (120 g) unsmoked slab bacon, cut into 1-by-1-by-1½-inch (2.5-by-2.5-by-4 cm) pieces

1 tablespoon olive oil (optional)

FOR THE POACHED EGGS:

½ cup (125 ml) distilled white vinegar

4 or 8 large eggs

Fine sea salt and freshly ground black pepper

Fresh flat-leaf parsley sprigs or chives for garnish

1. Prepare the sauce: Melt 2 tablespoons of the butter in a medium heavy saucepan over medium heat. When it is melted and frothing, add the onion and shallot, and

(continued)

ASTUCES:

- Use a flavorful red wine for the sauce, such as a pinot noir or a cabernet sauvignon; anything with imperfections will just be amplified when it is reduced.
- Rinsing the eggs in clear water after poaching in the highly vinegared water isn't indispensable, but it does remove any hint of vinegar from the egg, and it's a simple step.

cook, covered, stirring regularly, until the onion is tender through, about 10 minutes. Add the remaining sauce ingredients, whisk, and bring to a boil over medium-high heat. Lower the heat so the wine is simmering merrily and reduce until there is about ¼ cup (60 ml) in the pan. Remove from the heat and keep warm.

2. Prepare the carrots: Place the carrots in a separate medium saucepan and cover by 2 inches (5 cm) with water. Add the salt and garlic and bring the water to a boil over medium-high heat. Lower the heat so the water is simmering merrily, cover partially, and cook until the carrots are very tender, 20 to 25 minutes. Drain the carrots and puree them in a food processor along with the butter, until they are very, very smooth. Return the puree to the pan and keep it warm over very low heat.

3. Place the bacon in a large heavy skillet over medium heat and cook until it is golden on the edges, 5 to 6 minutes. If the bacon doesn't give off enough fat to make it sizzle, add the oil. Transfer the bacon to a plate lined with either a brown paper bag or paper towel to absorb excess fat (if there is any).

4. Poach the eggs: Bring a large pot of water to a boil over high heat. Fill a large bowl with hot water and set it by the stove. Add the vinegar to the boiling water and return the liquid to a boil. Lower the heat so the boil is vigorous but not wild. Break an egg into a small bowl to be sure it is fresh, then gently add it to the boiling water, and cook it, spooning the water over the yolk and trying to corral the white as best you can, until the egg is set, about 3 minutes. Using a slotted spoon, gently remove the egg from the boiling vinegar water, dip it into the bowl of hot water, then carefully set it on a plate or platter. Repeat with all of the eggs (you should be able to do three or four eggs at a time).

5. Before assembling the dish, trim any unkempt pieces of egg white from around the egg with kitchen scissors.

6. Evenly divide the carrot puree among four shallow soup dishes. Set an egg—or two—atop the carrot puree, then drizzle the red wine sauce around and over the egg. Season with salt and pepper, garnish with the bacon and parsley sprigs, and serve immediately.

Potato and Chive Soufflé with Chive Cream

SOUFFLÉ AUX POMMES DE TERRE À LA CIBOULETTE, CRÈME CIBOULETTE

Leave it to the French cook to invent the soufflé, the lighter-than-air creation that, no matter how dated it can seem, is always a thrill. The soufflé is making a reappearance in France as a plat du jour, scrawled on menus throughout the country. In Paris, it's never gone out of fashion—there are restaurants devoted to this singular dish.

This recipe is a combination of different ideas, with the result being light and hearty at the same time, simple to put together, and truly impressive to serve. The difference between this soufflé and others is that the potato keeps it from collapsing, so you can present it at the table and wow your friends and family, and it will stay puffed while you serve it. Serve this with the seasoned cream, or simply with a big sprinkling of freshly chopped herbs, and a green salad alongside, such as A Classic Green Salad (page 265). I love this with a lovely Réthoré Davy red from the Loire Valley. Tip: If there are leftovers, this is delicious, warmed, the next day.

SERVES 4 TO 6

EQUIPMENT: one 3-quart (3 L) soufflé mold or 4 to 6 ramekins depending on their size, medium saucepan

PREPARATION TIME: about 10 minutes

COOKING TIME: 34 minutes

DIFFICULTY LEVEL: simple

FOR THE SOUFFLÉ:

16 ounces (600 g) starchy potatoes, peeled, rinsed, and cut into quarters

1 teaspoon coarse sea salt

2 fresh or dried imported bay leaves

¾ cup (185 ml) crème fraîche

5 large eggs, separated

¾ teaspoon freshly ground nutmeg

1 large bunch fresh chives, divided in half

Generous 0.5 ounce (19 g) Parmigiano-Reggiano, finely grated

Fine sea salt and freshly ground black pepper

FOR THE GARNISH:

1 scant cup (about 200 ml) heavy cream, chilled

Pinch of fine sea salt

Several grinds of black pepper

1. Butter a 3-quart (3 L) soufflé mold, or four to six ramekins. Preheat the oven to 425°F (220°C).

2. Place the potatoes in a medium saucepan, cover them by 2 inches (5 cm) with water, add 1 teaspoon of coarse salt and the bay leaves, and bring to a boil over medium-high heat. Lower the heat to a simmer and cook the potatoes until they are very tender through, about 20 minutes.

(continued)

3. When the potatoes are cooked, drain them, remove and discard the bay leaves, and return the potatoes to the pot. Crush them with a potato ricer or a fork. They don't need to be entirely smooth, but there shouldn't be any large chunks. Whisk in the cream, egg yolks, and nutmeg.

4. Mince half of the chives, then fold them into the potatoes along with the cheese. Taste for seasoning and add salt and pepper to taste.

5. Place the egg whites in a large bowl or the bowl of an electric mixer fitted with the whisk attachment and whisk to soft peaks. Fold the whites into the potato mixture until thoroughly combined, adjust the seasoning, then carefully pour the mixture into the prepared soufflé mold or the ramekins. Place in the center of the oven and bake until the soufflé is golden on top, and nearly but not quite cooked through, about 14 minutes.

6. While the soufflé is cooking, whisk the heavy cream in a bowl until it makes soft peaks. Mince the remaining chives and fold them into the cream, then season it with salt and freshly ground black pepper.

7. Remove from the oven and serve immediately with the cream alongside.

ASTUCES:

- The amount of nutmeg you use will depend on its freshness, and your taste. If you are grating a nutmeg, 1/2 teaspoon should be fine. If you're using pre-grated nutmeg, you'll probably want to add more. Go ahead and taste the batter and decide. You definitely want to taste the nutmeg in the cooked soufflé.
- When you whisk the egg whites, stop *before* they develop stiff peaks— softer peaks allow for easier folding, and they puff just as well.
- If you like, you can bake this in four or six individual buttered ramekins (depending on their size). The cooking time will be a bit less than if you bake it in a soufflé mold.

Mushrooms with "Broken Eggs"

CHAMPIGNONS AUX "OEUFS CASSÉS"

As legend has it, Louis XIV discovered the button mushroom at Versailles and fell in love with its woodsy flavor. His royal gardeners made certain the king had an endless supply. More than one hundred years and a revolution later, Napoleon I shared the royal obsession with mushrooms and had his gardeners develop their cultivation in the catacombs of Paris, which is why today the button mushroom is called *champignon de Paris*. With the construction of the Métro, mushroom cultivation was moved to Anjou in the Loire Valley, where they are produced in abundance. But their production has spread throughout the country, so that fresh and flavorful mushrooms are available nearly everywhere, all the time.

Here, they are teamed with the poached egg which, right before serving, is broken so that its soft yolk runs throughout, creating an elegant dish fit for . . . Louis XIV! This is a lovely plat du jour when served with a green salad, such as A Classic Green Salad (page 265), and plenty of baguette. Or it can be an entrée to another plat du jour. Up to you to decide. A Saint-Véran is perfect here.

SERVES 2 TO 4

EQUIPMENT: medium skillet, fine-mesh sieve, slotted spoon or ladle, food processor, small saucepan, large saucepan, kitchen scissors

PREPARATION TIME: 8 minutes

COOKING TIME: 15 minutes

DIFFICULTY LEVEL: simple

FOR THE MUSHROOMS:

1 pound (500 g) wild or cultivated mushrooms, stems trimmed

2 tablespoons (30 g) unsalted butter

¼ cup (60 ml) water

Fine sea salt and freshly ground black pepper

FOR THE POACHED EGGS:

½ cup (125 ml) distilled white vinegar

4 or 8 large eggs

FOR SERVING:

Fleur de sel

Piment d'Espelette

Fresh chervil or flat-leaf parsley sprigs for garnish

1. Prepare the mushrooms: Brush the mushrooms clean with a pastry brush or a paper towel. Wipe them, if necessary, to remove all the grit, then thinly slice the mushrooms.

2. Melt the butter in a medium skillet, add the mushrooms, and toss them in the butter so they are completely coated. Add the water to the pan, season with salt and pepper,

(continued)

cover, and let the simmer until the mushrooms begin to turn tender, about 5 minutes.

3. Transfer three-quarters of the mushrooms from the skillet to a fine-mesh sieve, using a slotted ladle or spoon. Continue to cook the remaining mushrooms until they are tender, about 5 additional minutes.

4. Place the fully cooked mushrooms with their cooking juices in a food processor and blend. Taste for seasoning and transfer this mixture to a small saucepan.

5. Sauté the partially cooked mushrooms until they are golden and heated through. Season with salt and pepper.

6. To poach the eggs, bring a large saucepan of water to a boil over high heat. Fill a large bowl with hot water and set it by the stove. Add the vinegar to the boiling water and return the liquid to a boil. Lower the heat so the boil is vigorous but not wild. Break an egg into a small bowl to be sure it is fresh, then gently add it to the boiling water, and cook it, spooning the water over the yolk and trying to corral the white as best you can, until the egg is set, about 3 minutes. Using a slotted spoon, gently remove the egg from the boiling vinegar water, dip it into the bowl of hot water, then carefully set it on a plate or platter. Repeat with all the eggs (you should be able to do three or four eggs at a time).

7. Before assembling the dish, trim any unkempt pieces of egg white from around the egg with kitchen scissors.

8. Reheat the mushroom sauce over low heat, without bringing it to a boil. Taste for seasoning.

9. To serve, divide the mushroom sauce among four plates, spreading it in a small round in the center of the plate. Arrange the sautéed mushrooms on and around the sauce, mounding them slightly in the center. Slip an egg atop each mound of mushrooms, then season with fleur de sel and piment d'Espelette. Cut each egg so the yolk drizzles out over the mushrooms. Garnish with the chervil and serve immediately.

CHAPTER 9
SIDE DISHES

PLAT DU JOUR is a one-dish meal; that's clear enough. But what is also clear is the French meal protocol, which insists on time at the table to enjoy more than one dish. Thus, at the café and bistro, a plat du jour might be served with a side dish. If it isn't, the option is available. At home, there is always at least one side dish. As the dishes in this chapter illustrate, side dishes are weighted toward the potato, a vegetable beloved to the French. (*Merci*, M. Parmentier!). This chapter contains a varied and delightful assortment of side dishes to enjoy with your favorite plat du jour, or simply on their own. *Bon appétit!*

Braised White or Green Asparagus with Herbs

ASPERGES BLANCHES OU VERTES BRAISÉES AUX AROMATES

The asparagus season is ephemeral, lasting about six weeks if the weather is propitious. Asparagus is ubiquitous on plat du jour menus during that season so that chefs, cooks, and diners alike can take advantage of its charms.

Because asparagus is about 94 percent water, it cooks to tenderness in the blink of an eye. The French tradition holds for asparagus to be boiled, and the French have special tall, cylindrical pans just for this purpose; the asparagus is tied into a bundle and stood up tall, with the heads just poking out of the water. To my mind, however, it is best when braised as here. With the addition of a few herbs, this dish offers a whole new spring temptation, because the flavor of the asparagus is concentrated during braising and enhanced with the addition of herbs.

This also makes a wonderful plat du jour all on its own, thanks to the addition of ham and eggs.

SERVES 4 TO 6

EQUIPMENT: large heavy skillet with at least 2-inch (5 cm) sides, fine-mesh stainless-steel sieve

PREPARATION TIME: 10 minutes

COOKING TIME: about 12 minutes

DIFFICULTY LEVEL: simple

---

2 pounds (1 kg) white or green asparagus, trimmed and peeled (if using white), and cut on the diagonal into 2-inch (5 cm) lengths

2 tablespoons (30 ml) olive oil

½ cup (125 ml) water

2 fresh bay leaves

1 tablespoon fresh tarragon leaves

½ teaspoon fresh thyme leaves

Sea salt and freshly ground white pepper

6 very thin slices air-cured ham, cut crosswise into thin strips (optional)

2 large eggs, hard-cooked and cut in half lengthwise

Chive or other edible flower blossoms for garnish (optional)

1. Sort the asparagus by thickness.

2. Place the olive oil, water, and herbs in a large heavy skillet over medium-high heat and add the thickest asparagus pieces first. Turn the asparagus so it is coated with the oil mixture. When the liquid comes to a boil, lower the heat to medium-low, cover, and cook the asparagus until it begins to turn tender, about 5 minutes. Add the thinner asparagus stalks and tips, toss, and stir gently so they are coated with the oil mixture, season with salt and pepper, then continue to cook until all the asparagus is almost tender, an additional 4 to 5 minutes.

3. When the asparagus is nearly tender through, remove the cover and continue to cook the asparagus, shaking the pan and stirring it, until any liquid in the pan evaporates.

PEELING WHITE ASPARAGUS

If you cannot find white asparagus, use thick green asparagus stalks. If you are using white asparagus, peel off the outer skin, beginning just at the base of the leaves. Once you've peeled it, hold the stalk up to the light to be sure you've removed all the tough skin. You may need to peel each stalk twice to be sure. Trim off the end of the stem where it was separated from the roots, then carefully rinse the stalks with the heads up, so that if there is any grit, it won't lodge in the leaves.

4. Remove the pan from the heat, and remove and discard the herbs. Gently transfer the asparagus to a warmed platter. Sprinkle it with the ham slices, if using.

5. Use a spoon, fork, or pestle to firmly press each egg half through a sieve held over the asparagus. Garnish with chive blossoms and serve immediately.

ASTUCES:

- *Mimosa* is a term with double meaning when it comes to eggs. It can refer to the French version of deviled egg, or to this preparation here, where hard-cooked egg is pressed through a fine-mesh sieve, to "rain" down upon whatever it is garnishing.
- Always use a stainless-steel utensil and sieve with the egg, or it may turn black and take on a metallic taste.
- We call air-cured ham prosciutto, which is a misnomer. *Prosciutto* is the Italian word for ham of any kind.
- Refrigerate the ham slices before and after slicing them, so they aren't meltingly soft. You can sprinkle the slices over the warm asparagus so that they are warmed and softened by the time the dish gets to the table.

WHY FRENCH VEGETABLES HAVE SO MUCH FLAVOR— A LITTLE STORY ABOUT A MARKET GARDENER

Published in the New York Times, *April 9, 2013*

Baptiste Bourdon, 42, wipes muddy hands on his jeans and shakes the curls out of his eyes, which are aimed at the sky. "*Merdouille,*" he says heavily. "*C'est de la merdouille.*" Roughly translated, he is saying that the weather is simply terrible and it's beginning to annoy him.

Mr. Bourdon is naturally cheerful. His lively good mood and his market banter, along with produce that has more flavor than anyone else's, which he attributes to good soil and lots of singing as he works, have turned him into what the French refer to as a *phénomène*, or phenomenon. He burst onto the local farmers' market scene in Louviers, a town an hour west of Paris, about ten years ago, and has become the grower everyone wants to buy from. Mr. Bourdon grew up in the tiny town of Saint-Didier-des-Bois near Rouen, deep in lush Upper Normandy where tractors outnumber cars on the road. He trained as a civil engineer, but the politics of the job discouraged him. "My colleagues complained all the time," he said. "Nothing seemed fair, and nothing seemed fun."

Mr. Bourdon's maternal uncle was, meanwhile, struggling to keep the family farm. As the charm continued to wear off public engineering, the troubles of the farm loomed large. "I love the land," he said. "My uncle was driving the farm into the ground, so I decided to quit my job and help him."

When he took over the ten-acre farm, it included a couple of decrepit greenhouses. He jury-rigged them back into shape, and planted them with tomatoes, beans, peas, and eggplant. He reserved a stand at two different markets and showed up with full crates of gorgeous vegetables and a hungry look in his eye. It's not easy to break into a market because customers have their loyalties, but gifted with natural charm, he simply sweet-talked people into trying his wares, and with one taste they were convinced.

Farmers' markets are the backbone of rural France. Every single village, town, and city has its own, from Paris down to wide spots in the road. They help keep small market gardeners on the farm by providing direct access to customers. Mr. Bourdon took immediate advantage of local markets, and he's never looked back.

Except for today, which is the 40th in a string of gray, wet days when it's supposed to be the opposite, sunny and dry. Mr. Bourdon emerged from asparagus season, where he lost 50 percent of his crop to cold and rain. He worries for his turnips and onions, broccoli and multicolored carrots, which are growing slowly. "The weather is a catastrophe," he said, shaking his head. "We just have to move on."

Losing 50 percent of one crop and worries about others are common in farming. Mr. Bourdon is relatively philosophical, and he's accustomed to risk. When he decided to specialize in asparagus, a traditional crop in the Loire Valley, where temperatures tend to be more stable, he knew he was taking a risk, which he did again when he invested in Belgian endive as his major winter crop, another atypical vegetable for the region.

Why did he choose these two crops? "I knew I had to do something different to be a success. My grandparents grew small plots of asparagus and endive, and they did well," he said. "They're popular vegetables, and they're not typical to this region. I figured if I could make it work, I'd do well with them both."

His gamble usually pays off in spades. "Take endive," he said. "I was one of the first here to grow it commercially. It's the hardest thing I do

because everything happens outdoors in winter, when it's wet and freezing." But, when those ivory, torpedo-shaped vegetables are ready to sell, the lines form. Endive made his clients come; it and a host of other unusual produce—for Normandy—keep them returning.

Other things that set Mr. Bourdon apart include investing in two more huge greenhouses, which give him a jump on the season with no sacrifice in flavor. So just when the Norman palate is hungering for tender, sweet green peas, Mr. Bourdon is there with basketsful. Well before any of his colleagues have tomatoes at their stands, Mr. Bourdon has boxes of them, and they taste like heaven. His eggplants are earlier, bigger, and meatier than others, his zucchini shinier and more tender. And outside in the fields his salads grow better, his onions sweeter, his herbs more lush. Good soil, good farming, good employees, and smart thinking and planting have made Mr. Bourdon a successful market grower in a relatively short period of time.

Mr. Bourdon also has a nose for what's chic. So he grows multicolored carrots that fly off his stand; he's the only local grower to offer new garlic, and his heirloom tomatoes create an unbelievable buzz among local cooks. "I see what people in Paris are eating," he said. "Then I try to grow that."

His vegetables have attracted the area's Michelin-starred chefs, who come from as far away as Rouen to pick up produce early Saturday mornings. Mr. Bourdon can be found there with them, having coffee and sharing jokes in a rare moment of leisure. "They place their order, I get it ready, they're happy, and so am I," he says. Serving chefs gives him cachet. The fact that he also accepts orders by text message does, too. "Not before 7:30 on the morning of the market though," he cautions a client. "Otherwise, it's too confusing."

Mr. Bourdon, who until a couple of years ago also played the bass guitar in a rock band and still occasionally does a riff or two of air guitar between clients, is undeniably modern. While preceding generations have always offered fine and flavorful produce, Mr. Bourdon immediately realized he had to offer more variety, though not too much because the Norman cook doesn't want to be challenged, just excited by something a little different. He understood that attractively arranged produce was important, which in his case means piling vegetables that still have their muddy roots attached into lovely mounds. He knew, too, that the soil on his farm, the fact that he harvests just 12 hours before he gets to market so his vegetables are truly fresh, and the fact that he only picks at peak ripeness would seduce clients. But even all that wasn't enough because, he says, "I have to know my clients; they're my business. I treat them right."

Another thing that makes Mr. Bourdon undeniably modern is his work schedule. Up early and at his post six days a week, he nonetheless takes Sundays off and, unheard of in his profession, takes regular vacations. "A man has to live," he says. "And if I didn't take time off, my girlfriend probably wouldn't stay with me. I'm realistic."

Mr. Bourdon is the face of the new French market gardener. Motivated by making a good living and keeping the family land, he works hard but is no slave to his job. He also loves to have a good time, cook, and bring friends into his kitchen and his dining room. He gets teased about his aversion to olive oil, and his propensity to add cream to every dish that emerges from his kitchen.

He takes all of this in stride, just as he does the vagaries of his profession. Those who know him well know the debt he labors under, and the risks he takes in uncertain economic times. Despite these, he remains incurably cheerful, charming, and optimistic. "I watch what's going on, I try new things, and they usually work," he says. "I have found that there is always a solution."

Baptiste's New Potato Fries

LES FRITES AUX POMMES DE TERRE NOUVELLES DE BAPTISTE

French *frites* are ubiquitous worldwide, and the French continue to make them better than anyone else (sorry, Belgium), using fine and fresh potatoes, frying them twice in peanut oil, and seasoning them with sea salt. They're never too thin, never too fat, always just the right blend of crisp and meltingly tender, and served with just about every dish under the sun.

And then there are these unconventional fries, the brainchild of *maraîcher* (market gardener) Baptiste Bourdon (see page 248), whose eyes were on fire one morning at the market because he was so excited about this recipe that he couldn't wait to share it. And then he bagged up 2 pounds (a kilo) of new potatoes, thrust them into my hands, and said, "You've got to make these; they're life changing." In some ways, he was right, for these are the frites of frites, baked in the oven, seasoned with slightly spiced pepper, and so crisp and delicious yet tender on the inside that, once you've made them, you'll never look back.

SERVES 4

EQUIPMENT: large pot, cotton tea towels, large baking sheet

PREPARATION TIME: 15 minutes

COOKING TIME: 26 minutes

DIFFICULTY LEVEL: simple

1½ pounds (750 g) new potatoes, scrubbed but not peeled, cut into ¼-inch- (6 mm) thick rounds

3 tablespoons olive oil

Fleur de sel

Piment d'Espelette or freshly ground black pepper

1. Preheat the oven to 425°F (220°C).

2. Combine 8 quarts (8 L) of water with 1 tablespoon of coarse salt in a large pot and bring to a boil. When the water is boiling, blanch the potatoes for 1 minute. While they're blanching, lay out a double thickness of cotton tea towels on a work surface. This will allow the potatoes to dry so they can crisp in the oven.

3. Brush a baking sheet with about 1 tablespoon of the olive oil.

4. Transfer the potatoes from the boiling water to the tea towels, laying them out in a single layer. They'll dry quickly. Transfer them to the oiled baking sheet, then brush them evenly with the remaining 2 tablespoons of oil. Sprinkle them with salt and pepper, and bake in the center of the oven until they are golden and crisp, 20 to 25 minutes.

5. Remove from the oven, transfer to a serving dish, and enjoy!

Eggplant Disguised

AUBERGINE DEGUISÉE

I was walking down rue du Cherche-Midi the other day when I practically bumped into Sébastien Leroy, chef at the trendy restaurant Sauvage. We were having an exceptionally hot late summer and early autumn, and while it meant fewer clients for restaurants, we agreed it resulted in vegetables with unparalleled flavor.

We were talking eggplant, and he asked whether I'd ever steamed it. It wouldn't have occurred to me to steam such a water-rich vegetable. "Try this," he said and went on to give me the bones of this recipe, which I immediately tried at home. I find this a transformative dish, taking the glory of eggplant, which is a chameleon depending on how it is prepared, and turning it into something that has the taste and feel of a freshly picked wild porcini. And it requires so little oil that you'll find it light as air.

Sébastien uses the technique *snacké* to cook this eggplant once it has steamed, which is a trendy way of saying stir-fried, in very little oil over high heat. This seizes the pieces of eggplant, allowing them to develop a slight crust while retaining a tender moistness inside. He then douses it with soy sauce, shakes and shimmies it, and voilà, a gorgeous side dish. I love it alongside roast chicken or fish, though I sometimes serve it with fat slices of tomato seasoned with olive oil, shallots, and salt and pepper, plus a big green salad, and call it dinner. Try a rosé alongside, preferably from Bandol.

SERVES 4

EQUIPMENT: steamer, large skillet

PREPARATION TIME: 5 to 7 minutes

COOKING TIME: 20 minutes

DIFFICULTY LEVEL: simple

---

2 large eggplant (about 1 pound; 500 g each), rinsed

1 tablespoon untoasted peanut or other neutral oil

1 tablespoon tamari or soy sauce

½ cup (5 g) fresh basil or flat-leaf parsley leaves for garnish

1. Place 3 cups (750 ml) of water in the bottom half of a steamer and bring to a boil over high heat. Place the eggplant in the steamer basket, cover, and steam until the eggplant is tender through and slightly soft when you touch it, about 15 minutes. Remove the eggplant from the steamer and let cool to room temperature.

2. Cut the eggplant into ½-inch (1.3 cm) cubes.

3. Right before serving, heat the oil in a large skillet over medium-high heat. When the oil is hot but not smoking, sauté the eggplant slices, turning them regularly, until

(continued)

they are golden on all sides, 4 to 5 minutes. Just before you remove the eggplant from the heat, drizzle the tamari over the slices and shake the pan to move them around, or flip them using tongs, rubbing them in the soy sauce as you do, so the sauce is completely blended with the eggplant.

4. Transfer the eggplant cubes to a large platter.

5. Coarsely chop the basil or parsley and sprinkle it over the eggplant. Serve immediately.

ASTUCES:

- You don't need to trim the eggplant before you steam it, but you may need to trim off the stem end if you've got an eggplant too long for the steamer.
- If you put a metal skewer through the middle of the eggplant, it will steam more evenly.
- I always prefer tamari, a sauce that results from pressed and fermented soybean paste (miso), which is more richly flavored than soy sauce. But you can use soy sauce, which is a mixture of fermented soybeans, water, salt, and wheat.

Tender White Beans

HARICOTS BLANCS TENDRES

Fresh shell beans are delicious, and if you can find them, I recommend enjoying them often during the season, then shucking and freezing them raw for an off-season treat. If it's impossible for you to find them, and you cannot grow them (Johnny's Selected Seeds can help you!), then go ahead and use dried beans. Here are the cooking methods for both versions.

SERVES 4 TO 6

EQUIPMENT: heavy saucepan

PREPARATION TIME: 1 hour sitting time for the dried beans

COOKING TIME: 40 minutes for dried beans; 15 minutes for fresh beans

DIFFICULTY LEVEL: simple

FOR DRIED BEANS:

2 cups (12.5 ounces; 375 g) dried white beans, rinsed

2 fresh savory or oregano branches

1 fresh or dried imported bay leaf

2 tablespoons olive or walnut oil

Fine sea salt and freshly ground black pepper

1. Place the beans in a heavy saucepan, cover with water, and bring to a boil. Remove from the heat and let sit for 1 hour.

2. Drain the beans and return them to the pot. Add the herbs, then cover the beans with about 2 inches (5 cm) of water. Bring the water to a boil over medium-high heat, lower the heat to low, and cook the beans until they are just tender, about 40 minutes, depending on the freshness of the beans. Test them regularly after 30 minutes of cooking time. You want the beans tender, not at all mushy.

3. Spoon out ¼ cup (60 ml) of the cooking water from the beans and reserve. Drain the beans, discard the herbs, and place the beans in a warmed bowl. Pour the oil over the beans, toss, and season with salt and pepper to taste. If the beans are a bit dry, add some of the reserved cooking water and toss. Serve immediately.

(continued)

ASTUCES:

- The best shell beans in France are *haricots blancs*. The Coco de Paimpol from Brittany are considered the finest version of these, and are the only bean with an AOP (Appellation d'Origine Controlée), which is a hard-won pedigree. In the United States, the Great Northern bean is a good equivalent. Most edible beans are *Phaseolus vulgaris*.
- The weight for the fresh shell beans is for shucked beans.

FOR FRESH BEANS:

2 cups fresh shell beans (10 ounces; 300 g), rinsed

2 fresh savory or oregano branches

1 fresh or dried imported bay leaf

2 tablespoons olive or walnut oil (optional)

Fine sea salt and freshly ground black pepper

1. Place the beans in a heavy saucepan and cover the beans by 2 inches (5 cm) with water. Add the herbs and bring the water to a boil. Lower the heat to low so the water is simmering and cook until the beans are tender but not mushy, about 15 minutes. You can keep the beans in their cooking liquid until ready to serve, or spoon out ¼ cup (60 ml) of the cooking water and drain the beans, reserving the cooking water and discarding the herbs.

2. Place the cooked beans in a warmed bowl, add the oil (if using), toss, then season with salt and pepper to taste. If the beans are a bit dry, add some of the reserved cooking water. Serve immediately.

Parsley, Green Olive, and Almond Salad

SALADE DE PERSIL, OLIVES VERTES, ET AMANDES

The flavors of this gorgeous salad are so intense that they simply leap from the plate. The French cook is open to influences from around the globe, and this salad has its roots in Turkey, where parsley isn't just considered a condiment, but a green of worth. I recommend this salad with the tuna-stuffed peppers, but I also serve it with grilled meats or poultry, or any steamed or grilled fish. It's so "green" tasting, and so unusually delicious.

SERVES 6

EQUIPMENT: medium bowl, small bowl

PREPARATION TIME: 15 minutes

COOKING TIME: none

DIFFICULTY LEVEL: simple

---

3 scallions or 1 small spring onion (about 1 ounce; 30 g), trimmed and cut into paper-thin rounds or slices (for ⅓ cup sliced)

3 cups (30 g) firmly packed fresh flat-leaf parsley leaves

1 cup (155 g) brined green olives, pitted, coarsely chopped

⅓ cup (50 g) raw almonds, coarsely chopped

1 tablespoon fresh lemon juice

1 teaspoon balsamic vinegar

Pinch of fine sea salt

Several grinds of black pepper

3 tablespoons olive oil

1. Place the scallions, parsley, olives, and almonds in a medium bowl and toss. In a small bowl, whisk together the lemon juice, vinegar, salt, pepper, and olive oil until thoroughly combined.

2. Pour the dressing over the salad ingredients and toss until thoroughly coated. Evenly divide the salad among six salad plates and serve separately or use as an accompaniment. Serve immediately.

ASTUCES:

- Always try to use organic herbs for their flavor and overall "cleanliness."
- Why flat-leaf parsley? Because its flavor is more nuanced than that of curly-leaf parsley, and its leaves more tender.
- The almonds are delicious here, but you can substitute walnuts or hazelnuts.

Crisp, Golden Potato Cake from the Dordogne

LA GALETTE DE POMMES CROUSTILLANTE DE TERRE DE LA DORDOGNE

How many times did I watch my friend Danie Dubois prepare this potato cake for a tableful of diners? More than I can count over the period of many years. It is a standby at her Dordogne table, made with potatoes from her garden and goose fat from her geese. And it is a "délice," absolutely delectable, that appeals to everyone because it is golden and crisp on the outside, meltingly tender inside.

Normally served as a side dish, this potato wonder can easily be transformed into a plat du jour if you lay slices of cured duck breast on top right before serving, or add some crisp, air-cured ham that you've cut in strips and baked in a hot oven for a few minutes. Serve a green salad alongside, such as A Classic Green Salad (page 265). You can even top it with a fried egg, to make a very French dish. This dish merits a wine suggestion, and I like a good Corbières for the job!

SERVES 6 TO 8

EQUIPMENT: vegetable peeler, large nonstick skillet with 3-inch (7.5 cm) sides

PREPARATION TIME: 25 minutes

COOKING TIME: 45 minutes

DIFFICULTY LEVEL: simple

---

6 garlic cloves

1 cup (10 g) loosely packed fresh flat-leaf parsley leaves

5 tablespoons (75 g) fat, such as lard, goose, or duck fat

3½ pounds (1.6 kg) waxy potatoes, peeled

Fine sea salt and freshly ground black pepper

Fresh flat-leaf parsley sprigs for garnish (optional)

1. Mince the garlic with the parsley and transfer to a small bowl. Add 3 tablespoons (45 g) of the fat and mix thoroughly, to make a sort of paste. You may prepare this ahead of time and refrigerate it, covered.

2. Place the remaining 2 tablespoons (30 g) of fat in a large nonstick skillet. Melt the fat over medium heat. You will need to slice the potatoes paper-thin for this dish, and the best way to do that is to use a European-style vegetable peeler. "Peel" (or slice) the potatoes right into the hot fat, stirring them occasionally so they don't stick and seasoning them regularly with salt and pepper as you go (see Astuces). It will take about 20 minutes to slice all the potatoes into the pan, and the potatoes will cook evenly as long as you remember to stir them from time to time. They will stick together somewhat, so gently break them apart as you stir. After "peeling" the potato, you will have a core that remains and is too difficult to "peel." Simply reserve for another dish.

3. When all of the potatoes are sliced into the pan, season them one more time with salt and pepper, and stir so they are all coated with fat. Add the parsley mixture and stir so that it melts evenly throughout the potatoes, then cook until the potatoes are deep golden on the underside, a generous 10 minutes.

4. Carefully invert the potato galette onto a large plate and slide it back into the pan, golden side up, and cook until the underside is deep golden, about 15 minutes. To serve, place a serving plate on top of the pan and invert so the galette falls onto the serving plate. Garnish with flat-leaf parsley sprigs, if desired, and serve.

ASTUCES:

- A typical vegetable peeler removes a very thin layer of peel that is too thin for this recipe; if you have an OXO brand or the Swedish-style peeler, use that. Alternatively, you may use a mandoline, or simply slice the potatoes as thinly as you possibly can. If using a vegetable peeler, peel the potatoes right into the hot fat; if using another method, spread the potatoes so they evenly cover the bottom of the pan.
- If you cannot find lard or goose or duck fat, use either unflavored coconut or olive oil.
- If you want to make extra of the garlic and fat mixture, do so and refrigerate it. You can add it by the tablespoon to everything from an omelet to pasta to morning toast. It will keep, refrigerated, for 2 weeks.

New Potatoes with Cream and Chives

POMMES DE TERRE NOUVELLES À LA CRÈME

The French are addicted to potatoes, and the French cook knows just how to bring out their flavor with simple preparations like this one, which originally hails from Normandy. It makes a perfect side dish to so many plats du jour.

SERVES 4
EQUIPMENT: saucepan
PREPARATION TIME: 5 minutes
COOKING TIME: 15 minutes
DIFFICULTY LEVEL: simple

1 pound (500 g) new potatoes, scrubbed

2 teaspoons coarse sea salt

1 bunch fresh chives, rinsed and patted dry if necessary

¼ cup (60 ml) crème fraîche

Freshly ground black pepper

1. Place the potatoes in a saucepan and just cover with water. Add the salt and bring to a boil over medium-high heat. Lower the heat so the water is simmering and cook the potatoes until they are just tender through, about 15 minutes.

2. Mince the chives and stir them into the crème fraîche.

3. Drain the potatoes and transfer them to a warmed serving bowl. Crush them lightly with a fork and pour the crème fraîche mixture over them. Season generously with pepper. Serve immediately.

ASTUCES:

- The cream here retains its fresh flavor because it is poured over the hot potatoes, then served immediately. This is the best way to use cream, because you get all of its flavor.
- Mince the chives and immediately stir them into the cream, so all of their flavor is captured.

Buttered New Potatoes with Thyme, Parsley, and Lemon

POMMES DE TERRE NOUVELLES AU THYM, PERSIL, ET CITRON

Sometimes potatoes are boiled and tossed in butter, sometimes left plain, sometimes crushed with a fork and drizzled with oil . . . obviously the options are endless, and this version here is one of my favorites. It dresses up the potato and takes it out on the town. These go so well with Mme. Lambert's Lemon-Scented Seasonal Veal Stew (page 130), Golden Roast Chicken with Shallots and Apples (page 38), Steamed Cod with Melted Leeks and Caper Sauce (page 84), or all on their own.

SERVES 4 TO 6

EQUIPMENT: saucepan

PREPARATION TIME: 10 minutes

COOKING TIME: 15 minutes

DIFFICULTY LEVEL: simple

1½ pounds (750 g) new or waxy potatoes (e.g., Yukon Golds), peeled, and cut into 2-inch (5 cm) chunks if the potatoes are large

1 teaspoon coarse sea salt

1 teaspoon fresh thyme leaves

½ cup (5 g) fresh flat-leaf parsley leaves

Zest of ½ lemon, preferably organic

2 tablespoons (30 g) unsalted butter

1 to 2 teaspoons fresh lemon juice

Fine sea salt and freshly ground black pepper

1. Place the potatoes in a medium saucepan, cover by 1 inch (2.5 cm) with water, add the coarse salt, and bring to a boil over medium-high heat. Lower the heat so the water is simmering and cook until the potatoes are tender through, about 15 minutes. Remove the pan from the heat.

2. Just before serving, mince together the thyme, parsley, and lemon zest. Drain the potatoes and transfer them to a warmed serving bowl. Add the herbs and butter and toss the potatoes until the butter has melted and the herbs are thoroughly mixed with the potatoes. Season with the lemon juice and salt and pepper to taste. Serve immediately.

ASTUCES:
- To peel brand-new potatoes, simply twist their tender new skin off under running water. What remains goes unnoticed.
- To remove thyme leaves from the stem, pull on the leaves against the growing direction, then pinch off the little "bouquet" of leaves at the end of the stem.
- Use organic lemons for their zest, or at least lemons that are untreated after harvest.

Perfect Mashed Potatoes with Crème Fraîche

LA PURÉE PARFAITE À LA CRÈME FRAÎCHE

Purée (mashed potatoes) accompanies a French eater all of his or her life, from the very first moment solid food is introduced. Because, as the French know, there is nothing better than the potato when it's mashed and softened like this! This recipe is so flavorful that you'll make it all the time, serving it alongside some dishes, incorporating it into others.

SERVES 4 TO 6

EQUIPMENT: large saucepan, potato masher, large balloon whisk (optional)

PREPARATION TIME: about 15 minutes

COOKING TIME: 20 minutes

DIFFICULTY LEVEL: simple

- 2 pounds (1 kg) starchy potatoes, such as russet
- 1 fresh or dried imported bay leaf
- Coarse sea salt
- 4 to 6 tablespoons (60 to 90 g) unsalted butter
- ¼ cup (60 ml) crème fraîche or heavy cream
- Fine sea salt and freshly ground black pepper
- Freshly ground nutmeg

1. Peel the potatoes and cut them into large chunks. Place them in a medium saucepan and cover them by 1 inch (2.5 cm) with water. Add the bay leaf and a scant teaspoon of coarse salt. Bring the water to a boil over medium-high heat and cook until the potatoes are tender, about 20 minutes.

2. Drain the potatoes, reserving ½ cup (125 ml) of the cooking liquid. Return the potatoes to the saucepan and mash them with a potato masher or fork until they are crushed. Add the butter and crème fraîche and mash these into the potatoes until they are smooth—there may be a few chunks, which is fine unless you want a completely silken puree. If this is the case, keep mashing, finishing up with a large balloon whisk.

3. Season the puree with salt, pepper, and nutmeg to taste. Serve immediately.

ASTUCES:

- Always save some of the potato cooking water, in case you need to dilute your mashed potatoes once the butter and cream are incorporated.
- To avoid gluey mashed potatoes: Don't use waxy potatoes and never puree the potatoes in a food processor with the knife blade. Mash potatoes by hand or in a stand mixer fitted with the paddle attachment.
- If you have leftovers, they reheat perfectly if you do so *very gently*.

Simple Boiled Potatoes
POMMES DE TERRE CUITES SIMPLEMENT

Never mock the boiled potato—it is a cornerstone of life and meals in France, often served with no dressing at all. I generally like to boil and either season them with olive oil, salt, and pepper, or do as my Norman neighbors do, and add a big nob of butter to them right before serving. If you want them plain for, say, Anchoïade with Seasonal Raw Vegetables (page 72), just boil and serve!

SERVES 4 TO 6

EQUIPMENT: medium saucepan

PREPARATION TIME: 10 minutes

COOKING TIME: 15 minutes

DIFFICULTY LEVEL: eyes-closed simple

1½ pounds (750 g) small potatoes, peeled or unpeeled, rinsed

1 teaspoon coarse sea salt

1 fresh or dried imported bay leaf

½ cup (5 g) fresh flat-leaf parsley leaves

1 tablespoon (15 g) unsalted butter or olive oil

1. Place the potatoes in a medium saucepan. Cover them by 2 inches (5 cm) with water, add the coarse salt and bay leaf, and bring the water to a boil over high heat. Lower the heat so the water is boiling merrily and cook until the potatoes are just tender through, about 15 minutes.

2. Remove the pan from the heat. You can keep the potatoes warm in the water, with no danger of them overcooking.

3. If you're going to serve the potatoes as a side dish, mince the parsley. Drain the potatoes and place them in a warmed serving bowl, add either the butter or oil and toss, then add the minced parsley and toss. Season them to taste and serve immediately.

ASTUCES:

- If you're going to serve potatoes with their peel, make sure the potatoes have been cultivated organically and be sure to thoroughly wash them.
- Note that the French rarely—if ever—serve a potato with the skin on.
- You can make these an hour or two ahead and keep them hot in the cooking water.

A Classic Green Salad

SALADE VERTE

The simple vinaigrette here is delicious as is, though it can serve as a base for more flavored dressings as well: add minced shallot or garlic, minced fresh herbs, lemon zest and juice, cracked black pepper. Use this vinaigrette with grated carrots or beets, fresh tomatoes, or any other vegetable mixture.

SERVES 6

EQUIPMENT: whisk, salad servers

PREPARATION TIME: 10 minutes

COOKING TIME: none

DIFFICULTY LEVEL: simple

---

2 teaspoons Dijon mustard

4 teaspoons red wine vinegar

Fine sea salt

3 tablespoons (45 ml) neutral oil, such as untoasted peanut or safflower oil

1 tablespoon extra virgin olive oil

Freshly ground black pepper

1 small bunch chives

1 head of butter, oak leaf, or your favorite lettuce (preferably not a crisp one like romaine), leaves separated, carefully rinsed, and spun dry (or about 12 cups lettuce leaves)

1. In a large salad bowl, whisk together the mustard, red wine vinegar, and a pinch of sea salt. Slowly whisk in the 3 tablespoons of neutral oil until the mixture has emulsified, then whisk in the olive oil. Taste for seasoning.

2. Mince the chives and stir them into the vinaigrette. Adjust the seasoning as needed.

3. Add the lettuce to the bowl and toss, toss, toss with salad servers until the leaves are thoroughly coated with the vinaigrette. Serve immediately.

ASTUCE:

- Tear lettuce leaves into bite-size pieces before dressing them, so your guests get lettuce they can maneuver into their mouths.
- Mince the chives right before you serve the salad, to capture all their flavor.
- Always toss lettuce right before serving

Quinoa with Herbs

QUINOA AUX AROMATES

Quinoa, the flower of an amaranth, arrived in France just over a decade ago in restaurants that were looking for the unusual. Today, it is often a side dish to a plat du jour and its popularity is edging rice out of the picture. This is saying something, because white rice is vital to the French, who consider it a comfort food and a sign from the heavens that the world is turning on its axis. Quinoa's nutty flavor provides a tasty alternative, and it ends up on the French plate because it is so delicate and versatile. That it offers nutrition, considered the major benefit by many, is a side benefit to the French. Serve this often, with roasted meats or fish, or on its own.

SERVES 6

EQUIPMENT: medium saucepan with lid, one ½-cup (125 ml) ramekin

PREPARATION TIME: 3 minutes

COOKING TIME: 12 minutes

DIFFICULTY LEVEL: simple

---

1 cup (195 g) quinoa

2 cups (500 ml) filtered water

1 bay leaf

¼ teaspoon fine sea salt

1 cup (about 10 g) mixed fresh herbs, such as tarragon, sweet cicely, parsley, chives, and fennel fronds

Fine sea salt and freshly ground black pepper

1. Rinse the quinoa under cold running water until the water runs clear. Place the quinoa in a medium saucepan and add the water, bay leaf, and salt. Cover, bring the water to a boil over medium-high heat, lower the heat so the water is simmering merrily, and cook until the quinoa is tender, about 12 minutes. Remove the quinoa from the heat and let it sit, covered, to "plump" and absorb any remaining water. The quinoa will stay warm for up to 20 minutes.

2. Just before serving, mince the herbs and fold them into the quinoa. Season to taste.

3. To serve, using a ½-cup (125 ml) ramekin as a mold, mold the quinoa by simply packing it into the ramekin and turning it out onto a very warm dinner plate.

ASTUCES:

- If you follow this recipe to the letter, your quinoa will be light and fluffy, the way it should be.
- Quinoa easily holds a shape. I have heart-shaped ceramic cheese molds I like to use for quinoa—I gently pack the grain into one, then quickly turn it out onto a plate. I call for using a ramekin here, but you can use the mold of your choice.

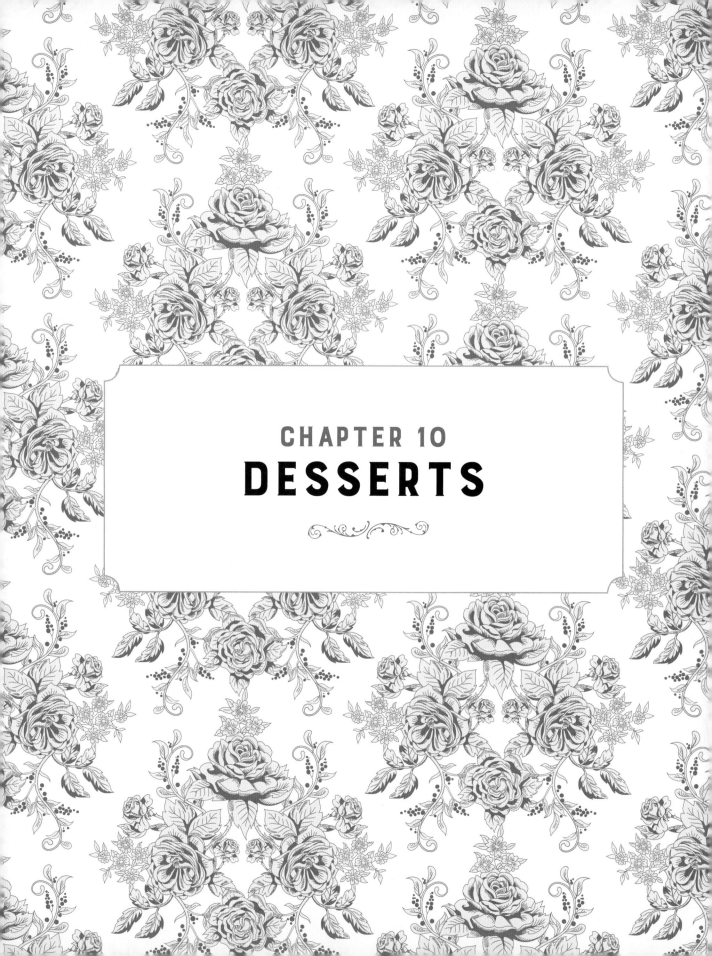

CHAPTER 10
DESSERTS

OH BOY, the best chapter! Because we all know the French gift with dessert, from delicate choux pastry to the fruit tart, ice cream to sweetened fresh cheese and berries. Dessert is a given at any French meal, regardless of whether you've enjoyed a single plat du jour or a multicourse affair. Why? The French have a sweet tooth, but more important than that, they turn the simplest ingredients into the most wonderful sweet finishes with ease. And even more than that, time at the table in France isn't just for sustenance—it's for pleasure, for discussion, for spending time with people you care about. Dessert prolongs the moment, and it adds an element of surprise, sometimes of luxury, often of a sweet celebration of the season.

So make, serve, and enjoy this selection of very special desserts, each a perfect finish to a plat du jour.

Individual Apple Tarts

TARTES AUX POMMES INDIVIDUELLES

The French love apples. They stuff and bake them, caramelize them, wrap them in pastry and serve them whole, make tarts and cakes with them. This, though, is one of the crowning glories of French apple use. Elegant and simple, the tarts come to the table like a birthday gift, and because they are ethereally light, nary a crumb will be left on the plate. They are professional to look at, easy to make, and you'll dazzle each time you serve them.

I drizzle each tart with a touch of honey to bring out the floral flavor of a good apple, which gives these tarts an added dimension!

SERVES 6

EQUIPMENT: 2 baking sheets, one 7-inch (17.5 cm) lid for template

PREPARATION TIME: including pastry, about 25 minutes

BAKING TIME: 25 to 30 minutes

DIFFICULTY LEVEL: simple

---

1 recipe Tender Tart Pastry (page 314)

5 medium apples (about 5.5 ounces; 165 g each), such as Cox's Orange Pippin, Reine de Reinette, or Jonagold

2 tablespoons (25 g) light brown sugar

3 teaspoons mild honey, such as lavender (optional)

1. Line two baking sheets with parchment paper.

2. Roll out the pastry as thinly as you possibly can. Using a lid as a template, cut out six 7-inch (17.5 cm) rounds and transfer them to the prepared baking sheets. Refrigerate for at least 30 minutes, and up to several hours. If you plan to refrigerate them for several hours (or overnight), cover them with parchment paper, then aluminum foil, so they don't dry out.

(continued)

3. Preheat the oven to 450°F (230°C).

4. Peel, halve, and core the apples. Cut them crosswise into paper-thin slices. Remove the pastry rounds from the refrigerator and arrange one-half apple's worth of slices on each of the pastry rounds, overlapping the slices slightly and mounding them attractively in the center. Sprinkle each tart evenly with 1 teaspoon of the brown sugar, then bake until the pastry is golden, the apples are golden at the edges, and the sugar has begun to caramelize, 25 to 30 minutes. If you have the baking sheets on two racks, you will need to switch them at about the 15-minute point, so the tarts bake evenly.

5. Remove the tarts from the oven and immediately drizzle each tart with ½ teaspoon of the honey, if desired. Transfer to a wire rack and let cool slightly, or to room temperature, before serving. If you've made them in the morning, warm them briefly in a very hot (425°F; 220°C) oven, so they're just lukewarm.

ASTUCES:

- If the weather is dry, make these the morning of the day you serve them. If the weather is humid, make them closer to when you'll serve them, as you want the pastry crisp. Whenever you make them, reheat them just slightly so they come to the table lukewarm, not cold.
- You will have leftover apple, because not every slice will be perfect. Use the leftovers to make a compote (page 313).

Upside-Down Apple Tart

TARTE TATIN

Tarte Tatin is the benchmark of a fine establishment, and when it is perfect like this one here, it is a glory to behold. Although the dessert originated in the Loire Valley, it has become a dessert every region claims and is one of the most popular in the French repertoire. Many make their tarte Tatin with sliced apples, caramelizing them quickly, then baking them under pastry. The version here takes more time and is much better. In fact, it is the only recipe that should be allowed for a true Tarte Tatin! Apple halves caramelize slowly on top of the stove, then bake to a melting tenderness under their pastry blanket, which turns shattery. You will love this, and you'll make it often.

MAKES ONE 10-INCH (25 CM) TART; 6 TO 8 SERVINGS

EQUIPMENT: baking sheet, very heavy 10- to 10½-inch (25 to 26.5 cm) ovenproof skillet (preferably cast iron) or a Tarte Tatin mold, turkey baster

PREPARATION TIME: 15 minutes

COOKING TIME: 1½ hours

DIFFICULTY LEVEL: medium

---

1 recipe Tender Tart Pastry (page 314)

All-purpose flour for dusting

1½ cups (300 g) Vanilla Sugar (page 339)

10 tablespoons (1¼ sticks; 150 g) unsalted butter, cut into thin slices

4 to 4½ pounds (2 to 2.5 kg) tart cooking apples, peeled, halved, and cored

1. Line a baking sheet with parchment paper or lightly flour it.

2. Roll out the pastry on a lightly floured work surface to form an 11½-inch (29 cm) round. Transfer the pastry to the prepared baking sheet and refrigerate for at least 1 hour.

3. Spread the sugar evenly over the bottom of a very heavy, 10- to 10½-inch (25 to 26.5 cm) ovenproof skillet; a simple cast-iron skillet is perfect. Place the butter slices evenly over the sugar, then arrange the apple halves on top of the butter, beginning at the outside edge and standing the halves on their stem ends, packing the apple halves as close together as possible so they are held standing by pressure. Make a second circle of apple halves inside the first, packing them on their stem end as well, facing in the opposite direction (for eye appeal). Place one apple half right in the center of the second circle to fill in the small space that remains. The idea is to get as many apples into the pan as possible, while keeping them nicely arranged.

(continued)

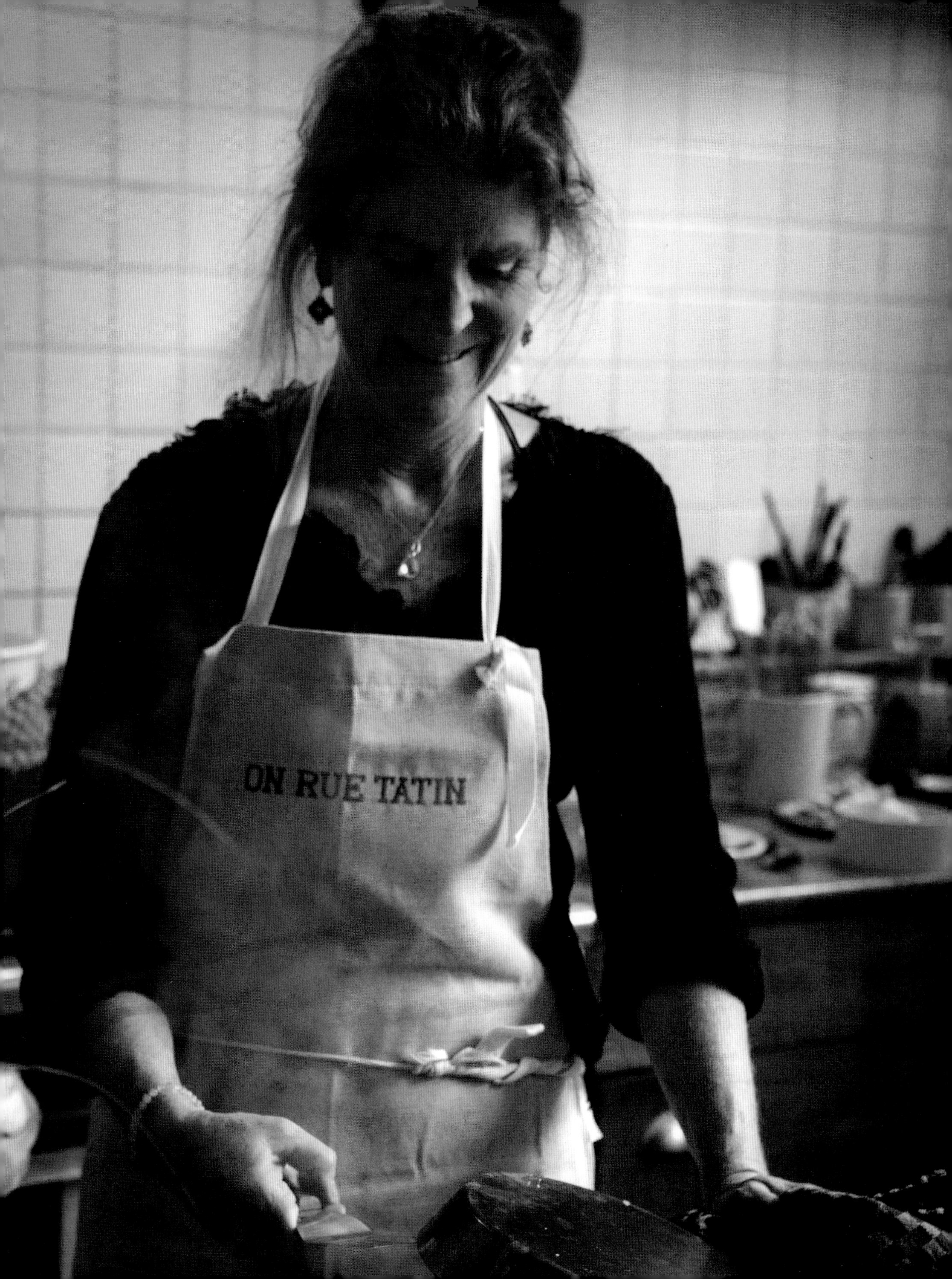
ON RUE TATIN

4. Place the skillet over medium-low heat and cook, uncovered, until the sugar turns golden brown, at least 1 hour. Watch the apples closely to be sure they don't stick; you may want to adjust the heat now and then, to slow down or speed up the cooking. As the sugar and butter melt and the apples give up some of their juices, baste the apples occasionally with a turkey baster. Gradually, the sugar will caramelize the apples nearly all the way through, though they will remain uncooked on top.

5. Preheat the oven to 425°F (220°C).

6. When the cooking juices are deep golden and the apples are nearly cooked through, remove the pastry from the refrigerator and quickly and carefully place it over the apples, gently tucking it down around them as though you were tucking them in bed.

7. Place the skillet on a baking sheet. Bake in the center of the oven until the pastry is golden, 25 to 30 minutes.

8. Remove the skillet from the oven. Immediately place a serving platter with a slight lip over the skillet. Quickly but carefully flip the two so the apples are on top. Remove the skillet. Should any apples stick to it, gently remove and reinsert them into their rightful place in the tart.

9. Let the tart cool to lukewarm before serving.

ASTUCE: You must use apples that will hold their shape throughout the cooking time. If you can find them, Cox's Orange Pippin are the absolute best, but Pink Lady, any apple that's been crossed with a Golden Delicious such as Jonagold, or Fuji will work as well.

Basil Sorbet

SORBET AU BASILIC

The flavors in this sorbet, inspired by Chef Frédéric Anton from Le Pré Catelan, pop and zing all over your mouth. They are intense, and the sorbet is intended to be served in small portions. I often accompany this with a bowl of fresh raspberries, or perfectly fresh sliced pineapple, though it is stunning on its own.

SERVES 4, LIGHTLY

EQUIPMENT: large heatproof bowl, small saucepan, citrus squeezer, immersion blender or food processor, ice cream maker

PREPARATION TIME: actual preparation is 10 minutes; cooling and sitting time is 1 hour 10 minutes

COOKING TIME: 3 to 5 minutes, 10 minutes cooling time

DIFFICULTY LEVEL: simple

½ cup (100 g) granulated sugar

2 scant tablespoons water

Juice of 4 limes (for a scant ⅔ cup; 150 ml)

2 cups lightly packed (20 g) fresh basil leaves

ASTUCE: Sometimes limes aren't very juicy, so get a few extra to be sure you have enough juice.

1. Fill a large heatproof bowl two-thirds full with ice cubes.

2. Place the sugar and water in a small saucepan, whisk them together, and bring to a boil over medium-high heat, occasionally shaking the pan gently. Not all the sugar will dissolve, but don't be concerned.

3. Place the pan in the bowl of ice to cool quickly. By the time the syrup cools, all but just the tiniest bit of sugar will have dissolved.

4. When the syrup is cool, whisk in the lime juice—the two liquids won't willingly combine at first, but don't worry. Mix them as best you can, then add the basil leaves, pushing them gently under the surface of the syrup. Cover and let sit at room temperature for 1 hour.

5. Blend the mixture either with an immersion blender or in a food processor until it is deep green with flecks of basil in it. Freeze it in an ice cream maker according to the manufacturer's instructions.

Salted Butter Caramel Ice Cream

GLACE CARAMEL AU BEURRE SALÉ

This recipe has its origins in Brittany, the land of salted butter. It is the only region where the butter is routinely salted, a habit that goes back centuries, a nose-thumb to Louis IX, who imposed a salt tax on the French, but not on the Bretons who harvested salt. When Louis needed money for his ships and wars and settled on a salt tax as a source of revenue, he needed the Bretons, who were the principle producers of salt at the time, so he left them salt tax–free. And because they had a near endless supply from the beautiful salt marshes of Guérande, they put it into everything. Ice cream may be a newer discovery than the sea salt of Brittany, but its spirit is born in that rugged region, and we can all be thankful to the salt rakers, who to this day spend their fine-weather days pulling salt from the marshes so it can drain and make its way into our ice cream (among other things!).

SERVES 8

EQUIPMENT: large bowl, one 2-quart (2 L) metal bowl, fine-mesh sieve, 3 small saucepans, ice cream maker

PREPARATION TIME: 10 minutes

COOKING TIME: 10 minutes, several hours chilling time, then 20 minutes to turn into ice cream in the ice cream maker

DIFFICULTY LEVEL: medium

---

2 cups (500 ml) whole milk

1 cup (150 ml) heavy cream

1½ cups (300 g) Vanilla Sugar (page 339)

4 tablespoons (60 g) salted butter

Scant ½ teaspoon fleur de sel

5 large egg yolks

1. Fill a large bowl about one-third full with ice cubes and add enough water (1 cup; 250 ml), so the cubes are floating but not drowning. Nest a smaller metal bowl that holds 2 quarts (2 L) in the ice cubes. Pour 1 cup (250 ml) of the milk into the smaller bowl and rest a fine-mesh sieve over the milk.

2. Place the cream in a small saucepan and heat over low heat to warm it.

3. Place the sugar in an even layer in a small heavy-bottomed saucepan over medium heat and cook the sugar until it begins to bubble up and turn golden. Move the pan around so the sugar shifts in the pan to caramelize evenly, and watch it so it doesn't become too dark. If the sugar clumps, don't be concerned; it will gradually all melt away, or you can use a chopstick to gently break it up. When the sugar is evenly caramelized, remove it from the heat and immediately whisk in the butter and salt, until thoroughly combined. Whisk in the warm cream. The caramel is likely to spit and squirm then seize up, but don't be concerned. Just keep stirring it, and the whole situation will gradu-

ally relax and become smooth. When that happens, whisk in the remaining cup (250 ml) of milk and remove from the heat.

4. Whisk the egg yolks in a small bowl. Gradually whisk in some of the warm caramel mixture, then pour this back into the caramel mixture and whisk until it is all combined. Return the pan to medium heat and, stirring in a figure-eight motion, cook the custard until the mixture thickens, 6 to 8 minutes. If it isn't thickening, increase the heat under the pan just slightly, but watch it like a hawk, so that it doesn't curdle.

5. When the custard is thickened, pour it through the fine-mesh sieve into the cold milk and stir the mixture until it is thoroughly cooled, then refrigerate until the mixture is chilled.

6. Freeze the mixture in an ice cream maker according to the manufacturer's instructions. Serve immediately.

ASTUCES:

- The operative word when making this ice cream is zen. It's all very simple, but you have to be relaxed and attentive, and don't listen to those voices that tell you that it is impossible to make caramel.
- I suggest making the mixture the day before you want to serve it, so it has a chance to chill overnight in the fridge. Or, once the ice cream is churned, put it in the freezer for about 30 minutes to firm up.

ASTUCES:

- Don't use chocolate wafers (the small rounds of chocolate often sold in bulk), as they are very waxy and will change the texture of the mousse. Instead, use Lindt, Scharffen Berger, Valrhona, or other high-quality chocolate in bar form.
- The pinch of salt in the egg whites is a French idea; French pastry chefs insist the salt helps break up the egg whites so they whisk up more easily.
- What is folding? It is what it says it is—literally folding one ingredient over another, to blend without deflating. A large silicone spatula is the best tool for this.

Chocolate Mousse

MOUSSE AU CHOCOLAT

There may be no more classic dessert in the French bistro, brasserie, or café than chocolate mousse. And it is almost always *fait maison* (homemade). Whether very light and creamy, more of a milk chocolate mousse, dense and chocolaty like a ganache, or a blend of those like this richly flavored dream, chocolate mousse is a crowd-pleaser.

I make this with lightly salted butter, a trick I learned from Breton friends. Brittany is the only region in France where the butter is salted—I think it makes everything better. But if you don't want the slight savory edge to your chocolate mousse, simply substitute unsalted butter here.

SERVES 6

EQUIPMENT: double boiler, large bowl or stand mixer

PREPARATION TIME: 12 minutes

COOKING TIME: 4 minutes

DIFFICULTY LEVEL: simple, as long as you know how to fold

- **3.5 ounces (105 g) semisweet (52% to 64%) chocolate, finely chopped**
- **3.5 ounces (105 g) bittersweet (70%) chocolate (see Astuces), finely chopped**
- **4 tablespoons (½ stick; 60 g) lightly salted butter, cut into several cubes**
- **4 large eggs, separated**
- **2 to 4 tablespoons brewed espresso, or the alcohol of your choice, to taste**
- **½ cup (125 ml) heavy cream, whipped to soft peaks**
- **Small pinch of salt**
- **Edible flower petals or fresh herb leaves for garnish**

1. Melt the chocolate and butter in a double boiler over medium-high heat, leaving it uncovered so condensed steam doesn't drip into the mixture. Remove from the heat and whisk in the egg yolks and at least 1 tablespoon of the espresso. Let cool.

2. Fold one-quarter of the whipped cream into the chocolate mixture, then fold in the remaining cream. Place the egg whites and salt in a large bowl, or the bowl of a mixer fitted with a whisk, and whisk until they form soft (not stiff) peaks. Fold one-quarter of the egg whites into the chocolate mixture, then fold in the remaining egg whites gently, until all the whites are incorporated. Taste for seasoning—you may carefully fold in additional coffee at this point, if you like.

3. Transfer the mousse to a serving dish or to six individual serving dishes and refrigerate for at least 2 hours and up to 24, tightly covered. Serve garnished with flower petals or herb leaves.

Choux Puffs

CHOUQUETTES

Chouquettes are the stuff of memories, little balls of choux pastry topped with tiny white pricks of sugar. Choux pastry is a cornerstone of French patisserie, and chouquettes are its most typical incarnation, displayed on every patisserie counter in the land, waiting for the after-school rush, when kids straight from school need a pick-me-up before they sit down for their homework. Like a *pain au chocolat* or a multilayered napoleon, they seem unmakeable in a home kitchen—but here, you've got the secret. And following this secret, you've got another for whipped cream and yet another for a chocolate sauce that will leave you licking your fingers, even if it's served on a porcelain plate at a fancy-dress ball.

MAKES 24 CHOUQUETTES

EQUIPMENT: baking sheet, large saucepan, pastry bag and ½-inch (1.3 cm) tip or small (1-inch; 2.5 cm) ice cream scoop

PREPARATION TIME: 15 minutes max

BAKING TIME: 15 to 18 minutes

DIFFICULTY LEVEL: simple

½ cup (125 ml) whole milk

½ cup (125 ml) water

7 tablespoons (105 g) unsalted butter

¾ teaspoon fine sea salt

1 tablespoon Vanilla Sugar (page 339)

1 cup (145 g) all-purpose flour, sifted

5 large eggs

FOR THE EGG WASH:

1 small egg

2 teaspoons water

¼ to ½ cup (25 to 50 g) crystal or pearl sugar

1. Preheat the oven to 425° F (220°C). Line a baking sheet with parchment paper. Mix together the milk, water, butter, salt, and sugar in a large saucepan over medium heat and bring to a boil. Mix in the sifted flour and, keeping the pan over the heat, stir constantly to dry out the mixture, until it is thick and sticky. Beat in the eggs, one at a time, mixing until they are thoroughly incorporated.

2. Prepare the egg wash: Whisk the egg with the water in a small bowl until foamy, then set aside.

3. Using a pastry bag fitted with a ½-inch (1.3 cm) tip, pipe out about 1 tablespoon of batter for each chouquette, leaving about 1½ inches (4 cm) between them. Paint each with egg wash and sprinkle with an equal amount of crystal sugar.

4. Bake in the center of the oven until the chouquettes are golden and puffed, 15 to 18 minutes. Remove from the oven, transfer to a wire rack, and eat when thoroughly cooled.

ASTUCE: The ambient atmosphere *can* affect the moisture in the pastry, so add one egg at a time and watch carefully—you want a dough that is soft but not liquid. If, after four eggs, you've got that, stop! Your pastry will be just fine.

Choux Puffs with Whipped Cream and Chocolate Sauce

CHOUQUETTES AU CHANTILLY ET SAUCE CHOCOLAT

What, you might ask, is the difference between this trio and profiteroles, the popular choux puffs filled with vanilla ice cream and drowned in chocolate sauce that one finds on every café and bistro menu in the land? Delicacy. Here, the choux pastry is lightly sweetened and topped with pearl sugar, then baked to a golden crisp. The whipped cream is flavored with vanilla and vanilla sugar, and the chocolate sauce is light yet richly flavored. All are combined to make a dessert that might be called "profiteroles deconstructed."

I had this at Girafe, an expansive restaurant overlooking the Eiffel Tower, which serves this as its signature. Once you make this dessert, your friends, family, neighborhood, and entire city will clamor for it. Note that it should be assembled right before serving.

SERVES 4 TO 6

EQUIPMENT: large bowl, electric mixer (optional), pastry bag and ½-inch (1.3 cm) tip

PREPARATION TIME: 15 minutes

COOKING TIME: none

DIFFICULTY LEVEL: simple, once you've mastered the piping

1½ cups (750 ml) heavy cream, chilled

2 tablespoons confectioners' sugar

½ teaspoon vanilla extract

1 recipe Choux Puffs (page 282)

1 recipe Chocolate Sauce (page 324)

1. Whisk the cream in the large bowl of an electric mixer fitted with the whisk attachment, or by hand, until it is thickened. Whisk in the confectioners' sugar and vanilla, and taste. Adjust the seasoning and the sweetness, if you like.

2. To fill the chouquettes, use a pastry bag fitted with a ½-inch (1.3 cm) tip. Fill the pastry bag with the whipped cream. Make a small slit in the bottom of a chouquette, and half-fill with cream, using the pastry bag. Continue until you've filled about 18 chouquettes, which is about how long the cream will last. If you want to fill all the chouquettes, then simply increase the amount of whipped cream.

3. To serve, either place three chouquettes on each of six plates with the warmed chocolate sauce alongside, or fill a platter or bowl with the cream-filled chouquettes. Let guests determine how much chocolate they want, and if there is sauce left . . . no problem!

ASTUCES:

- To whip the cream, chill the bowl and the whisk.
- If the weather is dry, you can make the chouquettes several hours before filling them. If it's humid, you'll need to make them, fill them, serve them. Note that you can make the chouquettes and freeze them.
- I use a pastry bag with a ½-inch (1.3 cm) tip to fill the chouquettes; you can use a crisp plastic bag with a corner cut off to do the same.
- Make sure your cream is chilled firm before filling the chouquettes, which has to be done at the last minute, so they hold their shape. Don't worry; it doesn't take much time to fill them.

Plum Clafoutis

CLAFOUTIS AUX PRUNES

Clafoutis (klah-foo-TEE), a simple, homey dessert from the Limousin region in southwest France, is perhaps the easiest, most familiar, and comforting dessert in the French repertoire. It is a fallback in the home, and a regular offering on every bistro and café menu in the land.

As I tested clafoutis recipes, I sorted through them like memories, for each evoked a moment, a snippet of conversation, a glint of light off a wineglass, an echo of laughter. Along with wonderful products, such memories are an essential ingredient in a clafoutis.

SERVES 6 TO 8

EQUIPMENT: nonreactive round or rectangular tart pan or baking dish, large mixing bowl

PREPARATION TIME: 10 to 15 minutes, depending on what fruit you use

BAKING TIME: 25 minutes

DIFFICULTY LEVEL: simple

About 1 teaspoon unsalted butter and about 2 teaspoons all-purpose flour for the pan

2 tablespoons light brown sugar

¾ cup (100 g) unbleached all-purpose flour

¾ teaspoon fine sea salt

2 cups (500 ml) milk, preferably whole

3 large eggs

¼ cup (60 g) Vanilla Sugar (page 339)

Seeds of 1 vanilla bean

1 pound (500 g) plums, rinsed, patted dry, pitted, and cut lengthwise into quarters

1½ tablespoons (22 g) salted butter, cut into 6 pieces (optional)

1. Preheat the oven to 450°F (230°C). Butter and lightly flour a 9½-inch (24 cm) nonreactive round or rectangular tart pan or baking dish. Sprinkle the pan with 1 tablespoon of the brown sugar.

2. Sift the flour and salt into a large mixing bowl. Make a well and whisk in 1 cup (250 ml) of the milk to make a smooth batter, then add the eggs, one at a time, whisking briefly after each addition. Whisk in the vanilla sugar and vanilla seeds until combined, then whisk in the remaining cup (250 ml) of milk.

3. Arrange the plums in the tart pan atop the sugar. Pour the batter over them. Dot the batter with the pieces of butter (if using) and bake in the center of the oven until the clafoutis is golden and puffed, about 25 minutes. Remove it from the oven and immediately sprinkle it with the remaining tablespoon of brown sugar, then let the clafoutis cool to lukewarm before serving.

ASTUCES:

- You can use so many fruits in a clafoutis, from apples to rhubarb, even raisins or dried plums.
- Note the use of both brown and vanilla sugar.

Vanilla Crème Brûlée

CRÈME BRÛLÉE À LA VANILLE

Crème brûlée is on the menu at every café and bistro in France, and there are good ones, not so good ones, and then there is this one. It is so good that you'll want to take tiny bites just to make the experience last longer. And when you serve it, you'll notice everyone at the table doing the same. The recipe is very simple, but the secret is in the baking—it needs to be baked gently, so the heat coaxes the custard together. Just follow the directions, which will lead you to perfection. This version is filled with the flavor of vanilla, which is the most traditional French version. If you want to vary the flavor, you can add 2 teaspoons of lime, lemon, or orange zest to the milk with the vanilla bean.

SERVES 6

EQUIPMENT: large heavy-bottomed saucepan, large bowl, one 2-inch- (5 cm) deep baking pan, six 6-inch (15 cm) round baking dishes with 1¼-inch (3 cm) sides, blowtorch (if you don't have a good broiler)

PREPARATION TIME: about 15 minutes (with infusing time, 1 hour 15 minutes)

BAKING TIME: 1 hour 15 minutes to 1 hour 30 minutes

DIFFICULTY LEVEL: simple

FOR THE CRÈME:

⅔ cup (150 ml) chilled whole milk

2 cups (500 ml) crème fraîche or heavy cream

½ plump, moist vanilla bean, split lengthwise, seeds scraped out with a small spoon

Zest from ½ lime, lemon, or orange, preferably organic (optional)

5 large egg yolks

½ cup (150 g) Vanilla Sugar (page 339)

FOR THE CARAMEL CRUST:

2 generous tablespoons granulated sugar

1. Whisk the milk and crème fraîche together in a large heavy-bottomed saucepan. Whisk in the vanilla seeds and the citrus zest if using. Add the vanilla bean, then scald the mixture over low heat (see Astuces). Remove from the heat and infuse, covered, for 1 hour. Remove and rinse the vanilla bean. Let dry and reserve for another use.

2. Whisk together the egg yolks and vanilla sugar in a large bowl until pale yellow and light. Whisk in the crème fraîche mixture until thoroughly combined.

3. Preheat the oven to 250°F (125°C). Line a 2-inch- (5 cm) deep baking pan with parchment paper.

4. Arrange the baking dishes in the baking pan. Pour boiling water around them, halfway up their sides. Pour equal amounts (½ cup; 125 ml) of the crème brûlée mixture into each dish. Place the baking pan in the oven and bake until the crèmes set, about 1½ hours. Check after about an hour and 15 minutes; you will know the crèmes are set when you jiggle the pan and they are tenderly solid throughout.

(continued)

ASTUCES:

- To scald, heat the milk and cream mixture over low heat until tiny bubbles form around the edge of the mixture, like pearls. Don't let it boil because boiling denatures the flavor.
- Why add the parchment to the baking pan? To keep the water from boiling up and into the crèmes!
- You can freeze the egg whites you'll accumulate and save them for another use.
- Finally, what difference does it make for the recipe to use crème fraîche or heavy cream? The difference is subtle, with the crème fraîche version being a bit richer in texture.
- Use a small blowtorch from the hardware store; they are more powerful than those sold in cookware stores.

5. Remove the crèmes from the oven and from the baking pan. Let cool to room temperature. Cover the cooled crèmes loosely with parchment paper and refrigerate for at least 2 hours.

6. At serving time, preheat the broiler or prepare a small blow torch.

7. For the caramel crust: Sprinkle equal amounts of granulated sugar over the crèmes and set them under the broiler until the sugar caramelizes and forms a crust, being careful to watch it so it doesn't burn. Alternatively, have some fun with the blow torch, using it judiciously to perfectly caramelize the sugar! Remove from the broiler (if using) and let the crust harden, then serve.

CRÈME FRAÎCHE VERSUS HEAVY CREAM

Crème fraîche or heavy cream—what is the difference? Crème fraîche is basically top cream, skimmed off the milk when it gets to the dairy, straight from the cow. In France, there are two versions of crème fraîche. One is simply chilled and, after a day or two, it will thicken and can be used in sauces, soups, or any manner of dishes. The other version has a fermenting agent added to it, which gives it a tang. This version is intended for serving fresh, along with Upside-Down Apple Tart (page 273), fresh berries, or Pear, Almond, and Nutmeg Crumble (page 296), though it isn't out of place in the same role as the unfermented version. Whatever version you choose, crème fraîche makes everything it touches just a little bit better!

Heavy or whipping cream? The FDA has words to say about these two ingredients. Heavy cream contains more than 36 percent fat; whipping cream contains 30 to 35 percent fat. The difference is subtle; the fattier cream whips up best.

Best Classic Lemon Tart

LA MEILLEUR TARTE AU CITRON CLASSIQUE

A more classic French dessert in any bistro, brasserie, or for that matter any patisserie, doesn't exist. And a better one than this doesn't, either. I taste Tarte au Citron everywhere I go, because it's one of those desserts that is a measure of the place where it is made. I've never found a better one than this, so you must add this to your repertoire—it's so simple to make, so luscious to eat. I usually reserve it for winter, the season of citrus, but also because it chases away the winter blues. It's the ideal end to a meal because, while sweet, it's also tart and refreshing.

SERVES 8 TO 10

EQUIPMENT: food processor, one 10½-inch (27 cm) removable-bottom tart pan, double boiler or a nonreactive metal bowl over a pan of water

PREPARATION TIME: 20 minutes

BAKING TIME: 12 to 15 minutes

DIFFICULTY LEVEL: simple to medium (the only trick is rolling out the pastry)

FOR THE PASTRY:

1½ cups (200 g) all-purpose flour

¼ teaspoon fine sea salt

7 tablespoons (105 g) unsalted butter, chilled, cut into 7 pieces

⅓ to ½ cup (80 to 125 ml) chilled water

FOR THE LEMON CREAM:

7 tablespoons (105 g) unsalted butter

1 cup (200 g) granulated sugar

4 large eggs

¾ cup (185 ml) fresh lemon juice (from about 3 large lemons)

Zest of 1 lemon, minced (about 2 teaspoons zest), preferably from an organic lemon

1. Make the pastry: Place the flour and salt in a food processor and process to mix. Add the butter and process until the mixture looks like coarse cornmeal. With the food processor running, drizzle in the water and process just until the mixture comes together; stop before it forms a ball. The pastry should be quite damp. Turn it out onto a work surface, form it into a flat disk, cover, and let sit for 1 hour. Roll it out and fit it into a 10½-inch (27 cm) tart pan, then refrigerate for 1 hour, or freeze for 20 minutes.

2. Preheat the oven to 425°F (220°C).

3. Prick the bottom of the pastry all over with the tines of a fork, then line it with aluminum foil and weight it with pastry weights. Bake in the center of the oven until the pastry is golden around the edges and on the bottom, 12 to 15 minutes. Remove from the oven, remove the aluminum foil and the weights from the pastry, and return the pastry to the oven to bake until golden all over, about 10 additional minutes. Remove the pastry from the oven and let cool.

4. Make the lemon cream: Place the butter and sugar in a double boiler set over medium heat so the water is gently boiling, and stir until the butter is melted. Add the eggs,

(continued)

one at a time, whisking well after each addition so they are thoroughly blended into the butter and sugar. Add the lemon juice, whisk, and cook, stirring gently, until the mixture is thickened, 6 to 7 minutes. Remove the double boiler from the heat, then remove the top pan holding the lemon cream and let it cool to room temperature. Stir in the lemon zest. If you have made this the day before serving, transfer it to an airtight container and refrigerate. Remove from the refrigerator at least 30 minutes before you assemble the tart, so the lemon cream is spreadable.

5. If you have made this the day that you're planning to serve it, spread the pastry with the lemon mixture and refrigerate for at least 2 and up to 3 hours before you plan to serve it.

ASTUCES:
- You can make the lemon filling the day before. Just make sure it's at room temperature before you spread it on the pastry.
- When baking the pastry, make sure it is golden on the bottom, so it can stand up to the lemon cream. You want the lemon cream and the pastry to meld without the pastry becoming soggy.

Rhubarb and Speculoos Tartlets

TARTELETTES À LA RHUBARB ET SPECULOOS

These tartlets, which are layers of crust, slices of nectarine or persimmon, cream, then rhubarb, surprise and delight everyone because they offer just the right combination of sweet, crisp, creamy, and tart . . . you'll see. The recipe makes use of the beloved Speculoos (page 319), though if you're not the baking kind, you can purchase speculoos and then it's a true snap to put this together. The advantage of making your own speculoos is that they are so crisp and flavorful, and there will be many left over to savor with tea or coffee!

Rhubarb grows primarily in maritime regions, from early spring to mid-autumn, depending on the variety and the seasonal temperatures. There are dozens of varieties, which come in an array colors, from vivid red to an almost pistachio green, with speckled varieties somewhere in between. Most people know the red variety, but the green variety not only grows better than its red cousins, it also offers the characteristic tartness of rhubarb with more flavor and a touch of sweetness. And if the plant in my garden is any indication, it produces several crops a year.

If you prefer to make a large tart so that you can cut slices, you will need a 10½-inch (27 cm) springform tart pan. These miniature versions are more dramatic—they look as if you spent all day making them, but actually they're so easy and they taste like cheesecake, only better!

SERVES 6

EQUIPMENT: baking sheet, food processor, medium bowl, 6 stainless-steel pastry rings about 3 inches (7.5 cm) in diameter, medium saucepan, large bowl

PREPARATION TIME: 20 minutes

COOKING TIME: 10 minutes for the rhubarb

DIFFICULTY LEVEL: simple

FOR THE CRUST:

7.5 ounces (225 g) Speculoos (page 319)

Pinch of fine sea salt

5 tablespoons (75 g) unsalted butter, melted (see Astuces)

FOR THE RHUBARB:

¾ cup (185 ml) water

½ cup (100 g) Vanilla Sugar (page 339)

One 1-inch (2.5 cm) piece fresh ginger, peeled and diced

½ vanilla bean

11 ounces (330 g) rhubarb, rinsed and trimmed, cut into ¼-inch (6 mm) half-moons

FOR THE CREAM:

1 cup (250 ml) crème fraîche

2 tablespoons Vanilla Sugar (page 339)

½ teaspoon vanilla extract

FOR ASSEMBLY:

1 just-ripe nectarine or other fruit, pitted and very thinly sliced

(continued)

1. Preheat the oven to 325°F (170°C). Line a baking sheet with parchment paper.

2. Prepare the crust: Place the speculoos in a food processer and process until finely ground. Add the salt, process once or twice, then turn into a medium bowl and mix in the melted butter until you have a sort of dough.

3. Place six 3-inch (7.5 cm) pastry rings on the prepared baking sheet and press equal amounts of the dough into each one, using a metal soup spoon to press them so they are even around the edges. Make a slight indentation in the center. Place in the center of the oven and bake until they are golden, 15 to 20 minutes. Remove from the oven and let cool.

4. Prepare the rhubarb: Place the water, sugar, ginger, and the half vanilla bean in a medium saucepan and bring to a boil over medium-high heat. Lower the heat so the syrup is boiling, whisking from time to time, until the sugar is dissolved. Add the rhubarb, stir gently so it is mixed with the syrup (it may seem there is too much rhubarb—don't worry, it's just fine), and return the syrup to a simmer. Shake the pan and watch the rhubarb as it cooks, stirring if necessary. Depending on its texture, the rhubarb will cook in about 1½ minutes, though it can take up to 5 minutes. You can tell because it begins to turn color, and if you touch a piece, it will have begun to soften. Remove from the heat and leave the rhubarb in the syrup to cool.

5. Prepare the cream: Place the cream, sugar, and vanilla in a large bowl and whisk until it forms stiff peaks.

6. To assemble the tartlets, leave them in their metal rings. Lay equal numbers of nectarine slices atop each crust with the skin against the edge, so it's pretty when you unmold them. Top with cream, evening it out so it completely covers the nectarine and is even against the edges of the mold. Refrigerate for 30 minutes to 1 hour.

7. To serve, unmold a tartlet on each of six plates. Spoon the rhubarb over the tartlets, leaving excess syrup in the pan so it doesn't drown the tartlets. Serve immediately.

Pear, Almond, and Nutmeg Crumble

CRUMBLE AUX POIRES, AUX AMANDES, ET AU NOIX DE MUSCADE

The French love a good crumble, which is a sweet, crisp import from their British cousins. While much between the French and the Brits is contentious, they come together over food and fashion, and this dish is a perfect example. Depending on the time of year, one can find crumbles of all sorts in the French patisserie, restaurant, and home, from those made with apples or pears to berries and bananas. This is my all-time favorite and will highlight any plat du jour you choose to serve in the fall and winter, when pears are at their finest. Although this crumble needs no adornment, it is delicious with crème fraîche or homemade Vanilla Ice Cream (page 302).

SERVES 6

EQUIPMENT: baking sheet, one 8-by-9 inch (20-by-23 cm) nonreactive baking dish, food processor

PREPARATION TIME: 10 minutes

COOKING TIME: 50 minutes

DIFFICULTY LEVEL: simple

---

2 generous pounds (1.2 kg) pears, such as Bartlett or Anjou, peeled, cored, and cut lengthwise into thin (¼-inch; 6 mm), slices

2 tablespoons fresh lemon juice

¾ teaspoon freshly grated nutmeg

½ cup (100 g) Vanilla Sugar (page 339)

⅓ cup (50 g) toasted almonds

Generous pinch of fine sea salt

½ cup plus 2 tablespoons (100 g) all-purpose flour

7 tablespoons (105 g) unsalted butter, cut into ½-inch (1.3 cm) pieces, chilled

1. Preheat the oven to 425°F (220°C). Line a baking sheet with parchment.

2. Place the pears in an 8-by-9 inch (20-by-23 cm) nonreactive baking dish. They will almost fill it up. Drizzle the pears with the lemon juice, then sprinkle them with ½ teaspoon of the nutmeg.

3. Place the vanilla sugar and almonds in a food processor and process until the almonds are unevenly chopped. Some of the almonds will be almost powder; other pieces will be the size of an oat flake. Add the salt, remaining ¼ teaspoon of nutmeg, and flour and process until combined. Add the butter and process until the mixture is the texture of coarse cornmeal (there will still be some larger almond pieces, which is fine).

4. Pour the mixture over the pears in an even layer, then gently press it into the pears. The baking dish will be very full.

5. Place the baking dish on the prepared baking sheet and put it on the center rack. Bake until the crumble is golden on top and the pears are cooked through, about 50 minutes.

6. When the crumble is baked, remove it from the oven and let it cool to room temperature before serving.

ASTUCES:

- To core the pears, use a vegetable peeler to cut out the stem end before you peel the fruit, then a melon ball maker to remove the seeds and what surrounds them, remembering to dig just deep enough, but not so deep you waste a lot of pear flesh. Then, with a very sharp knife, cut out the fibrous stem that runs through the "neck" of the pear.
- Let the crumble cool substantially before serving, as it is blistering when it comes out of the oven.
- Try substituting mace—the lacy covering of the nutmeg with a slightly more intense nutmeg flavor—for the nutmeg here.

Rhubarb Poached in Vanilla Syrup with Fromage Blanc

RHUBARBE POCHÉE À LA VANILLE AU FROMAGE BLANC

It is safe to say that everyone in France north of Lyon who has a *potager* (home garden) grows rhubarb. And anyone who does not rushes to buy it at the farmers' market at the first sign of spring. Rhubarb is so universally loved that it is turned into jams and compotes, shaved over seafood, tucked into pastry, folded into custard. Here, poached in vanilla syrup and combined with fromage blanc, it is one of life's simple pleasures.

SERVES 6

EQUIPMENT: large saucepan, fine-mesh sieve, cheesecloth

PREPARATION TIME: 10 minutes

COOKING TIME: 25 minutes

DIFFICULTY LEVEL: simple

1¼ cups (250 g) Vanilla Sugar (page 339)

¾ cup (65 ml) filtered or bottled water

½ vanilla bean, seeds removed

1½ pounds (750 g) fresh rhubarb, peeled and cut into small dice (about ¼-inch [6 mm] square)

1½ to 1¾ cups (375 to 430 g) Fromage Blanc (page 312) or drained yogurt

Fresh mint, basil, or tarragon leaves for garnish

1. Mix the sugar, water, and vanilla bean and its seeds together in a large saucepan and bring slowly to a boil over medium-high heat. Boil gently, stirring often, until all the sugar is dissolved, about 5 minutes. Fold the rhubarb into the boiling syrup. It will seem as though there is too much rhubarb for the amount of syrup, but continue to fold it gently as it cooks, and you will see that the rhubarb will decrease in volume and release liquid into the syrup.

2. Cook the rhubarb just until it is tender, 3 to 10 minutes, folding it almost constantly until there is enough liquid for the rhubarb to be fully covered, and checking frequently to be sure it doesn't cook for too long. As soon as it is cooked, remove from the heat and let cool to room temperature.

3. To serve, divide the Fromage Blanc among six dessert bowls. Pour equal amounts of rhubarb with its syrup over the Fromage Blanc. Garnish each bowl with a mint leaf and serve immediately.

ASTUCES:

- Fromage blanc is available in some specialty markets, or you can make your own (page 312). Or substitute with Greek yogurt by lining a colander or sieve with cheesecloth and draining for an hour or two
- If the rhubarb skin is very tough—and it can be so tough a knife will hardly go through it—peel the stalks.

Fresh Strawberries with Crème Chantilly

LES FRAISES À LA CHANTILLY

Come late spring, this is a typical "dessert du jour," a no-fuss, no-muss recipe that pleases everyone. All you need, of course, is the best strawberries you can find, some crème fraîche or heavy cream, a bit of sugar, and then perhaps some Speculoos (page 319) to serve alongside.

SERVES 6

EQUIPMENT: strawberry huller, medium bowl, whisk or electric mixer, large bowl

PREPARATION TIME: 10 minutes

COOKING TIME: none

DIFFICULTY LEVEL: simple

---

3 pounds (1.5 kg) strawberries, hulled

2 tablespoons (25 g) Vanilla Sugar (page 339)

FOR THE CRÈME CHANTILLY:

2½ cups (625 ml) crème fraîche

2 to 4 tablespoons (25 to 50 g) Vanilla Sugar (page 339)

1. Cut the berries lengthwise into thin slices and place them in a medium bowl. Add the sugar, toss gently, and let macerate for at least 1 hour.

2. Just before serving, make the crème Chantilly: Using a whisk or electric mixer, whisk the crème fraîche in a large bowl until it doubles in volume, then whisk in the sugar and transfer it to a serving bowl.

3. To serve, pass the strawberries and the crème Chantilly separately.

ASTUCES:

- Strawberries can be had year-round, but they're not delicious year-round—if you've ever had a strawberry in December you understand. So make this wonderful dessert in the fullness of local strawberry season, to get the most from it.
- In France, the strawberry season has been extended so that we have wonderful berries from May through July, depending on the year.
- Mixing the berries with a bit of sugar after cutting them allows them to exude some juice, which makes them all the more delicious!

Buttery Almond Tile Cookies

LES TUILES

There are tuiles and then there are tuiles, and these crisp, not-too-sweet and very almond-rich tuiles are the best I've ever tasted. I have been making them for many years, after getting the recipe from Odile Engel, an Alsatian cook who wound up in Normandy. She had a way with everything, and was generous enough to share her lovely recipe, which inspired my own creation here. These are simple and absolutely delicious served alongside sorbet, ice cream, a simple fruit salad, or on their own with coffee. They're a staple of the French bistro and patisserie, and so much fun to make!

MAKES 40 TUILES

EQUIPMENT: small bowl, medium bowl, baking sheet, clean broomstick, wine bottles or rolling pins

PREPARATION TIME: 15 minutes

BAKING TIME: about 12 minutes

DIFFICULTY LEVEL: medium (these are simple to make; you just need to be quick!)

---

6 large egg whites

Pinch of fine sea salt

2¼ cups (8 ounces; 250 g) sliced almonds

½ cup plus 2 tablespoons (130 g) Vanilla Sugar (page 339)

Scant ½ teaspoon cardamom seeds, finely crushed

7 tablespoons (105 g) clarified butter (see Astuces)

Neutral oil (untoasted peanut) for the baking sheet

1. Whisk the egg whites with the pinch of salt in a small bowl, just to break them up. Mix together the almonds, sugar, and cardamom in a medium bowl, then stir in the egg whites, using a wooden spoon. Stir in the clarified butter and mix until the batter is homogeneous. Refrigerate, covered, for 1 hour.

2. Preheat the oven to 350°F (180°C). Oil a baking sheet. You may want to use a nonstick baking sheet, which you still need to lightly oil. Prepare a clean broomstick, series of wine bottles, or rolling pins for shaping the tuiles.

3. Place about 1 tablespoon of batter on the baking sheet and flatten it into a 4-inch (10 cm) round, using the back of the tines of a fork. If the batter sticks, simply dip the fork into a glass of water between each use. Repeat with the remaining batter, leaving a ½-inch (1.3 cm) space between the rounds. Bake in the center of the oven until the tuiles are deep golden on the edges and pale gold in the center, about 12 minutes.

4. Remove the tuiles from the oven and quickly remove them from the baking sheet, using a spatula or offset spatula, and transfer them to the broomstick or other mold, pressing them very gently to give them a rounded shape. Once

the tuiles have taken the shape, gently transfer them to a plate or platter. Once they are cooled, serve immediately. Tuiles stay fresh and crisp for about 4 hours.

ASTUCES:

- To clarify butter the simple way, melt the butter in a small saucepan over medium-high heat, remove from the heat when it is melted, and skim off any impurities. Let the butter cool but not harden, then use just the golden butter that is above the settled milk solids, which you can either discard or add to bread dough.
- Regarding what you use to create the famed *tuile* (tile) shape, I highly recommend a rolling pin, but a wine bottle or a broomstick works, too. Note that the cookies harden very quickly, so you have to transfer and gently mold them as quickly as you can.

Vanilla Ice Cream

GLACE À LA VANILLE

The French love ice cream, and it is always on the menu at a café, bistro, or even starred restaurants—the perfect finish to a plat du jour! This particular ice cream is a study in frozen perfection, richly flavored and textured. It defines our dreams of French vanilla ice cream, the one with tiny dark spots in it. You will find those spots in this version; they're seeds from the whole vanilla pod, and they lend their delicate and dreamy flavor to the custard. Once you've got this recipe down, you can vary the flavor by adding spices and herbs to the custard to infuse, along with the vanilla.

MAKES 1 QUART (1 L) ICE CREAM

EQUIPMENT: large heavy-bottomed saucepan, large bowl, fine-mesh sieve, medium bowl, ice cream maker

PREPARATION TIME: 10 minutes

COOKING TIME: 10 minutes, with plenty of time for the mixture to cool to room temperature, then to chill

DIFFICULTY LEVEL: simple

---

4 cups (1 L) half-and-half

1 vanilla bean, split lengthwise

10 large egg yolks

1¼ cup (250 g) Vanilla Sugar (page 339)

Small pinch of fine sea salt

1. Place the half-and-half in a large heavy-bottomed saucepan. Scrape in the seeds from the vanilla bean and add the whole bean as well. Stir, then scald over medium heat. Remove from the heat, cover, and infuse for 20 minutes.

2. Whisk together the egg yolks, sugar, and salt in a large bowl, until pale yellow and light. Slowly whisk in the warm infused half-and-half along with the vanilla bean, then return the mixture to the pan.

3. Rest a fine-mesh sieve atop a medium bowl and set aside.

4. Cook the custard mixture over medium heat, stirring constantly in a figure-eight pattern, until it is thickened and coats the back of the spoon, and a line run through the custard on the back of the spoon stays clean. Pour the custard mixture into the sieve so it drains into the waiting bowl. Remove the vanilla bean from the sieve and return it to the custard.

5. Let the custard cool to room temperature, then refrigerate it until it is chilled through. Make the ice cream in an ice cream maker according to the manufacturer's instructions.

ASTUCES:

- Keep vanilla beans in an airtight container out of the light. If they develop crystals or a white powder on them, simply scrape it off, wash the jar, and leave the vanilla beans to air dry before returning them to the jar.
- When making the custard for ice cream, you must bring it very close to the curdling point for it to cook properly, so close that when you pour it through the sieve into the waiting bowl (don't omit this step), there may well be the beginnings of curdled egg in the pan.
- Homemade ice cream is absolutely best served the day it is made. It will be like soft-serve when right out of the ice cream maker, so I put it in the freezer for an hour or so to firm it up. It's delicious the following day, too, but you need to manage the texture by removing it from the freezer at least an hour before you plan to serve it. Keep it in the fridge; check on it. If it's rock hard, which will happen because there aren't any stabilizers in it, then remove it from the fridge about 15 minutes before you serve it.
- Consider making the custard the night before you plan to serve the ice cream, as it needs time to come to room temperature, then time to chill completely in the fridge.

CHAPTER 11
BASICS

WHERE WOULD ANY COOK BE without the basic recipes that provide the foundation for so many dishes? In a sad place, for certain. The basics here include some of the most fundamental sauces, such as béchamel; pastries, such as pâte à choux and pâte brisée; and mayonnaise. They are the recipes that give French cuisine its elegance, its subtle but indispensable layering of flavor, its inimitable structure that makes for such finesse.

Basics like the recipes here are the "secret" to French cuisine. If you have a wonderful pastry recipe like the one here, your tarts will wow everyone who samples them. Béchamel? It's a simple sauce, but the one here is simply divine, better than most. Stocks, mayonnaise, bread dough . . . the better they are, the more refined, the better every dish they touch will be. And the recipes in this chapter are the best basics you'll find. *Alors, allons-y*—let's go—into the Basics!

ASTUCES:

- Dry yeast, such as SAF brand, available at specialty shops and online, requires very hot water to blossom and grow.
- Note that if you use a mixer, don't over-knead the dough or it could be tough.

Tender Bread Dough

PÂTE À PAIN TENDRE

This is a no-fail recipe that makes a tender, light loaf. I use it as a base for just about all my recipes that call for bread dough, such as "Bathed" Bread (page 182) or Alsatian Bacon, Onion, and Cream Pizza (page 146). It's a winning recipe, and once you've made it, you'll put it in your "favorites" file.

If you're making this bread for pan bagnat, use olive oil as indicated, and be sure to brush the rolls with egg wash to make them shine. If you want to use this recipe to make a fruit or other sweeter bread, consider substituting butter for the olive oil.

MAKES ONE 1-POUND (500 G) LOAF OR 6 INDIVIDUAL BUNS (FOR PAN BAGNAT)

EQUIPMENT: electric mixer (optional), tea towel, baking sheet or 9-by-5-by-3-inch (23-by-12.5-by-7.5 cm) loaf pan

PREPARATION TIME: 10 minutes, plus 1 hour 20 minutes for rising

BAKING TIME: 18 to 25 minutes

DIFFICULTY LEVEL: simple

- 1 teaspoon active dry yeast (I like SAF brand)
- 2 cups (500 ml) very warm (almost hot) water
- 3 to 5 cups (400 to 666 g) unbleached all-purpose flour
- 2 teaspoons fine sea salt
- 3 tablespoons olive oil or unsalted butter (45 g), at room temperature
- 1 egg plus 2 teaspoons water for egg wash (optional)

1. Whisk together the yeast, water, and ½ cup (70 g) of the flour in a large mixing bowl or the bowl of an electric mixer fitted with the paddle attachment. Let the mixture sit just until it begins to bubble, then add the salt and stir. Gradually add 2 cups (265 g) of the flour, then stir in the olive oil. Add enough of the remaining flour to make a dough that is firm but not at all dry. Knead the dough until it is smooth and satiny, 5 to 6 minutes.

2. Place the dough in a bowl, cover with a clean, dampened tea towel, and let it rise at room temperature (68° to 80°F; 20° to 27°C) until doubled in bulk, about 1 hour. (At this point, the dough is ready to be shaped as you like, after punching it down.)

3. Punch down the dough and shape it into a round loaf 5 inches (12.5 cm) in diameter or an oblong loaf 9 inches (23 cm) long. Set it on a floured baking sheet, or parchment-lined loaf pan (9-by-5-by-3 inches; 23-by-12.5-by-7.5 cm), cover, and let rise again until almost doubled in bulk, about 20 minutes. Alternatively, if you are making buns for pan bagnat, cut the dough into six equal-size pieces and set them about 3 inches (7.5 cm) apart on a flour-dusted or parchment-lined baking sheet. Pat the dough into rounds that measure about 5 inches

(continued)

(12.5 cm) across and let them rise until nearly doubled in bulk, about 20 minutes.

4. Preheat the oven to 400°F (200°C).

5. Prepare the egg wash (if using): Whisk together the egg and water in a small bowl until foamy. Paint the top of the formed bread dough or buns with the egg wash.

6. If you're making one loaf, you'll want to slash it several times with a very sharp knife, making your cuts about ¼ inch (6 mm) deep, to allow the steam to escape during baking. Bake until the loaf is golden and sounds hollow, about 30 minutes. For buns, bake until they are golden and puffed, about 20 minutes.

7. Remove the bread or buns from the oven and turn out onto a wire rack. Let cool thoroughly before slicing.

Pain d'Épices

SPICE BREAD

Pain d'épices (spice bread) is like fragrant, tender, living history. Charlemagne insisted his troops eat a similar bread, to keep up their health as they marched throughout Europe. Legend has it that Genghis Khan, too, fed his hordes on a version of this bread. Henry IV created a corporation in the 14th century called Le Pain d'Épiciers (Grocers' Bread) that was responsible for making the rye flour and honey loaf that is now called pain d'épices, and it is thought that this is the root of its name, since many versions of pain d'épices don't actually include spices.

Today, spice bread hails from two French regions, Alsace and Burgundy, both of which claim to have invented it. Likely both regions are correct, given that an idea in one place can be had simultaneously in another. That is true today and surely was hundreds of years ago.

Wherever it originated, pain d'épices is different in the hands of everyone who makes it. This very traditional version is compact and flavorful with hints of honey, anise, and very little sweetness. It is ideal to season Carbonnade (page 137), and you'll find all sorts of other uses for it, such as lightly toasted with your morning coffee, thoroughly toasted with a slice of sautéed foie gras on top, served with cheese, or dried and crumbled atop roasted leg of lamb. Once you've tasted and put your imagination to it, a loaf will disappear in no time. In case it doesn't, don't be concerned, because it keeps a long while due to the honey, and it gets better each day.

MAKES 1 LOAF

EQUIPMENT: medium saucepan, small saucepan, electric mixer (optional), one 9-by-5-by-3-inch (23-by-12.5-by-7.5 cm) loaf pan, baking sheet

PREPARATION TIME: 20 to 30 minutes

COOKING TIME: about 1 hour 40 minutes

DIFFICULTY LEVEL: simple

Unsalted butter and all-purpose flour for the loaf pan

1 cup (250 ml) whole milk

1 tablespoon ground cinnamon, preferably from Vietnam

½ teaspoon ground cloves

½ teaspoon ground cardamom

1 tablespoon whole aniseeds

1¼ cups (310 g) mild honey

6 tablespoons (90 ml) orange marmalade

3¾ cups (about 1 pound; 500 g) all-purpose flour

1 teaspoon baking soda

1 tablespoon warm water

(continued)

1. Preheat the oven to 325°F (165°C). Butter and flour the loaf pan.

2. Combine the milk and the spices in a medium saucepan over medium-high heat and whisk gently. As soon as bubbles have formed around the edges of the milk, remove it from the heat, cover, and let the spices infuse for 10 minutes.

3. Heat the honey in a small saucepan over low heat just until it is liquid; do not let it boil. Transfer it to a large mixing bowl or the bowl of an electric mixer fitted with the paddle attachment, add the milk, and mix well. Then mix in the marmalade. Slowly add the flour, stirring until the mixture is thoroughly combined.

4. Stir together the baking soda and warm water in a small bowl; the mixture will fizz and bubble. Stir this into the dough and continue to mix (at medium speed, if using a mixer) until the dough is satiny, at least 10 minutes by hand or 5 minutes in a mixer.

5. Transfer the batter to the prepared loaf pan—it will come almost to the edges of the pan. Place the pan on a baking sheet, then place them in the center of the oven. Bake until the loaf is puffed and golden and springs back when you touch it, 1 hour 20 minutes to 1 hour 40 minutes.

6. Remove the pain d'épices from the oven and turn out the loaf onto a wire rack. Once the loaf is cool, wrap it in parchment paper, then either aluminum foil or, as my French neighbors would do, in a cotton tea towel. Let it sit for 24 hours to ripen before cutting into it. If you can avoid the temptation, that is.

ASTUCES:

- Scalding the milk with the spices encourages them to give up more of their flavors into the hot milk.
- Use a mild honey, such as spring flower or even acacia, so that it doesn't overpower the other ingredients.

Fromage Blanc

FRESH, CREAMY CHEESE

Fromage blanc (also called fromage frais) is a staple in the French refrigerator, the way cottage cheese is in the American refrigerator. Fromage blanc is either a *gouter* (snack food), or it is served as dessert with jam mixed in, fresh berries piled atop, and honey drizzled all over. It's also used in savory dishes, such as the Alsatian Bacon, Onion, and Cream Pizza (page 146).

Because fromage blanc is tough to find in the United States, I'm including this recipe. It makes a very worthy substitute for French fromage blanc, and I suspect you'll find yourself making it often. It makes a wonderful addition to your repertoire, and it will keep for several days in the refrigerator. You can get rennet online at many shops, either animal- or plant-based.

MAKES 2 CUPS (500ML)

EQUIPMENT: medium saucepan, cheesecloth, fine-mesh strainer

PREPARATION TIME: 3 hours

COOKING TIME: none

DIFFICULTY LEVEL: simple

---

1 quart (1 L) whole milk

⅓ cup (80 ml) heavy cream

1 tablespoon fresh lemon juice

8 drops rennet

1 teaspoon fine sea salt

ASTUCES:

- The lemon juice (or white wine vinegar) is essential in this recipe to get the requisite acidity.
- When you've made fromage blanc once, you can determine how much acidity you desire and how much cream you want to use, depending on the acidity and the richness you're looking for.

1. Place the milk, cream, and lemon juice in a medium saucepan, whisk to blend, and place over low heat until it reaches 100°F (38°C). If you blink and the mixture heats to a higher temperature, just remove it from the heat and wait for it to come back down to 100°F (38°C). Do not let it boil! Remove the saucepan from the heat.

2. Whisk in the rennet, cover the saucepan, and wrap it in a towel or set it in a warm spot (68 to 70°F; 20 to 21°C) for about 3 hours. Check it occasionally to see when the solids have formed and separated from the whey, and then tip the solids into a cheesecloth-lined strainer set over a bowl and let drain.

3. You can decide at this point how firm you'd like your fromage blanc. If you want it loose, like thick cream, then when it gets to that texture simply pour it into a container. If you want it more firm, let it drain longer until it's the texture you prefer. I like it best when it's become like a very, very soft fresh goat cheese, and that's when it's best for flammekueche, too.

Apple Compote

COMPOTE DE POMMES

Compote is a favorite in France, for dessert or *gouter* (snacktime), or even served as vegetable alongside roasted meats. Nothing could be better or simpler because all you need are wonderful apples, vanilla bean, and a touch of water. No sugar is needed, and without the sugar, the true flavor of the apple comes through. Depending on the apple variety, you will either end up with lovely golden and tender chunks, or a wonderful chunky puree.

MAKES 4 TO 6 SERVINGS

EQUIPMENT: large saucepan

PREPARATION TIME: 10 minutes

COOKING TIME: 18 to 25 minutes

DIFFICULTY LEVEL: simple

½ **vanilla bean**

2 **pounds (1 kg) sweet/tart apples, such as Cox's Orange Pippin, Pink Lady, or Jonagold, cored, peeled, and diced**

ASTUCES:

- When you core the apple, make sure to remove all of the tough "fingernail" that surrounds the seeds, so you don't wind up with any in your compote.
- Watch this carefully and stir often, as the apples have a tendency to stick to the bottom of the pan.

1. Slit the vanilla bean down the center and scrape out the seeds inside.

2. Place the apples in a large saucepan. Add the vanilla seeds, the bean, and the water. Stir, cover, and place over medium heat. When the liquid begins to boil, lower the heat to medium-low and continue cooking, stirring frequently, until the apples are soft through. Remove from the heat and serve.

Tender Tart Pastry

LA PÂTE TENDRE

Tender, buttery, and crisp, almost like puff pastry, this simple recipe will change your life. I know this because so many of my students have told me so! It's very quick to make, and the trick to its success is handling it as little as possible.

MAKES ENOUGH PASTRY FOR ONE 10^1/$_2$-INCH (26.5 CM) TO 12^1/$_2$-INCH (31.5 CM) TART
EQUIPMENT: food processor
PREPARATION TIME: 5 minutes
COOKING TIME: 15 to 25 minutes
DIFFICULTY LEVEL: simple

1½ cups (205 g) unbleached all-purpose flour

¼ teaspoon fine sea salt

12 tablespoons (1½ sticks; 180 g) unsalted butter, chilled and cut into 12 pieces

5 to 6 tablespoons (80 to 95 ml) ice water

1. Place the flour and salt in a food processor and process once to mix. Add the butter and process until the mixture resembles coarse meal. Add the 5 tablespoons ice water and pulse just until the pastry begins to hold together. If the pastry seems dry and dusty, add the remaining 1 tablespoon water.

2. Tip out the pastry from the food processor to your work surface and form it quickly, without touching it too much, into a flat round. Cover it with a bowl and let it rest on the work surface for at least 30 minutes. The pastry can sit several hours at room temperature, as long as the room isn't warmer than 68°F (20°C). The pastry is now ready to use as desired.

ASTUCES:

- This is made in a food processor, so the ingredients stay cold while they're being put together.
- Once the pastry is made, it needs to sit at room temperature for at least 30 minutes so it can relax before being rolled out.

Steamed Couscous

LE COUSCOUS À LA VAPEUR

Couscous, prepared as this recipe instructs, is a privilege to eat. Light, fluffy, buttery but not too buttery, it drifts like powder snow onto your plate, into your mouth. I love to make this—the process is meditative, perfect for this stressful era, as it takes time and concentration, care, and a certain derring-do as you plunge your hands into some pretty hot couscous. You've got to focus and you've got to pay attention. At first it can seem intimidating, but once you've done it a couple of times, you'll get the hang of it. And when you serve this to your family and friends, they most likely won't believe that simple couscous can be taken to these heights!

You most likely will have leftover couscous. Simply store it in the refrigerator and reheat it in the steamer—for breakfast (with cinnamon and raisins), lunch (with leftover couscous soup or by itself with a big green salad), for dinner (with leftover soup). It also freezes well.

SERVES 8 TO 10

EQUIPMENT: large shallow bowl, couscous steamer or other two-part steamer, cotton tea towel, rubber spatula

PREPARATION AND COOKING TIME (impossible to separate the two): 1 hour 50 minutes

DIFFICULTY LEVEL: simple, but takes some time

---

6 cups (2 pounds; 1 kg) fine couscous

1 tablespoon olive oil

3¾ cups (930 ml) warm water

2 teaspoons fine sea salt

9 tablespoons (130 g) unsalted butter

1. Pour the couscous into a large shallow bowl or onto a work surface. Drizzle the olive oil over the couscous. Thoroughly blend the oil into the grain with your fingers and between your palms, gently rubbing and working until the oil is completely incorporated into the couscous.

2. Place 1¼ cups (310 ml) of the water in a small bowl, add the salt, and stir until it is dissolved. Sprinkle the salted water over the couscous 2 to 3 tablespoons at a time, then work the water into the couscous with your fingers and palms as you did with the oil, only even more gently, until the water disappears into and slightly softens the grain. Let the couscous sit for 10 minutes.

3. Prepare the couscous steamer by wrapping a wet cotton tea towel around the seam where the top and the bottom come together, to prevent steam from escaping. Bring the water in the bottom to a rolling boil and place the couscous in the top of the steamer. Steam, uncovered, for 30 minutes.

(continued)

- Step 1 urges you to proceed gently, so please do. As you use your fingers and palms, urge rather than rub the liquids and fats into the couscous, very lightly, very gently. Use a scraper as you work the butter and water into the hot couscous, to save your hands.
- It is very important that the couscous steams uncovered. If it steams covered, condensation falls from the cover onto the grain, causing lumps and making it soggy.
- Wrap a towel around the seam of the steamer to make sure steam doesn't escape into the atmosphere.
- If you do not have a couscous steamer, you may use a traditional two-part steamer.

4. Turn out the steamed couscous into a large shallow bowl or onto a work surface and, using a wooden spoon, a plastic dough scraper, or your fingers (the couscous is very hot, so be careful), gently break up any clumps in the couscous without mashing it. At this point, if you do not plan to serve the couscous immediately, you may let it sit for several hours. If you plan to serve it soon, spread out the couscous slightly on the work surface, then sprinkle it with an additional 1½ cups (375 ml) of warm water, 2 to 3 tablespoons at a time. Work it in, using a wooden spoon and your fingers, by lifting up the couscous and letting it fall through your fingers or from the bowl of the spoon. As soon as the couscous is cool enough for you to handle, work only with your fingers, handling the couscous very lightly until all the water is absorbed. The couscous should be inflated and feel slightly tender, though it will still be quite firm. Let it rest for 10 minutes.

5. Check the cloth tied around the steamer—if it needs moistening, remove and moisten it, then retie it around the steamer. Return the couscous to the top of the steamer, bring the water in the steamer to a boil over medium high heat, and steam the couscous for 30 minutes. Turn out the couscous into a shallow bowl or a work surface. Add the remaining 1 cup (250 ml) of warm water, 2 to 3 tablespoons at a time, working it as before, and let sit for 10 minutes. Return the couscous to the steamer to steam until it is fluffy and tender, about 15 additional minutes.

6. Turn out the couscous into a large shallow bowl or onto a work surface. Cut the butter into tablespoon-size pieces atop the couscous. Gently work the butter into the couscous with your fingers and a wooden spoon, breaking up any lumps and urging the butter into the grain the same way you urged the oil and the water into it. When all the butter has been absorbed, transfer the couscous to a warmed shallow platter, mounding it in the center, or a large shallow bowl. Serve it with Saffron-Scented Lamb, Vegetable, and Chickpea Soup (page 115).

Speculoos

SPICE COOKIES

Originally from Belgium, this cinnamon-scented cookie has seduced the normally non-cinnamon-inspired French populace. Today, speculoos are not just served with coffee at nearly every café in the land, nestled against your cup of *express*, but they are ground and turned into a crust for cheesecakes or other desserts requiring an easily made crisp crust, ground and folded into chocolate mousse, and ground and used as a dusting for foie gras, duck breast, or steak destined for the hot pan. They have become, in other words, a cornerstone of the French culinary landscape. This is a simple recipe but not an easy one to perfect. I was on the train to Cap Ferret and had a bag of three different versions with me, which I'd planned to roll out for the friends I'd be visiting, to get their opinion. My seat partner on the train was enjoying a picnic lunch, and when she got to her dessert—a chocolate bar—she offered me a piece. I, in turn, offered her a version of each speculoos to taste. She was so cute—delighted to taste them all. This was the version that won her approval, as it did mine!

MAKES ABOUT 40 COOKIES

EQUIPMENT: 2 baking sheets, electric mixer (optional)

PREPARATION TIME: 10 minutes

BAKING TIME: 12 minutes

DIFFICULTY LEVEL: simple

1½ cups (220 g) all-purpose flour

½ teaspoon baking soda

2 teaspoons ground cinnamon, preferably from Vietnam

½ teaspoon fine sea salt

10 tablespoons (150 g) unsalted butter, at room temperature

⅔ cup (92 g) gently packed light brown sugar

1. Preheat the oven to 400°F (200°C). Line two baking sheets with parchment paper.

2. Sift together the dry ingredients onto a piece of parchment or waxed paper.

3. Cream the butter and the sugar together in a large bowl or the bowl of an electric mixer until it is pale yellow and light.

4. With the mixer set at low speed, add the flour mixture to the butter mixture and mix just until a dry, crumbly dough is formed. Otherwise, add the dry ingredients all at once to the butter mixture and mix with a wooden spoon, until they are combined.

5. Turn out the dough onto a piece of parchment paper and shape it into a rectangle with your hands. Lay another piece of parchment paper over the dough and carefully roll

(continued)

out the dough until it is about ¼ inch (6 mm) thick. Even out the edges of the rectangle as best you can, then cut the dough into 3-by-1-inch (7.5-by-2.5 cm) strips. Don't be concerned if some of the rectangles aren't *exactly* that size, nor if your edges aren't perfectly straight. Any "imperfect" cookies are for the ones you love.

6. Transfer the dough rectangles to the prepared baking sheets, leaving ½ inch (1.3 cm) between each rectangle, and bake in the center of the oven until they are golden, about 12 minutes. You may need to rotate the baking sheets to bake the cookies evenly.

7. Remove the cookies from the oven and transfer to a wire cooling rack. The cookies will become nice and crisp as they cool.

ASTUCES:

- If you're a cinnamon fanatic and want more here, simply add an extra ¼ to ½ teaspoon to the flour. And be sure to check the freshness of your cinnamon—it should be rotated in your spice cupboard each year.
- If you want your cookies to look more like the commercial version with their lightly scalloped edges, cut them with a ravioli cutter.
- These keep for at least a week in an airtight container.

Buckwheat Galettes

GALETTES AU SARRASIN

What's the very best reason to go to Brittany, the farthest west region of France? All reasons. But I suppose if I had to rank them, I'd put buckwheat galettes right near the top. Buckwheat has grown in Brittany since time immemorial and maybe even before that. Traces of buckwheat have been found in caves; the Breton soil is such that wheat had a hard time bearing fruit, but buckwheat, the wheat of the poor, flourished. And so its dark seeds were ground into dark flour that, because it contains no fat, doesn't spoil and could be stored even during times of famine. Thus, the Bretons had food when other wheat-based regions didn't.

MAKES ABOUT 10 GALETTES

EQUIPMENT: nonstick flat skillet or crêpe pan, one ⅓-cup (80 ml) measuring cup, baking sheet

PREPARATION TIME: 5 minutes

COOKING TIME: about 20 minutes to use up all the batter

DIFFICULTY LEVEL: simple, once you've made your first galette

---

1 cup plus 5 tablespoons (240 g) buckwheat flour

2¼ cups (560 ml) water

2 large eggs

½ teaspoon fine sea salt

1 tablespoon (15 g) clarified butter (see Astuces, page 301)

1. Place the flour in a medium bowl. Slowly whisk in the water to form a smooth batter, then whisk in the eggs and salt. Whisk vigorously for several minutes, until the batter is smooth and the ingredients are thoroughly combined. The batter will be quite thin but elastic; when you lift the whisk, the batter will drop off in "ropes." You may use it immediately or let it sit, loosely covered, for up to 2 hours. If it sits, whisk to blend it before using.

2. Heat a 10½-inch (26½ cm) nonstick or cast-iron skillet or crêpe pan over medium-high heat. Brush it lightly with clarified butter.

3. Pour ⅓ cup (80 ml) of the batter in the center of the skillet and quickly rotate the skillet to spread the batter as evenly as possible across the bottom. It is fine if the batter is thicker in the center than at the edges.

4. Cook the galette until it begins to curl up on the edges, about 1½ minutes. If it is browning too quickly, lift the pan off the heat while you lower the heat slightly, so it won't burn. Using your fingers, carefully pick up the edge of the galette, gently pull it from the skillet, flip it over, and continue to cook just until it is set on the other side, about 30 seconds. As the galettes are cooked, stack them on a baking sheet and cover them with a cotton tea towel. Keep in a low-heat oven (about 200°F; 100°C), as you cook the remaining batter.

ASTUCES:

- The secret to good galettes is that the batter should be very thinly spread over a hot—but not too hot—pan. I use a nonstick crêpe pan that I oil with clarified butter.
- You want to use medium-high to high heat so the batter sizzles when it hits the pan, but it doesn't bounce or bubble. You'll lose the first galette or two as you adjust the heat and your skill.
- Here's the trick to the even spreading of batter: pour the batter in the pan, then rotate the pan while you shake it, so the batter shimmies across the bottom of the pan. There might be a few holes in your galette, and it will be thinner at the edges than in the center, but this is just fine!
- Buckwheat doesn't contain gluten, so there is no need to let the batter sit before you use it.

Chocolate Sauce

SAUCE CHOCOLAT

This is a delicately light chocolate sauce, perfect for the Choux Puffs with Whipped Cream and Chocolate Sauce (page 284), though you'll find this a very useful sauce for serving alongside everything from simple cakes to ice cream. Once you've got this sauce under your belt, you'll make it often, because it's ridiculously easy and, while richly flavored, is satisfyingly light. And on a dark winter day, if you're looking for a perfect hot chocolate, this is your recipe—just add more milk.

MAKES ABOUT 1^1/$_2$ CUPS (375 ML) SAUCE

EQUIPMENT: medium heavy-bottomed saucepan, medium heatproof bowl, heatproof silicone spatula

PREPARATION TIME: 5 minutes

COOKING TIME: 10 minutes max

DIFFICULTY LEVEL: simple

⅓ cup (80 ml) filtered water

⅓ cup (80 ml) heavy cream

⅓ (80 ml) whole milk

5.5 ounces (165 g) semisweet chocolate, very finely chopped

Pinch of fine sea salt

1. Combine the water, cream, and milk in a medium heavy-bottomed saucepan over medium heat. Be very careful not to let the liquids boil.

2. Place the chocolate in a medium heatproof bowl

3. When the liquids are hot, pour them over the chocolate, stirring gently with a heatproof silicone spatula as you pour. Keep stirring until the chocolate is melted. Stir in the salt and then remove from the heat.

4. Serve immediately, or whenever you feel it is necessary!

ASTUCES:

- The addition of milk here makes the sauce slightly "light" in the French sense, in that you can eat more of it and still feel great afterward.
- "Finely chopped" here means into slivers so that, when you pour the hot liquids over the chocolate, it will melt entirely.
- Use high-quality chocolate, such as Lindt, Scharffen Berger, or Valrhona.

Mayonnaise

Mayonnaise is a fundamental sauce in the French repertoire. And every French cook makes her or his own, as do most chefs. You've got to try it—once you've made it, you're likely never to use any other kind! Try this basic recipe, always beginning with a neutral oil, and finishing off with a flavored oil, such as a nut or olive oil. Once you've got the mayonnaise you can spice it up with minced herbs and capers, extra mustard or lemon juice, minced garlic ... you can see, the possibilities are manifold.

MAKES ABOUT 1¼ CUPS (310 ML) MAYONNAISE

EQUIPMENT: wet towel, medium nonreactive bowl

PREPARATION TIME: 10 minutes

COOKING TIME: none

DIFFICULTY LEVEL: simple

---

1 teaspoon fine sea salt

1 teaspoon Dijon mustard

1 tablespoon red or white wine vinegar

2 large egg yolks

1 cup (250 ml) untoasted peanut oil or other neutral oil

¼ cup (60 ml) fine-quality olive oil

1. Place a wet towel under a medium nonreactive bowl to keep it from sliding around on the work surface. Place the salt, mustard, and vinegar in the bowl and whisk them together. Whisk in the egg yolks until thoroughly combined.

2. Then, *very slowly* and in a very fine stream, whisk in the oils. The mixture will thicken as you whisk. You may stop adding oil when it gets to the thickness you desire. Taste the mayonnaise for seasoning.

MAYONNAISE MYTHS: TRUE AND FALSE

- All ingredients need to be at the same temperature—false.
- Chilled ingredients won't work—false.
- Only whisk in one direction—false.
- Whisk in the oil slowly—true. This is the real secret to mayonnaise success every time, along with the addition of mustard. If you have both of these elements—slow and mustard—you'll have gorgeous mayonnaise.
- Mayonnaise made by hand is more tender than that made in a food processor or blender—true!

Béchamel

Béchamel is a fundament of French cuisine, considered a Mother Sauce because it is the basis of so many dishes, sauces, wonderful concoctions. And this is the best béchamel you will ever make.

MAKES 4 CUPS (1 L) BÉCHAMEL
EQUIPMENT: 2 medium saucepans
PREPARATION TIME: 5 minutes
COOKING TIME: 10 minutes
DIFFICULTY LEVEL: simple

3½ cups (880 ml) whole milk

1 fresh or dried imported bay leaf

8 tablespoons (1 stick; 125 g) unsalted butter

½ cup (70 g) all-purpose flour

Fine sea salt

ASTUCES:

- Be sure to cook the flour in the butter for at least 2 minutes, which allows the flour to lose its "floury" taste.
- If your béchamel is thicker than you want it to be, simply add more milk to the sauce, tablespoon by tablespoon.

1. Pour the milk into a medium saucepan. Add the bay leaf and set the pan over medium heat. Scald the milk, remove it from the heat, and keep it warm.

2. Melt the butter in another medium saucepan over medium heat until completely melted. Whisk in the flour and let the mixture foam and cook, whisking occasionally, for at least 2 minutes. Whisk in the hot milk mixture and cook, whisking regularly, until the sauce thickens, about 5 minutes. If the sauce isn't thickening, increase the heat slightly and whisk occasionally.

3. Season the béchamel to taste and remove from the heat. Remove the bay leaf. The sauce is ready to use immediately.

Sauce Gribiche

TARRAGON SAUCE

Sauce Gribiche is one reason to make the Ham Hock, Smoked Sausage, and Vegetable Stew (page 158), because this tangy sauce is the special ingredient that makes the dish so exceptionally tasty! I publish the sauce as a separate recipe because it's good on so many different dishes, from poached fish to the Pork, Chicken, and Beer Terrine (page 150). Once you've made and loved it, you'll find lots of uses for it!

MAKES 2 CUPS (500 ML) SAUCE

EQUIPMENT: medium bowl

PREPARATION TIME: 10 minutes

COOKING TIME: none

DIFFICULTY LEVEL: simple

---

2 tablespoons capers,
    preferably packed in salt

¼ cup (60 ml) best-quality red
    wine vinegar

Fine sea salt

1 teaspoon Dijon mustard

¾ cup (185 ml) olive oil

19 cornichons (tiny dill pickles),
    diced

½ cup loosely packed fresh
    tarragon leaves

1. If you are using capers packed in salt, place them in a small bowl, cover with warm water, let sit for 30 minutes, then remove them from the water and pat dry.

2. Place the vinegar in a medium bowl and whisk in a generous pinch of salt. Whisk in the mustard, then add the oil very slowly, whisking all the while, until all of it is incorporated into the sauce. Stir in the capers and the cornichons.

3. Right before you serve the sauce, mince the tarragon and stir it into the sauce.

ASTUCES:

- You can make this sauce several hours in advance, but don't add the tarragon until right before you serve it, because the acid will "cook" the tarragon, turning it a dull color and usurping some of its flavor.
- As for capers, the very best are packed in salt. They need to be soaked in warm water for at least 10 minutes, so include this in your timing. If you can only find capers packed in vinegar, rinse and pat them dry before using them.
- If your taste goes for the tart, add more cornichons to this lovely sauce.

Sauce Verte

CAPER SAUCE

This is a lovely little sauce to make and serve with all manner of dishes: roast meat or fish, steamed or roasted vegetables, even over slabs of toasted bread rubbed with garlic. I use it on the Happy Toasts with Chicken Livers (page 50). You'll be happy you have this little sauce in your repertoire.

MAKES ABOUT $^2/_3$ **CUP (160 ML) SAUCE**

EQUIPMENT: bowl

PREPARATION TIME: 5 minutes

COOKING TIME: none

DIFFICULTY LEVEL: simple

⅓ **cup (80 g) capers, preferably packed in salt**

1 bird's eye chili, crushed, or ½ teaspoon piment d'Espelette (optional)

½ **cup (125 ml) olive oil**

ASTUCE: Sauce verte will keep for about a week in the refrigerator, and it is wonderful to have on hand. Remove it from the refrigerator about 30 minutes before you plan to use it, so the oil can relax and return to its liquid state.

1. If you are using capers packed in salt, place them in a small bowl, cover with warm water, let sit for 10 minutes, then remove them from the water and pat dry. If using capers in vinegar, rinse them, pat them dry, and proceed.

2. Mince the capers and bird's eye pepper, if desired, and place them in a bowl. Add the olive oil and whisk to blend. If using piment d'Espelette instead of the chili, whisk it in after adding the olive oil. The sauce is ready to use immediately.

Beef Stock

FOND DE BOEUF

Making stock can be intimidating, but it's actually very simple. The results will give life and a depth of flavor to dishes, and stock is delicious on its own as a pick-me-up, or with a drizzle of vinegar. In fact, this was one of the first "dishes" ever to be served in a restaurant in France, where broth was believed to *restaure* (restore the life to) those who were in need of fortification.

ABOUT 6 CUPS (1¹/₂ L) STOCK

EQUIPMENT: 2 ovenproof baking dishes, large stockpot, colander, flat strainer or large spoon

PREPARATION TIME: 15 minutes

COOKING TIME: 3 to 5 hours

DIFFICULTY LEVEL: simple

---

4 pounds (2 kg) beef or veal bones, cut into 2-inch (5 cm) lengths (ideally a mix of marrow and other bones)

3 large onions (7 ounces; 210 g each), peeled and cut in half

4 medium carrots (3 ounces; 90 g each), peeled and cut into chunks

Four 9-inch (22.5 cm each) celery stalks, trimmed and cut into chunks

1 medium fennel bulb (6 ounces; 180 g), trimmed and cut into quarters (optional)

4½ to 5½ quarts (4.5 to 5.5 L) water

1 large Bouquet Garni (page 338; see Astuces)

20 black peppercorns

5 garlic cloves

1. Preheat the oven to 450°F (230°C).

2. Place the bones in an ovenproof dish large enough to hold them in a single layer. Lightly oil a baking dish that is large enough to hold the vegetables in a single layer and place them in it.

3. Place the dish of bones in the center of the oven and roast for 15 minutes. Then add the dish of vegetables to the oven. Roast the vegetables until they are browned, and the bones until they have given up most of their fat, about 45 minutes more for each.

4. Place the bones (leaving the fat in the pan) in a large stockpot. Add 2 cups (500 ml) of the water to the vegetables to help disengage them from the dish and scrape up any browned bits. Add the vegetables and and their juices to the stockpot. Add the bouquet garni, peppercorns, garlic, and enough water to cover the bones and vegetables—at least 4 quarts (4 L) and as many as 5 quarts (5 L).

5. Bring to a rolling boil over medium-high heat and skim any impurities that foam to the surface. Lower the heat and simmer partially covered, until the liquid looks rich and brown, 3 to 5 hours. You may want to taste the vegetables and look closely at the bones. If the vegetables have no flavor, they will contribute nothing more to the stock. If the bones look as though they've given their all, then they

(continued)

ASTUCES:

- Your butcher can give you beef bones; ask him or her to cut them to the required size. As they cook, a white foam (impurities) will float to the surface of the water, so follow the directions and skim it off, using a flat strainer or spoon.
- A fennel bulb adds an intriguing anise flavor to your stock, which you may or may not want, thus the "optional."
- Note that when you make the bouquet garni here, you want to double the amount of ingredients in the recipe on page 338.

have. However, it won't hurt the stock to continue cooking all day long, and you can even add more vegetables or bones as it cooks—all will contribute to its richness. If the liquid level drops below the bones, add water to keep them covered.

6. Let the stock cool so it isn't boiling hot, then strain it, discard the bones and vegetables, and taste the stock. If it isn't quite as intensely flavored as you'd like, return it to the pot and reduce it to concentrate its flavor.

7. Let the stock cool completely, then store it in the refrigerator overnight. The next day, use a flat strainer or large spoon to remove and discard the layer of fat from the top of the stock. Either use the stock or freeze it for future use.

FREEZING STOCK

I freeze about 2 cups (500 ml) of stock in ice cube trays, then pop the cubes out of the trays and put them in freezer bags or containers (each cube is approximately 1½ tablespoons of stock). This way, if I need a bit of stock, I add a cube! Also, if you've made a great deal of stock and still have extra after filling the ice cube trays, freeze it in 1-cup (250 ml) quantities for ease of use—most recipes call for relatively small amounts of stock.

Chicken Stock

FOND DE VOLAILLE

This is a wonderful base for soups and stews, and a restorative on a cold winter day. The first restaurant in Paris made its name serving cups of stock like this that were believed to strengthen (*restaure*), thus giving rise to the word *restaurant*.

ABOUT 6 CUPS (1½ L) **STOCK**

EQUIPMENT: large heavy-bottomed stockpot, flat strainer or large spoon, strainer

PREPARATION TIME: 10 minutes

COOKING TIME: 3 hours

DIFFICULTY LEVEL: simple

---

1 medium onion (5 ounces; 150 g), cut in half

2 whole cloves

One 3½- to 4-pound (1.8 to 2 kg) chicken, cut into serving-size pieces

1 medium carrot (3 ounces; 90 g), trimmed and diced

2 leeks, trimmed 2 inches (5 cm) above the white part, well rinsed, and diced

1 Bouquet Garni (page 338)

2 garlic cloves, cut in half lengthwise

10 black peppercorns

10 cups (2.5 L) filtered water

1. Brown the cut sides of the onion over a gas flame or under the broiler until they are a very dark brown color, almost black.

2. Stick 1 clove in the uncut side of each onion half, making a little slit in the onion first if necessary, so the clove will fit in easily.

3. Place all the ingredients in a large heavy-bottomed stockpot and bring to a boil over high heat. Skim off any foam that rises to the top. Lower the heat to medium so the stock is boiling gently but steadily and cook for 3 hours, partially covered.

4. Strain the stock and discard the vegetables. Allow the stock to cool, then refrigerate it. The following day, remove the layer of fat on top of the stock with a flat strainer or a large spoon, discard it, then use or freeze the stock.

ASTUCES:
- Searing the onions gives the stock depth of flavor.
- The foam that rises to the top is protein, and if left in the pan will cause the stock to be cloudy. There is nothing harmful about it, however.
- Note that if you want to remove the fat from the stock, it's best to make it the night before you plan to do this and refrigerate it. The fat will float to the surface and solidify, making it easy to remove and discard.

Fish Stock

FUMET

I always have fish stock in my freezer, for making a quick soup or adding to a sauce. Often I freeze the bones from white fish (don't use bones from oily fish for stock) until I have enough for stock.

MAKES 8 CUPS (2 L) STOCK

EQUIPMENT: large heavy-bottomed saucepan, flat strainer or spoon, strainer

PREPARATION TIME: 10 minutes

COOKING TIME: 19 minutes

DIFFICULTY LEVEL: simple

---

2 pounds (1 kg) bones from white fish, such as snapper, sole, or rockfish

2 tablespoons (30 g) unsalted butter

2 medium carrots (3 ounces; 90 g each), peeled and coarsely chopped

10 cups (2.5 L) water

1 large onion (6 ounces; 180 g), coarsely chopped

Leaves from 2 celery stalks, or 2 lovage leaves

1 fresh or dried imported bay leaf

1 bunch fresh flat-leaf parsley

5 fresh thyme sprigs

12 black peppercorns

2 teaspoons coarse sea salt

1. Rinse the fish bones well under cold running water until the water runs clear.

2. Melt the butter in a large heavy-bottomed saucepan over medium heat. Add the vegetables and stir to coat with butter. Add the water, herbs, peppercorns, salt, and fish bones; bring to a boil, then lower the heat to low so that the liquid is simmering. Simmer the stock for 18 minutes, skimming off any foam that rises to the surface.

3. Remove the stock from the heat. Strain, discarding the solids. When the stock is cool, either refrigerate or freeze it.

ASTUCES:

- Be sure to skim away any foam that rises to the surface of the stock— the foam is protein and harmless, but if left in the stock, the stock will be cloudy.
- Be very attentive while making fish stock; once you've added the water, you want to cook the mixture for 18 minutes, not more, or your stock risks becoming bitter.
- The trick to this recipe is getting good fish bones. Make sure they smell sweet, of sea brine. Rinse them well before using to remove any blood, which will make the stock bitter.

BROTH, STOCK, OR WATER . . .

The classic French basis of sauces and soups is a chicken, veal, or beef stock or broth. These add flavor, texture, and depth, which are hallmarks of French cooking.

What's the difference between a stock and a broth? Stock is made from beef, chicken, or veal bones, vegetables, herbs, and water that simmer together for hours until all the flavor is extracted from the ingredients. *Fond brun* (brown stock) is beef and/or veal bones and vegetables that are roasted before being simmered with herbs in water, resulting in a deeply flavored stock. *Fond blanc* (white stock) is veal or beef bones that are simply simmered with herbs in water, giving a full but less intense flavor than fond brun. Roasting and long, slow simmering encourage the gelatin out of the bones, making for stock or broth that thickens when it's cool.

A broth, or *bouillon*, is similar, but it cooks for much less time, and it can be made with bones from previously cooked meat, such as a roast bird, or meat and no bones at all. The results are lighter than stock.

The keys to good stocks or bouillon are high-quality ingredients, skimming the foam (proteins) that will rise to the surface as the mixture simmers and which can cloud a stock, and a final filtering once the mixture is cooked. You can follow the recipes on pages 329 and 332, always keeping in mind to adjust the flavor and the vegetables to your own taste. Remember, though, that any brassica (cabbage/cauliflower/broccoli) or a root vegetable such as turnip will not make a good addition to a stock or broth because their flavors turn funky after several hours. The more carrots you add to your stock or broth, the sweeter it will be, so keep this in mind as well. Favored herbs for stock or broth are thyme, bay leaf, pepper, and parsley.

Herb broth is an alternative to meat-based stocks, and it's quick and simple to make. Follow the recipe on page 336, using your favorite herbs. You can also add coins of fresh ginger, aromatics such as star anise or cloves, or whatever suits the taste you're after.

I'd like you to consider water as a base for soups and sauces, too. Water makes for light, bright soups and sauces that allow the flavor of whatever is being "sauced" to come through.

So, what to use in a soup or a sauce? Stocks and broth add depth and texture; herb broth adds a subtle dimension of flavor; water allows the flavor of the individual ingredients to come through. I offer alternatives in recipes that call for stocks or broths, so the decision is yours.

Herb Broth

BOUILLON D'AROMATES

This broth is a wonderful base for soups and stews, whether you have vegans or vegetarians at your table, or just want a fragrant base to your dish.

MAKES 6 CUPS (1½ L) BROTH

EQUIPMENT: stockpot, fine-mesh sieve

PREPARATION TIME: 5 minutes (not including picking the herbs . . .)

COOKING TIME: 15 minutes cooking; 15 minutes sitting time

DIFFICULTY LEVEL: simple

---

20 fresh thyme branches

10 fresh sage leaves

4 fresh or dried imported bay leaves

4 garlic cloves, unpeeled

1 teaspoon sea salt

6 cups (1.5 L) water

1. Place all the ingredients in a stockpot over medium-high heat. When the mixture boils, lower the heat so it is simmering, then simmer for 15 minutes. Remove from the heat. You may let the broth sit for 15 minutes before straining, for a more intense herb flavor. Otherwise, strain and use immediately.

ASTUCES:

- You can experiment and add such herbs as fennel blossoms, anise hyssop, or star anise to give a slight anise flavor to the broth, ginger for a bite, turmeric root for a bit of color. Have fun; be judicious.
- Note: If you add rosemary, add very little, as it can become bitter as it cooks.

Cumin Salt

SEL AU CUMIN

I like to have seasoning mixtures on hand to dress up a meal, and this is a favorite. I strew it over freshly sliced cucumbers, on avocados drizzled with pistachio oil, fish fillets, eggplant, a potato gratin straight from the oven, or I use it in the Egg Flowers with Kuri Squash (page 232). It is universal and universally appealing.

MAKES 3 MOUNDED TABLE-SPOONS

EQUIPMENT: small heavy skillet, mortar and pestle or spice/coffee grinder

PREPARATION TIME: 7 minutes

COOKING TIME: 3 to 4 minutes

DIFFICULTY LEVEL: simple

---

2 tablespoons very fresh cumin seeds

4 teaspoons fleur de sel

1. Place the cumin seeds in a small heavy skillet over low heat and toast them until they turn golden and begin to emit a fragrant aroma, 3 to 4 minutes, shaking the pan regularly. Remove them from the heat and transfer them to a mortar, or a spice or coffee grinder. Add the salt and grind the spices together until they are uniformly but coarsely ground. It should be very "sprinklable."

2. Place the mixture in an airtight jar and keep in a dark, cool spot.

ASTUCES:

- Watch the cumin carefully while it is toasting, as it can burn in a thrice.
- I keep this mixture in an airtight jar in my spice drawer, but it still doesn't last forever, which is why I make it in small quantities. This way it is always fresh and sprightly with flavor.
- I prefer to grind the cumin and the salt with a mortar and pestle, because it gives a mixture that is nicely combined but still has much of its delicate "crunch." If you don't have a mortar and pestle, use a spice or coffee grinder, but be gentle about it—you want a full-textured mixture, not fine dust.

Bouquet Garni

A bouquet garni is as important to French cooking as is salt and pepper. A small bundle of herbs wrapped in leek leaves, a bouquet garni adds poetry to a dish—that indescribable and underlying flavor of herbs that makes you settle into the gorgeous flavor of whatever you are eating.

MAKES 1 BOUQUET GARNI
EQUIPMENT: kitchen twine
PREPARATION TIME: 3 minutes
COOKING TIME: none
DIFFICULTY LEVEL: simple

5 fresh flat-leaf parsley stems

2 fresh or dried imported bay leaves

12 fresh thyme sprigs

2 green leek leaves, well rinsed

1. Make a small bundle of the parsley, bay, and thyme, and nestle them into one of the leek leaves. Place the other leek leaf over the bundle so that the herbs are hidden inside the leek leaves. Tie the bundle together, gently but firmly, wrapping the twine around it several times.

ASTUCE: If you don't have leek leaves on hand, use just the herbs.

Vanilla Sugar

SUCRE VANILLÉ

This recipes makes a lot of vanilla sugar, but you'll want plenty on hand. It's very easy to make and will add the gentlest but most vital hint of vanilla to all of your recipes that call for vanilla and sugar.

MAKES 8 CUPS (1.6 KG)

SPECIAL EQUIPMENT: large airtight jar (for storing)

PREPARATION TIME: none

COOKING TIME: none

DIFFICULTY LEVEL: simple

---

8 cups (3½ pounds; 1¾ kg) granulated sugar

1 fresh vanilla beans or 2 previously used vanilla beans

1. Pour the sugar into an airtight container and push the vanilla beans down into the sugar. Cover and let sit for at least 1 week.

2. Replenish the sugar as you use it, pouring out the sugar that is already flavored, adding new sugar to the container, and topping it with the flavored sugar. Replace the vanilla bean once every 4 months.

ASTUCES:

- You can make vanilla sugar using vanilla beans that you've used in another recipe. Just rinse and thoroughly dry.
- You know the vanilla in the sugar is ready to be changed when the beans turn pale brown. That means they're no longer adding anything to the sugar. Generally a bean will contribute flavor to the sugar for at least 4 months.

ACKNOWLEDGMENTS

Every book project is an adventure. Before the work begins—the *real* work that comes after submitting a proposal, getting the thumbs-up, then actually fulfilling the promises you've made—it is impossible to know just how the adventure will unfold. This is part of the delight of creating a book because, although a proposal is the road map, it is impossible to know in advance who will be alongside the road, the colors of the landscape, the tenor of the wind, the warmth of the sun. It is these details, these unknowns, that keep me writing books, because each book is such a voyage of discovery that I wonder: How is it that I didn't know this, or this, or that before, when I've devoted so much of my life and time to food?

Plat du Jour has been no exception, and I have a boatload of people to thank for assisting me, accompanying me, dining with me, all with the goal of making this book the best it can possibly be for you.

Thank you, then, my friends Edith and Bernard Leroy in Louviers, who are constant and always ready to come have supper at On Rue Tatin to taste and test; Baptiste Bourdon for his inspiration and amazing vegetables; Mathilde, Nadine and Christian Devisme; Betty and Louis Garcia; Hervé Lestage; Marie-Hélène and François Bourdon; Nathalie and Arnaud Souchet-Heridon for their particular enthusiasm; Alain Madonna and Philippe Sainjean; Lena Sodergren; Sarah Thu Ly; Dalila Bourras; Nicholas Lebas; Therese Leduc and Bernadette Goehl for their Irish laughter; Arguine and Tigrane Begoyan; and Christophe Guégan for his cheerful fixes, even if he doesn't care for peanut butter!

Thanks to chefs Eric Georget and Jordan Fouchet, for the early-morning advice and ideas over coffee with Baptiste.

I owe so much to Francis Hammond, photographer par excellence, for his skill, his talent, his appetite, his good judgment, his friendship, and his ridiculous sense of humor that makes the work such fun!

Karen Kaplan has held my hand throughout this book, suggesting, taking so much time, even testing a recipe or two. Thank you, Karen, for your invaluable help and friendship. Thank you, Cat Burgett, for your pastry expertise, and thank you, Roscoe Betsill, for your friendship and cocked eyebrow. You three, my fellow *stagiaires*, are my culinary backbone!

Thank you, Cathy Arkle, for being my conscience when it comes to recipes (and other things!), and for testing.

Thank you to dear Shannon Lemon for being there each step of the way to test and submit marvelously lucid evaluations; thank you Isolde O'Hanlon for your generosity and your frank appraisals . . . you're each one in a million and I'd be lost without you!

To the friends who simply keep me going: Charles and Karen Malody, Patricia and Walter Wells, Ellen Cole and Michael Daum, Judy Kao and Heidi McWorkman, Tricia Rogers, David and Beverly Crofoot, Carolyn Johnson, Christian Laporte, David Lebovitz, Bruno Richomme, Betsy and Alon Kasha, my sweet Halkawt Hekem, Dries Van Ingen for his eternal appetite and joy, and, of course, the Overs. You know who you are . . .

As always, music plays a huge part in my work

as encouragement, solace, delight. I thank Pink Martini, particularly Timothy Nishimoto; Leonard Cohen; Wolfgang Mozart; and Harry Nilsson.

And to Joe and Fiona, my children who are now adults—sorry, kids, you'll always be my children and the center of my world!

INDEX

*Italics are used to indicate illustrations.